The Chronic Illness Experience

I found your book to be the best in frankly dealing with the many issues confronting someone with a chronic illness. —Bill, Michigan

Thanks for writing such a supportive, encouraging book that flows without getting dragged down in frustrated feelings. It's about coping and moving beyond your problems while dealing with them. —Jean, New York

You have comforted me more than anyone else in my life. Now, I never feel so isolated and alone thanks to you and your "characters." —Victoria, California

Even though I've read other books on chronic illness, yours is the only one that really gets to how it feels to be stuck in a malfunctioning body. On every page I saw my life. —Theo, Oregon

After fifteen years of living with rheumatoid arthritis, my feelings have finally been validated. You have given me back a part of my self. —Karla, Texas

I have had rheumatoid arthritis for thirty-five years and discovering your book was like having a support group anytime I wanted. I have a collection of such books, but none can touch the quality of yours—no easy answers or "shoulds," just much understanding and companionship. I dip into it often, at random, and laugh and cry and nod my head and somehow am energized once more. —Margarita, Missouri

You were able to put into words feelings I have had for years and was unable to express. I will forever be grateful for this. Thank you for helping me to adjust and accept my disease. —Carol, Colorado

As I began reading with a sense of detachment, distant from the text, I soon discovered that it was speaking to my own personal experiences in very intimate ways. It speaks to the fears, hopes, and questions of "who I am," "what should I do/not do," that are common to all of us. —Dolores, Minnesota

Your openness to the problems faced by chronically ill persons is to be treasured. —Mark, Ohio

I've avoided "illness books" for years. By chance, I opened your book and read the same evasions I use to pass as healthy. I was hooked. —Rachel, New York

Never have I read anything as concise and insightful as your writing. I especially appreciate your open-ended approach. Too many books like yours try to answer questions where there are no answers, or glorify illness as an exalted state. Thank you for writing such a thoughtful and probing book. —Joan, California

You have not only touched me deeply but have put into words what I believe is one of the most important perspectives on life. Your ability to allow your pain and suffering to transform into insight and wisdom about the human condition has been a gift to me and all your readers. —David, Connecticut

I just finished reading your book. I feel as if I had eaten my first home-cooked meal after subsisting on snack food on a long, long journey. —Aileen, Pennsylvania

The Chronic Illness Experience
Embracing the Imperfect Life

CHERI REGISTER

HAZELDEN®

INFORMATION & EDUCATIONAL SERVICES

Hazelden
Center City, Minnesota 55012-0176

1-800-328-0094
1-651-213-4590 (Fax)
www.hazelden.org

The Emily Dickinson poem on page 265 is reprinted by permission of the publishers and the Trustees of Amherst College from *The Poems of Emily Dickinson,* Thomas H. Johnson, ed., Cambridge, Mass.: The Belknap Press of Harvard University Press, copyright © 1951, 1955, 1979, 1983 by the President and Fellows of Harvard College.

Library of Congress Cataloging-in-Publication Data
Register, Cheri, 1945–
    [Living with chronic illness]
    The chronic illness experience : embracing the imperfect life / Cheri Register.
      p. cm.
    Previously published under the title: Living with chronic illness : days of patience and passion.
    Includes index.
    ISBN 1-56838-346-0
    1. Chronic diseases—Psychological aspects.   I. Title.
  RC108.R44   1999
  362.1'9—dc21
                          99-32734
                          CIP

03 02 01   6 5 4 3 2
Cover design by David Spohn
Interior design by Donna Burch
Typesetting by Stanton Publication Services, Inc.

To Linda DeBeau-Melting for forty years of chronic friendship,

and for my sisters,
Nancy Register Wangen
JoAnn Squires (in memoriam, 1937–1998)

Contents

Preface

This book is an updated version of *Living with Chronic Illness: Days of Patience and Passion,* first published by The Free Press of Macmillan in 1987. When I first wrote the book, there was almost no literature available on chronic illness and little attention to chronicity in the health care field. I wrote with an intensity of purpose that might be less necessary now, but I have chosen to preserve that tone. The text has been altered somewhat to reflect changes in the way chronic illness is perceived and treated, and I have updated the account of my own illness. Stories told by the people I interviewed have been left intact in the confidence that they contain timeless truths that will speak to readers coming to terms with illness today.

In the last twelve years, I have met with many groups of chronically ill people and their families and with health care professionals, and I have heard some challenging accounts of life with illness. What I have learned has found its way into this edition, but the basic message of the book remains the same.

The greatest reward for writing about this subject comes in letters and phone calls from readers who say, in various ways, "You've told my story." They have become a vast support group that understands this agonizing yet enlightening experience of life's imperfections. We welcome you, the new reader, to join us.

Acknowledgments

Many, many people—friends, family, and innocent bystanders—have offered practical and moral support as I have lived the experience that underlies this book. All of them deserve a hearty thanks. Special recognition goes to Dr. Michael Levy, who has retired after maintaining a close watch on my health for twenty-four years. A smaller group of people encouraged the writing by reading the original manuscript at various stages in its evolution: Ellen Babinsky, Linda DeBeau-Melting, Gail Dekker, Carol Frenning, Susan Geiger, Betsey Hulstrand, Kent Jones, Linda Mack, M. J. Maynes, JoAnn Miller, Ardis Register, John Sayer, Naomi Scheman, Janet Spector, Nancy Register Wangen, and my former husband. There would have been no book without the sisterly discipline imposed by the Friday morning breakfast-and-work group at the New Riverside Café: Sara M. Evans, Amy Kaminsky, Elaine Tyler May, and Riv-Ellen Prell. The revised edition owes its existence to poet Richard Solly, a reader turned friend, who nudged me to get the book back into print and whose reflections on personal suffering have enhanced my vision. My first editor, Laura Wolff at The Free Press, gave thoughtful, respectful, and prompt advice, and Corrine Casanova of Hazelden provided generous and courteous assistance with the revision. I owe thanks and best wishes for good health to the fellow sufferers who entrusted me with their stories. They have been given pseudonyms to protect their privacy, and any resemblance of these names to the names of actual people, living or dead, is coincidental. Finally, a hearty thank-you to the many readers who have let me know that this effort was truly worthwhile.

Introduction

Chronic illness is at the same time a personal misfortune and a sign of progress. Had we been born a few decades earlier, many of us who are chronically ill would not be alive at thirty or forty or fifty. Earlier and more precise diagnosis, more effective remedies against acute problems, and better means of maintaining health have slowed the course and limited the impact of some diseases that used to be quickly terminal. No longer illnesses to *die of*, but still not thoroughly curable, they have become illnesses to *live with*. As more and more people learn to live hopefully and purposefully with the daily awareness of interminable disease, popular notions about the experience of illness are necessarily challenged. People can and do find ways to accommodate physical suffering without either denying its reality or letting it govern their lives.

The interminably ill hardly form an exclusive society. Estimates have it that nearly fifty-nine million people in the United States have cardiovascular disease, sixteen million have diabetes, more than two million have lupus, and fifteen million have asthma. Since 1987, when the first edition of this book was published, new illnesses have been identified and new counts taken: more than four hundred thousand people have been diagnosed with chronic fatigue and immune dysfunction syndrome, five million show symptoms of fibromyalgia, and nearly four million have hepatitis C. People once thought to be cured of polio have turned up with neuromuscular disorders in middle age, and people once doomed to death by AIDS or by certain cancers have responded to new treatments and now live with illness as an ever-present companion. Readers of my book have introduced me to Ehlers-Danlos syndrome, inclusion body myositis, reflex sympathetic dystrophy syndrome, and other relative rarities. Add to the list arthritis; hemophilia; a variety of liver, kidney, and intestinal disorders; multiple sclerosis; physiologically based mental illnesses; and many other painful, degenerative, and/or life-threatening diseases, and hardly a family in America is left untouched by chronic illness.

I have chosen to focus on "invisible" illnesses, those with few outward signs. "You'd never know it to look at you" is a phrase familiar to many of us. Though we can avoid some of the stereotyping and discrimination that those with obvious disabilities encounter, illness is still a constant presence, with a profound impact on emotional health, self-image, relationships, work habits, aspirations, and overall outlook on life. Most of us prefer to pass as healthy, living as normally and fully as we can under the circumstances. We hesitate to inflict our private anxieties on a health-conscious world that sees illness as a temporary abnormality and has little understanding of chronicity.

It is difficult to describe what a lifetime of illness is like. The most common images of illness draw on the language of combat: We *battle* cancer, *fight* infections, *overcome* paralysis. Illness is an *enemy* to be *struggled with* and finally *defeated*. A *victory* over cancer may be due to an *advance* of medical science or a *triumph* of the will. Even inevitably fatal illnesses are to be resisted. The dying patient who wages a valiant battle to the death wins the resounding eulogy. While the constant vigilance that a chronic illness requires may be reminiscent of war, how many of us can tolerate being at war with our own bodies over a lifetime—even a somewhat shortened one? Is truce or détente the best we can hope for, or do we strive for a negotiated peace?

The way we speak about illness does affect how we live with it. The war imagery obligates us to resist. On the other hand, euphemisms such as "challenged" and "differently abled" pretend away the pain and suffering involved and turn the natural sorrow and anger and anxiety into character defects. Even those of us who work with language and are sensitive to its subtleties are restrained by it. Susan Sontag, in her extraordinarily insightful book *Illness as Metaphor*, still clings to metaphors that are inadequate to describe the experience of chronic illness:

> Illness is the night-side of life, a more onerous citizenship. Everyone who is born holds dual citizenship, in the kingdom of the well and in the kingdom of the sick. Although we all prefer to use only the good passport, sooner or later each of us is obliged, at least for a spell, to identify ourselves as citizens of that other place.

So what is it like to be permanently exiled into that dark and onerous kingdom where battles are waged? That is the subject of this book, based on firsthand accounts of living with interminable illness. Its intent is to show that we do not spend our lives groping in the dark, nor do we see ourselves as isolated from the mainstream of human experience, nor are we constantly geared for war. While illness sets many of the terms by which we live, it need not do us in altogether.

The dark-as-night metaphors and the language that casts people as *victims*, or as *diabetics* and *arthritics*—walking embodiments of disease—emphasize passivity, when in fact illness demands an active response. It does not deprive you of free will, even though it may very well limit your range of choices. Above all, you must choose whether to fight the illness to the death or accept it as your own normal state of being. It is a choice that is made over and over again, with each change in your physical condition. Just where you see yourself fitting on the spectrum from perfectly healthy to hopelessly ill depends on how you make more particular choices. For example:

- You can tough it out, ignoring symptoms at the risk of getting worse, or you can check out every little quirk, at the risk of hypochondria.

- You can shop for miracle cures, at the risk of harming yourself, or you can trust one doctor's judgment, at the risk of selecting unwisely.

- You can keep your ailment secret, at the risk of deception, or you can talk openly about it, at the risk of self-pity.

- You can ask friends for help, at the risk of becoming a burden, or you can hold fast to your independence, at the risk of isolation.

- You can insist that your family treat you as normal and healthy, at the risk of denying them release for their own worries about you, or you can let them protect you, at the risk of becoming dependent and childlike.

- You can strain your body to its limit, at the risk of harming yourself, or you can play it safe, at the risk of becoming an invalid.

- You can live in terror of degeneration and death, at the risk of being immobilized, or you can look upon each good day as a special dispensation, at the risk of smugness.

- You can insist on controlling the course of your life, at the risk of frustration, or you can "go with the flow," at the risk of passivity.

- You can be angry about your fate, at the risk of bitterness, or you can focus only on your blessings, at the risk of self-delusion.

No one can say with absolute certainty which of each of these extremes is the healthier or exactly where the healthy medium lies. Only trial and error will reveal the most livable choice.

These choices are seldom made once and for all. Conditions change, for better or for worse, demanding new responses. Neither are the choices always conscious and deliberate. A pattern may emerge gradually and be discerned only in retrospect, or by others. "I went through all the stages of grief that the experts on death and dying talk about," says a woman whose long-controlled diabetes was unexpectedly complicated by neuropathy, "but I didn't know I was in the acceptance stage until my friends started commenting on it."

Free will is a treasure to be carefully guarded. We who live, always, with an awareness of our physical infirmities tend to think we know best how to manage our lives. Often that means leaving the invisible unacknowledged, and that may puzzle the concerned and caring people around us. The etiquette of behavior that governs acute illness is not necessarily appropriate to chronic illness. We who choose to pass as healthy fear loss of independence and self-esteem as much as we fear physical degeneration. Whatever coping mechanisms we use, we want them to be respected. Those of us who strive for normality in all we do and constantly test our limits will resist warnings that we are denying reality and endangering our health. If, on the other hand, we have scaled down our ambitions to protect ourselves from pain, harm, and frustration, we may not see the glory in heroic legends about one-legged marathon runners and quadriplegics who paint with their teeth.

Nevertheless, however determined we are to be the arbiters of our own lives, the conviction that we are doing well occasionally falters. Doubts arise especially when our bodies go out of control in spite of our best efforts. Then we want acknowledgment—and sympathy—from family, friends, co-workers, and professionals: doctors, therapists, and clergy. We long, too, for genuine understanding—the assurance that "it's not just me." Organizations like the American Behcets Disease Association and the Celiac Sprue Association offer that assurance by providing both factual information and peer support through their newsletters and programs and Internet Web sites.

It was the absence of peer support that prompted me to write this book. As the only person in the Upper Midwest known to have Caroli's disease—a congenital defect of the liver also known as intrahepatic ductual ecstasia—I had never known anyone who could tell me truthfully, "I know exactly how you feel." Going public with a book has put me in touch with just two others with

Caroli's, both men in more serious condition than I am. When I first started having problems at age nineteen, well before the illness was diagnosed, the episodes of severe pain and malfunction that came on without warning terrified me, but eventually my record of survival reduced the terror to a mild, underlying worry. I learned to accept the illness as an unwelcome but usually tolerable feature of my otherwise normal life. Then, after seventeen years of growing accustomed to occasional frightening disruptions, I developed new symptoms that would not subside. For nine months, I ran a high fever that could be controlled only by heavy doses of antibiotic administered intravenously. There was little pain, but the fever and the accompanying anemia were debilitating in new, unfamiliar ways. My physical ailment had emotional consequences: irritability, depression, even suicidal fantasies. Because the source of the fever could not be located, even with the latest technology, I lost confidence in the medical profession. To someone whose very life depends on medical expertise, that can mean losing hope. This time, I *did* grope in the dark, I *did* feel isolated from normal human experience, I *did* feel at war with an enemy inhabiting my own body. I was driven, as in the beginning, to ask all the existential questions: "Why me? Why is this happening? What does it mean? How can I go on like this? What will become of me?"

I looked, first, for a book to read—a testimony by someone who had been through the worst and emerged with optimism intact. There was, at that time, virtually no literature on the distinctive nature of chronic illness. Posthumously published cancer narratives did not pick up my spirits, nor did the self-help guides that seemed to want me to feel responsible for somehow bringing the fever upon myself. Since my natural inclination is to write my way free of preoccupations and oppressive moods, I put my feelings into incomplete sentences in quaky handwriting in a journal. Then, when my doctor had found an oral antibiotic that worked and I had been transfused with blood from an obviously energetic donor, I began writing an account of my experience with chronic illness. I left out the medical details, concentrating instead on the ways in which illness had determined the shape of my life. The words came, appropriately enough, at a feverish pace, and I was amazed at the clarity of thoughts and feelings I never knew I had. It was pure catharsis. When I finished, I felt healthier than ever.

With that essential work done, I decided to interview other people who were invisibly and interminably ill. Finding them was, of course, a challenge, since you can't just spot them on street corners. Word of mouth worked best of all, but I also left cards in doctors' offices, put announcements in illness foundation newsletters, and placed ads in ethnic community newspapers in the hope of getting a diverse group. Rather than try to get a representative cross section of the population, however, I accepted those who volunteered. I was interested to know what motivated these people to want to talk about this otherwise private feature of their lives. The book was not intended to be a social science study. I thought of it, rather, as a work for solo and chorus, with my own story at the center, augmented by the voices of others— individual voices, still. It didn't take me long to notice, however, that my chorus was heavy on sopranos and altos. I would have to make a special effort to find some men. I asked a very gregarious acquaintance if he would pass on my cards to some of his friends. Though eager to be of help, he was stymied. He didn't know which of his friends were chronically ill. "That's not the sort of thing men like to advertise," he explained. Passing as healthy is apparently a more urgent matter for men than for women. Women have also been far more likely to write or call me after reading the book.

There were other surprises, as well. "Isn't it awfully depressing?" people would ask when I told them what I was working on, and I had fully expected that it would be. Instead, I was heartened by the human capacity to adjust to unwelcome change. I also expected to make comparisons, to be awed by the stamina of the most dangerously ill and perturbed by the self-pity of those with milder conditions. I soon learned that comparison is irrelevant, because there is no single basis for it—not the severity of pain or disability, not the number of years of ill health endured, not even the likelihood of death. How well people manage lives marked by illness depends not on the nature of the illness but on the strength of their conviction that life is worth living no matter what complications are imposed on it. One interviewee's proclamation, "The first day I ever realized you could be happy and still sick was a real red-letter day," can serve as an epigram for the major lesson I learned: Chronic illness, though ever present, is not what matters most in people's lives.

I did find sustenance for my optimism in the examples of the people I interviewed, as well as encouragement for my work. How affirming it was to hear, over and over again, "I'm so glad you're writing this book." At long last, I had found a peer group. Apart from the medical specifics of their illnesses, the configurations of their families, the nature of their work, their ethnic origins, and their religious persuasions, the people I interviewed have a great deal in common. Their voices sometimes join in unison, sometimes harmonize beautifully, and only occasionally break into discord.

This book is intended, first of all, to help others who are chronically ill to strengthen their resolve to live richly and fully. Second, it should help families, friends, and co-workers of the chronically ill become more understanding and better able to respond to their changing needs. Finally, it offers guidance to those who make their livings keeping us as healthy as we can be. Like any work grounded in individual experience, this one is limited in certain ways. Likewise, it is culturally specific, applicable to a sort of "mainstream" middle- and working-class American—even Midwestern—experience. Fortunately, some high-quality books have been written in the meantime. Arthur Kleinman of Harvard University Medical School, author of *The Illness Narratives,* continues to explore the meaning of illness cross-culturally. The recent immigration of refugees from Southeast Asia and East

Africa has challenged the U.S. medical system with unfamiliar concepts of illness and treatment. Anne Fadiman's best-selling book, *The Spirit Catches You and You Fall Down,* tells this story. My wish is that we will soon be reading first-person testimony about how a struggle between two cultures defines the experience of illness, by eloquent voices such as Mai Neng Moua, a young Hmong American writer whose decision to undergo kidney dialysis, an invasion of the body, put her at odds with her parents and her community. The more we know, the clearer we will see how chronic illness shapes us.

Chapter
1

Naming the Problem

"Thank God, I'm not crazy."

It started when I was in college. I was living in a house with
seven other women. I woke up one morning, and it was my
turn to go to the shower first. On the way, I stumbled across
the room and fell into a pile of boxes. I thought, "This is
strange. I've got to go back to bed and try this again." I did,
and I stumbled into the boxes a second time. So I sat on my
bed, and it felt like I had slept on my body funny. The left side
of me was kind of deadened. I lit up a cigarette, and I went to
take a puff of the cigarette in my left hand and it wasn't
there. I had dropped it, and I thought, "This is silly." So I sat
there for a while wondering what was going on, and then I
thought, "Well, I can't just sit here. Other people have to get
up and shower and go." I went into the bathroom and
grabbed my toothbrush and put toothpaste on it and lifted
it to brush my teeth, and it, too, had fallen out of my hand.
And then I started to worry: "Something's wrong with me."

In the years since her dramatic awakening, Louise Taylor, a professional woman with a promising career, has spent her sum-
mers perfecting her tennis technique and a month or more of
nearly every winter lying in a hospital bed, unable to stand without collapsing. The story she tells is remarkable, because few
people can point to a date on the calendar and say, "This is the
morning I woke up with multiple sclerosis." Getting sick for a
lifetime is seldom a single, discrete event. The symptoms are
more likely to come on gradually, altering your life in subtle ways
that can often be explained away as a temporary aberration. The

mild irritation—occasional dizzy spells, bouts of indigestion, throbbing aches that come and go—is far more common than the sudden, overwhelming catastrophe that tells you clearly, "Something's wrong with me."

The onset of Louise's multiple sclerosis was, in fact, less distinct than her vivid recollection of that one fateful morning suggests. She had already experienced some dizziness and fatigue and a temporary loss of vision. In telling me her story, she had simply rearranged the details of what actually happened, making that morning the dramatic focus. Each of us has such a story. When I describe the onset of my liver disease, what I remember most vividly is an eight-hour train trip back to college after spring break that I endured writhing in pain. I was experiencing the first in a continuing series of "liver attacks," known to the doctors as "ascending cholangitis." Yet the defect in my liver is congenital and has thus always been with me. My childhood was somewhat sickly, with digestive upsets, abdominal cramps, and anemia. Besides, this was not really the first attack, but the second. The first had come and gone with no explanation. The intensity of the pain this second time was great enough to convince me that something was seriously amiss with my body. I spent half the spring term in the hospital, undergoing diagnostic tests. In my memory, the trip back to Chicago has been transformed into a long, painful journey toward a new consciousness of my vulnerability and mortality. That single event changed everything, I tell myself. But was that really how it happened? Did I see things that clearly in those confusing circumstances? I doubt it.

Neither Louise nor I suspected at the time that our life stories were about to be revised. We still trusted that something could be done to restore us to health. At worst, an offending organ, preferably a vestigial one, would be operated away. Both of us continued to live as though our lives had been only temporarily disrupted. The realization that the underlying problem would never go away came later. "Acceptance"—the recognition that illness had become our normal condition—came later still.

We continue to tell these stories because it seems important to have a frame in which to contain the experience of chronic illness. The story needs a strong beginning because it has no structure otherwise. With chronic illness, there is no single climax, just the irregularly recurring ups and downs. And there is no certain conclusion, just faint hopes of cure and nearly fatal crises. Chronic illness does not fit the popular notion of how illness proceeds: "You get sick, you go to the doctor and get some medicine, and wait to get better. If there is no remedy for what ails you, you die." An illness that drags on for years, defying diagnosis, treatment, or cure is an anomaly. We would like life to be orderly and predictable, and we want to believe that science has solved all the mysteries of the human body. When we realize that is not so, the best we can do to clear up the chaos in our lives is to look back and say, "This is how it all began. *This* was when my life took an unfortunate turn."

Revising our stories makes them no less true. Indeed, they contain a more profound truth: that human beings, even when sick, seek order in chaos and purpose in apparent meaningless. Arthur Kleinman, in *The Illness Narratives*, proposes that the ways in which we narrate our stories contain clues for diagnosis and hints about the kinds of treatment that will be most beneficial to us. "Each patient is a story," he says, and physicians would do well to listen carefully not only to the content but to the structure. "You leave medicine behind and enter a life. . . . Medicine is concerned with the problem of keeping you alive; but serious illness asks the question for you, 'What is life for?'"

Here is another story about the onset of multiple sclerosis (MS), recast in a style that bears retelling. This one, however, highlights the confusion and uncertainty that make the beginning of chronic illness so difficult to recognize. In public speeches sponsored by the National Multiple Sclerosis Society, Gloria Murphy has had plenty of opportunity to test her story on an audience and hone it into a form that finds resonance in others:

It started about ten years ago, and my first symptom was a lot of dizziness. I spent about three months just crawling on the floor with my children. I went through the Mayo Clinic and was told that I had an inner ear disorder that I would just have to live with. Time went on and it got better and I forgot about it. Then other symptoms started appearing: numbness in my legs, inability to walk at times, double vision, a lot of bladder, kidney, and bowel problems. I was told that if I just got busy and away from my children, all of these things would clear up by themselves. The doctors called it "housewife's syndrome."

So, I became a supermom. I was the kind of mother who made her own noodles. I used to hang my noodles over the railing on the back porch to dry. Erma Bombeck [who died in 1996 while waiting for a transplant necessitated by polycystic kidney disease] says a supermom is one who has theme parties for her dog. I did that. I was a den mother for three of our boys. I chaperoned eighteen field trips in three years. I worked on school board elections and on any committee that asked for volunteers. I taught Sunday school. I worked for several years until one day I literally fell in a big heap and was carted off to the emergency room.

This all happened over a period of five years. It caused a great deal of struggle within our family, because I knew there was something wrong with me, and yet I felt I had to keep up. So rather than slow down, I tried to move faster. The faster I went, the sicker I got. My husband always stuck beside me. When I look back on it now, I wonder why he even stayed, because there were some times when it was really difficult for him and the boys. My attitude was one of sheer grit and determination: By God, if there's nothing wrong with me or if they can't figure it out, I will find more things to do. My husband could see that I was deteriorating, and the harder I pushed, the grumpier I got. The more things I took on to do, the less I could do for him and the children. I thought I was doing everything a good mother should do.

I spent a lot of time in the hospital. I had periods where exhaustion would take over and I would become so ill they would put me in just to run more tests. I often think about what my body went through as far as chemicals that were put in, medications, X rays, scans, surgeries I had that weren't necessary or at least didn't help. And I think of the emotional stress I put my family and myself and my friends through, although at the time there's no way of knowing that that's what's happening to you. I had bladder surgery several times, and they treated it as bladder and kidney problems. I went through three myelograms because they thought I had disc problems in my back. Throughout all this, I would see different specialists for different things, and none of them ever consulted with each other.

Finally, when I had my "big heap," I was introduced to my neurologist, who specializes in multiple sclerosis. He put me in the hospital and diagnosed me as having MS about two days later. And with that came this wonderful sense of relief. I giggled and laughed. I was joyous. My husband was the same way. We were just like two kids running through a park. We had a name for this. We could deal with it. I was not a neurotic lady. It was OKAY to slow down, to quit work. It was OKAY to say no to things.

Despite its special eloquence, Gloria's story is not atypical. It contains features that many people who have been through the initial phase of chronic illness will recognize:

- Diffuse symptoms that come and go over a period of time
- Attempts to find psychological or circumstantial causes for these symptoms
- False or partial diagnoses

- Determination to make the symptoms disappear by changing habits and behavior
- Strained relationships with family and friends
- Stress that is often not perceived as stress
- Changes in mood and personality
- Physical examinations and procedures that may be redundant, unnecessary, or even harmful
- Different and sometimes incompatible diagnoses and remedies from different specialists consulted
- Relief at having an answer that seems definitive

Sick Enough to Go to the Doctor?

The first challenge illness poses is in deciding just when you are sick *enough* to worry about it. Often, the initial problems are not that great a departure from your usual state of health. As annoying as they might be, you may be tempted to dismiss them, unless they are known to be danger signals, like the "warning signs" of cancer. Everyone has aches and pains, after all, and most of them subside on their own. For fear of being called hypochondriacs, many of us would rather wait out the discomfort than risk seeming excessively alarmed. Sometimes we depend on the people around us to get alarmed on our behalf and urge us to take action.

Contrary to popular belief, it is not so much fear and denial as it is confusion and embarrassment that keep people out of the doctor's office in the early stages of illness. Having no clear sense of the boundaries that divide illness from health, we redraw our own as needed to keep ourselves functioning. Soon enough we become inured to our ailments. Once you get used to a low hemoglobin level, for example, you don't consciously feel anemic. On the contrary, it is surprising to find, in periods of good health, how much difference a few red blood cells make in your energy level. Barring a cataclysm like Louise's awakening, my train trip, or Gloria's "big heap," it may be quite some time before you stop to reflect and realize how long it has been since you really felt well.

Like "hypochondriac," the word "psychosomatic" also has the force of taboo. And so, as new symptoms appear, we feel compelled to examine our circumstances and look for external causes. Duane Barber was an infantryman in Vietnam when he developed a tingling sensation in his feet and calves. In the alien atmosphere of war, he was subject every day to new, unfamiliar terrors. It hardly mattered that his feet felt like pincushions. Even people who are first afflicted in the security of their homes or in the routine of their jobs can usually identify a likely origin for the initial discomforts: a heavy work schedule, concern about a loved one's welfare, a minor injury. Rather than do without an explanation, you can always turn to the catchall, stress. Having accustomed ourselves to the multiple pressures of life in a fast-paced technological society, we add the pain, the numbness, the faulty digestion to the list and proceed as best we can, counting on spring or the completion of a project or a change in eating habits to bring relief. This tendency is reinforced by the fact that so often stress *is* at fault.

But Which Doctor?

A problem on its way to becoming chronic does not clear itself up, though it may subside for a while. Eventually it demands attention. When it impedes normal activity for too long, or recurs once too often, patience wears thin. Once you acknowledge that you are indeed sick and in need of treatment, you run up against the next challenge: Where should you turn for help? How the symptoms are perceived and treated may depend, as Gloria's story illustrates, on the specialty of the doctor you consult or are referred to. In extreme cases, the consequences can be deadly. When Donna Schneider asked a gynecologist to examine her swollen abdomen, he ordered an emergency hysterectomy. Fortunately, she took time to get a second opinion and learned that she was on the verge of kidney failure. The swelling was due to water retention. Susan Alm went for years believing the severe pain in her joints was rheumatoid arthritis and wondering why the proven remedies did her no good. It was only when her husband switched jobs and changed health plans that she chanced upon a rheumatologist familiar with the signs of lupus.

While we contemplate how best to get help, some of us "try on" various diseases by checking our symptoms against whatever we can learn about them. To healthy friends this may look like hypochondria or a foolish attempt at self-diagnosis. But a preliminary self-diagnosis is not folly. Limiting the field of options at the outset saves time, expense, frustration, and the discomfort of indiscriminate testing. Being actively involved in the diagnostic process is also a way of retaining control over a situation that otherwise leaves you feeling powerless and at the mercy of medical guesswork. Nine years after his feet began to tingle—an unusually long delay due, he says, to his great capacity for denial—Duane Barber finally told an internist about it. But before he could bring himself to that point, he spent a month reading medical books:

> I tried to correlate the symptoms I had with the possibilities of disease. I had it narrowed down to diabetes, a tumor on the spinal column, a thyroid problem, a vitamin B deficiency, and multiple sclerosis. I didn't think it was a tumor because I'd had these symptoms for years and a tumor would have affected me to a greater degree earlier. I have always been careful about nutrition, so I wasn't likely to have a vitamin deficiency.

The internist referred him to a neurologist, who put him in the hospital for tests that confirmed Duane's expectation that it was multiple sclerosis. Asked why he went to such great lengths to research his illness in advance, he explained, "I guess it's just a flaw in my makeup. You're always, oh, not afraid, but uncomfortable with the unknown. I knew what to expect when the neurologist examined me, so it wasn't a shock."

Many people guard against shock by preparing for the worst. Given the current folklore about illness, that usually means cancer. One man even told me he was disappointed to find out that he "only" had Crohn's disease, a chronic inflammation of the small intestine that can be very painful and may require corrective surgery:

> I was all ready for a valiant, death-defying battle with cancer and all I had was a dirty little intestinal disease. I was kind of depressed about not being more sick because I was psychologically prepared for the worst. When it turned out that I didn't have cancer, I lost my enthusiasm for finding out about what I did have.

Frustration and Doubt

When you declare yourself sick enough to consult a doctor, you are also expressing your faith in the likelihood of diagnosis and treatment. As a diagnosis eludes even the most competent specialist's efforts, that faith begins to wane. Either you lose your confidence in the medical profession or you begin to doubt the validity of your symptoms. Surrendering confidence in the medical profession is risky business. If doctors have no capacity to heal, what hope remains? Self-doubt may be easier to live with, and so you wonder if perhaps you are only imagining things. Doctors may even encourage those doubts. Trained as they are in the empirical method, they will interpret a series of negative tests to mean that everything is working correctly. If nothing is demonstrably wrong, the doctor must consider the possibility that the patient is malingering, or at least having delusions of illness. Women are especially subject to this suspicion. Gloria Murphy's "housewife's syndrome," treated with tranquilizers in the 1960s and 1970s, was the modern version of the nineteenth-century catchall—hysteria. People with chronic fatigue syndrome have had their suffering dismissed as "yuppie flu." While it is certainly legitimate to check for possible psychological causes, reverting to social stereotypes is not in the patient's best interest.

To persist in seeking a medical explanation in the face of skepticism takes strong will, an assertive personality, and a good measure of physical endurance. Those of us who have been through lengthy testing processes know that the warning "This may be a little uncomfortable" translates into "This is going to hurt like hell." JoAnn Berglund, whose mobility is now limited by multiple sclerosis, found herself growing impatient after a year of fruitless trips to a clinic for numbness, tingling, and vision problems:

> I was ice-skating over Christmas break and my leg just crumbled. Well, I was sick and tired of them telling me, "You're nervous," or "Lose weight," for everything you go in for. So I said, "What if I was cool as a cucumber and thin as a rail? Then what do you think I'd have?"

Without the benefit of JoAnn's confidence and sense of humor, many people see no recourse but to accept the doctor's word that examination shows no abnormalities. There is nothing to do but wait and see what happens. If you begin to doubt the validity of your problems, chances are you will do your waiting in private. Concerned that family and friends will grow weary of your company, you refrain from talking about the worries that are uppermost in your mind. Like Gloria, you may even overcompensate by acting superhealthy. But time solves nothing. The problems do not disappear. They *feel* real, no matter how hard you try to talk yourself out of them. Rosemary McKuen describes her desperation at the onset of ulcerative colitis, which was treated with "a pat on the head and a bottle of Librium":

> I had been feeling sick for maybe two months—having diarrhea pretty steadily. I lost a lot of weight, had pain in my

joints, and lots of cramping. That's what I remember about it: just how I would feel during those times, and how I would feel if I thought it was coming on. What would happen to me? Oh God, there wasn't anything I could do about it. There wasn't any way that I could stave it off. There wasn't anything I could pop. I couldn't talk it away. If it was coming, it came.

Going Crazy

If you are used to good health and reasonable control over your body, the continuing mystery of your illness produces an anguish that is difficult to express even to your most intimate confidantes. "I must be going crazy" is how you express it to yourself, as you begin a new round of self-probing. When the doctors labeled my nine-month bout of fever and anemia "FUO" for "fever of undetermined origin," I relied on a rigorous self-analysis to offset my fear of losing control of my body. I came up with a very elaborate diagnosis. The fever must be a psychosomatic escape from the turmoil caused by adopting a child and leaving a dead-end teaching job to pursue a writing career. Both of these decisions were, in all healthy respects, changes for the better. Because I thought it unnatural to be frustrated with motherhood and could not admit to a lack of confidence about my writing ability, I had converted my frustration to fever. Figuring out why the fever had to be 104 degrees instead of a bearable 99.5 was beyond my intellectual capacity.

Private anguish is not easily contained. It shows, despite your best efforts, in tension, irritability, sorrow, nervous behavior, absent-minded preoccupation, emotional withdrawal, or unfocused anger. The people around you notice the behavior and pass judgment on it without seeing the suffering person caught inside it. Feeling isolated and invisible, you can easily become self-pitying. Trapped in your private hell, you begin to think that no one could possibly comprehend your misery or offer you sympathy enough.

Given enough time, suppressed anguish threatens to become the core of your character. Phyllis Mueller, now middle-aged, has endured severe abdominal pain and muscle spasms since childhood, but no treatable abnormality has yet been identified. Were it not for the ironic wit that sees her through, she could easily be perceived as malcontent and hostile. She has reason to be. When she was ten, a doctor discovered that the food was not passing through her digestive tract correctly. Though that was description and not diagnosis, matters were left there. At thirteen, she had her stomach pumped in another attempt at diagnosis.

The end result was, "She has a nervous stomach." And once again it made no difference because the condition was still there, basically untreatable. I have had a lot of gastrointestinal tests, gall bladder X rays, and so forth. During the ensuing years there has been a lot of frustration, part of it with doctors. Some of them tend to zero in on the stomach as though it's just lying there in a body and there's absolutely nothing feeding into it or going out of it. You look at the stomach and if it looks good, there's nothing wrong with this lady. It must be emotional. I started hearing "neurotic," "emotional problems," "marital problems." In other words, they were looking for anything outside this "healthy" stomach as a reason for stomach dysfunction. But still I would get sick after I ate and I had no idea why. When you can say you've got MS or diabetes, you've got something to hang on to. But I think I was unfairly categorized as having emotional problems. I felt pigeonholed and unfairly treated as a result of that.

I seem to have developed some allergies, too. So I went to the university hospital and I said, "I have a list here of eighteen medications. I can't take any of them. Every time I take medications I get sick. What is it with chemicals and me? I don't drink well. Liquor doesn't agree with me. A lot of food doesn't agree with me. Is there something wrong with my chemistry or what?" Well, fifteen hundred dollars later they said, "You have a dysfunctional GI tract." Now I have a hunch that for another thousand dollars they would have given me some guesses as to what it was. But I still didn't have anybody saying, "I really care about trying to find out why this GI tract is dysfunctional." I felt very depressed after that. I guess it's a "nobody cares" feeling. I mean, this is my life, for God's sake. I would like to live it in a better way. I would like to have fewer limitations. And I have been willing to spend a lot of money in order to do this, but I don't think I have had a lot of cooperation. I think there was originally an emotional cause, and I have tried to put together what upset me, but is it possible that some of the physical problems in turn have caused some emotional problems, instead of always looking at it from the other direction?

In Phyllis's case, the original cause has become irrelevant. The illness has dominated her life. After lengthy psychotherapy, she still feels the pain. It's real. Her insight that the physical can affect the emotional as well as vice versa is a crucial one. Though she has survived, remarkably, with her basic spirit intact, it is hard for Phyllis to imagine an emotional life completely free and unburdened as long as she still hurts.

The Rigors of Research

Typically, university hospitals have a reputation for taking mystery diseases seriously. It was my dual fortune and misfortune to get sick while I was a student at a university with a highly respected medical school and research hospital. I say "fortune" because the people reviewing my case were on the leading edge of progress in the diagnosis and treatment of liver diseases. How thankful I am now that the train was taking me back to school rather than to my hometown! I say "misfortune" because I became accustomed to a type of care that was not in my long-term interest. Academic medicine is extremely open-ended and inconclusive. Every tentative answer raises more questions, each of which has to be tested by a different X-ray procedure or a different laboratory culture. In my case, treatment was delayed until the diagnosis was fairly certain, even though I was very uncomfortable in the meantime.

The impersonality of the hospital care was troubling, but it took quite some time and trial before I objected, shy undergraduate that I was. As I surveyed the circle of faces that gathered around my bed each morning, I was never sure who was who or whether they all had valid reasons for being there. I tried to relax as they took turns palpating my liver and asking me questions I had already answered several times over. I wanted to be cooperative, thinking that would get me a foolproof diagnosis. During one of my many incarcerations, I was put in the charge of a resident who could actually see the human being under my pallid skin. He had a bizarre sense of humor that kept my spirits up, and he took the time to sit on the edge of my bed and draw pictures of the biliary system. Thanks to him, I began to expect more personal consideration. Months later, the student health clinic director, Dr. Moy, told me that this resident had asked how I was doing. I was flattered that he remembered me. "Oh, no one ever forgets you," he told me. As I began imagining myself featured in the *Reader's Digest* as "The Most Unforgettable Character I've Ever Met," he added, "We hardly ever see a liver like yours."

Whether it was me or my liver he liked best, I was grateful to Dr. Moy for the special interest he showed in my case. He took on the role of my advocate, calling staff doctors to urge them to explain to me the procedures they had ordered and scheduling regular checkups just to keep tabs on my progress, including my emotional health. Having an advocate who is familiar with the system makes a great deal of difference both in enduring the physical rigors and in keeping hope alive. I wish everyone could have the moral support that Dr. Moy provided me.

In thinking back over the years I spent in and out of that hospital, I can recall horror upon horror: unnecessary surgery, ex-

cruciating examinations that still make my body recoil, screaming in pain with no one to comfort me. Yet I have to admit that I
was lucky. Anywhere else, I might have been treated as a bad case
of acute hepatitis, with no attention to the chronic nature of my
illness. But I have also learned, from the people who have told me
their stories, that the research hospital does not always deliver the
panacea its reputation promises.

I'm Not Crazy

For Phyllis Mueller and countless others, the lack of "something
to hang onto"—a name for the ailment—can be as unsettling as
the physical discomfort itself. They fear having to live out their
lives with a daily consciousness of illness that must be kept secret
because it does not have the medical profession's stamp of legitimacy. When you lose hope that the problem will go away, the best
consolation is to have something to call it—preferably a name
that others recognize. Then, when you are acting out of sorts,
they will attribute it to the illness rather than to your character:
She has arthritis, you know. She's probably in pain. As strange as
it may seem, Gloria Murphy's "wonderful sense of relief" upon
learning that she had a serious disease is not at all atypical. It is
echoed again and again in the stories told to me:

> One of my first reactions when the lupus was finally diag-
> nosed was, "Oh, thank God! I'm not crazy!" Because having
> strange symptoms for so long a time, you wonder if they're
> imaginary. And lupus has so many fuzzy things about it.

> There was great relief and a feeling of euphoria when they
> told me I had Crohn's disease. Gee, I was right. Something
> was wrong and this is what it was. I remember feeling kind of
> special and important. I could have just hugged that doctor
> for taking me seriously and deciding to get to the bottom of

this. He didn't say, "It's all in your mind. Go away and don't bother us."

———◈———

I felt good about being diagnosed as a manic-depressive because, number one, it meant that I was going to have some good periods as well as the bad—at least that's what I say when I'm joking around. The second thing is that the manic-depression is a biochemical disorder. It sort of takes the pressure off me to think, "Well, this isn't self-induced. It's just something that happens. You're not mentally ill because you made yourself crazy."

Giving the illness a name changes your perspective and allows you some control over its place in your life. The expression of relief, "It's not just me," means more than I'm not just imagining this, or "I'm not the only one who has this problem." It also means that there *is* still a "me" apart from the symptoms that have absorbed you for so long. *That* is the illness, you can say to yourself, and *this* is me, the healthy, real me I have always been. That reclamation of self may be what accounts for the euphoria.

Having proof of illness—something genuinely and demonstrably wrong with your body—gives you permission to let up on yourself, to come out from under the cloud of anguish, to stop feeling guilty about the hardship your complaints have imposed on the people around you. It allows you, in retrospect, a better explanation for all the peculiar developments in your life since the symptoms first appeared. Things that made no sense before begin to fall into place. The diagnosis gives you the perspective you need to revise your story.

Relief versus Grief

The feeling of relief is not always shared by the family and friends who have invested their emotions in your well-being. I remember a phone call from my sister who was concerned about a friend just diagnosed as diabetic. "He doesn't seem to be dealing with it," she said. "He's so cheerful, as though it hasn't fazed him a bit. We're worried that he's not facing up to how serious this is." I assured her that there was a sound reason for his cheerfulness: His general misery had a specific cause—a disease with a familiar name, a huge body of research, and standard treatments with proven rates of success. He would have plenty of time to "deal with it" later.

One person's consolation is another's grief, it seems. It is not unusual for friends and relatives to be crushed by the news that this person they care about is not just under stress, not just imagining things, but in real mortal danger. Before diagnosis, friends' awkward assurances that the problem will likely clear itself up in time can actually compound the anguish you feel by making you more reluctant to talk about your fears. No one understands how hard this is, you think to yourself. Ironically enough, euphoria after diagnosis may be equally isolating, with the moods reversed. How do you share your joy with such gloomy-faced visitors? As Delores Garlid recalls it:

> I remember having friends who were so uptight that I wasn't bent out of shape about having multiple sclerosis. And I kept saying, "I'm so relieved that I know. I'm so relieved." Rather than being extremely down, I was euphoric. It was a little unreal, but I kept saying to my friends and family, "I will get a little more balance after a while, but right now it's just such a high that I know what's going on. I don't like it, but I can't take it away, and I know that."

"High" is, of course, a relative term. Relief at diagnosis is only a plateau in what otherwise looks like a downhill course. It certainly is "a little unreal," because it makes no rational sense to those who can't *feel* the euphoria. Why should any sane person be joyful at the prospect of crippling or kidney failure or constant pain? It is precisely because the euphoria is so fragile that we insist on enjoying it to the fullest. We may resent well-intended efforts to bring us down to earth where we can deal more appropriately with the fact of serious illness. After all the discomfort and anxiety, the respite that certainty offers is to be cherished as long as it lasts.

There is more to euphoria than the thrill of solving a mystery, however. Diagnosis raises the hope of treatment and maybe even cure. Even a faint possibility of recovery may inspire fantasies about a whole new life in which values are shifted and outgrown patterns discarded. In this atmosphere, even the doctor's cautionary advice may go unheard. Robert O'Shea, who as a counselor has had plenty of opportunity to help people adjust to bad news, is amused at his own first response to heart disease:

> I wasn't fully aware that the doctor kept promising that open heart surgery wasn't a cure. It's only on reflection now that I can see what he really meant by that, because bypass surgery was simply removing the blockage in the arteries. There was absolutely no assurance that this would not return. A day and a half after surgery, I was reading and I was so aware that I was reading at a faster pace and comprehending more than I had before. So for me, it was a marvelous experience—kind of a new life. The physician would remind me that I now had to watch my diet, which had not been a problem before, but in my own mind, I was away and running. Even though he was saying, "We have just removed the blockage and it can come back," this was not going to happen to me because I was so perfect on all the other scores. "Euphoria" is a marvelous word for it, but it's also a kind of dishonest euphoria. You're on a motorcycle, you know, the wind is in your hair and you're really moving.

Whether it is honest or not, those of us who have experienced euphoria hardly regret it. It restores the energy expended in worry and allows our psyches a respite from pessimism. In all likelihood, it is a natural part of the "dealing" process. Yet, euphoria, like anxiety, is preoccupying, and it obscures the seriousness of our friends' and families' concern. How can they grieve adequately if the object of their grief refuses to cooperate and act grief-stricken? Leaving your gloomy friends stranded at your bedside while you float off on a cloud may look to them like selfishness. They need assurance that the dealing will come later. When Delores Garlid's friends suspected her of ignoring the hard truth, she told them bluntly, "I don't want to think about multiple sclerosis every minute of the day. Let me deal with this *my* way."

Sorrow, Shock, and Fear

While it is frequent and typical, euphoria is not a universal response to diagnosis. Many people are, on the contrary, overcome with sorrow at having their fears confirmed. Furthermore, diagnosis does not remove the uncertainty in every case. Having a name for what ails you brings little relief if the name is unfamiliar. Though I have had a good dose of euphoria each time I have recovered from an acute episode, I do not recall feeling relief upon diagnosis. The words "polycystic liver" elicited no sighs of "aha!" No one I talked to had heard of it. The indexes of the home medical guides listed other "polys" but not this one. The mystery had only become more embroiled. Even knowing what it was, the doctors were not sure how to treat it, nor could they predict how it would develop. Having heard over and over what an interesting case I was, I nurtured the peculiar, exalted sense of specialness that comes with having a rare disease. My later diagnosis of Caroli's disease brought neither clarity nor relief.

The psyche has other methods besides euphoria for protecting itself against the horror of degeneration and death. One of these is a seeming indifference that may be a type of shock response:

When the doctor told me I had multiple sclerosis, I sat there and said, "Oh, okay." No emotions did I show. He said, "I can't tell you what you can and can't do. We will let you know that sooner or later, but it's hard for me to explain." Nothing could really tell me that I had MS. He told me I should think about changing jobs because what I was doing was physically demanding. I said I wanted to stay where I was. He looked at me as if to say, "We'll see." It all felt very strange and very meaningless. I walked back out to my car to drive to my apartment, and that's when I broke down into tears. I just boohooed all over the place, not really knowing why, because I didn't know what it was he was saying to me.

Louise Taylor lived in this state for the first four years of her illness. Even when she accepted an invitation to join the National Multiple Sclerosis Society, reality had not yet broken through:

It was okay to serve on committees, but I didn't feel that it pertained to me. I met people who had exactly the same symptoms I did, but it still didn't feel like it was me. I had this wall separating me from the others. I was physically there, but that was about it.

Rosemary McKuen offers a similar description of that detachment:

It was like it wasn't really happening to me. I felt like there was part of me that was experiencing it and there was another part sitting on the outside watching what was going on with me. There was a real unreality about the whole thing.

Whether you are racing along on a motorcycle, drifting on a cloud, or sitting outside a wall, the reality of chronic illness, with all its inherent fears, eventually does catch you unawares. Gloria Murphy has a vivid recollection of when that happened to her:

And then after the flowers stopped coming and neighbors stopped baking cookies and the relatives stopped being quite so concerned, I started thinking, and it dawned on me that this wasn't going to go away, and that it was very likely to get worse. It was real frightening to wonder: Well, if I'm bad today, will I be bad next week or the next week or the next year? And so then I became angry—not angry at the Lord and not really too angry at myself and not angry at people around me. Just angry. I just wasn't happy with the world. About the time the anger started getting better, fear set in, and it was fear of the unknown. Fear of what would happen to me tomorrow, fear of what will happen to my children. I also had a fear of dying, that I would die very young, before my children were grown. People don't die from MS, but I was more worried about all the X rays I had had. Something else would happen.

The fear of a vague "something else" is understandable. Once your body, with its intricate systems of blood vessels, nerve networks, brain convolutions, and digestive passages, begins to malfunction, it seems as though anything can go awry. The involuntary mechanisms of heartbeat and breath command your attention in a new way, as though you don't trust them to continue. The disease seems to have a will of its own that resists efforts to contain it. In keeping with the military imagery used to describe illness, it does feel as if your body has been invaded by some sinister force. Not content with making your legs numb or shooting pains through your abdomen, it also saps your energy, makes you irritable, upsets your schedule, intrudes on your plans for the future, occupies your imagination—in short, takes over your life. The thought that the force exists *within* you, that it is a part of your own body acting in defiance of your will, is very hard to take.

Negotiating with Your Illness

The first step in accommodating yourself to chronic illness is, then, negotiating a coexistence with this sinister force that allows you some autonomy. The process of negotiation is seldom easy or pleasant. Most of us choose, at least in the beginning, to put our trust in a physician as mediator. If there is a standard remedy for the illness, the process may go smoothly, but a quick medical fix is no sure bet. What works in one case may be ineffectual in another, or may cause side effects that rival the original symptoms for pain and discomfort. Seeing your illness rage out of medical control is terrifying. The search for a remedy may be even harder to endure than the search for a diagnosis. When Bill Gordon learned that he has bipolar affective disorder, or manic-depression, caused by a chemical imbalance in his brain, he fully expected that the balance would be put aright with medication and he would be cured.

> They gave me one of the mainline drugs for depression and at the end of the first week I had a psychotic break. I just woke up in the middle of the night and started talking crazy. I thought I was going to be killed, and I shaved off my beard because I thought that was the one thing that could save me. Everything became very symbolic. My wife took me to the hospital and they locked me up in the psychiatric ward until they determined that the drug was responsible. Then they tried the other main line of drugs and I ended up in the hospital after a manic episode. I had a psychopharmacologist come in for consulting, and I spent just a miserable five-and-a-half-month period trying all different sorts of drugs and getting sick. I've had seven adverse toxic reactions. Nothing worked, and it was very discouraging. I had a lot of suicidal thoughts during that period. It wore me down psychologically because a drug might work for a little while and then give out, after I had gotten real hopeful. Finally I told the doctor, "I just can't take any more of this."

Four years later, after another hospitalization, Bill enrolled in an experimental treatment program and started on a new medication that he believes will keep him stabilized for a long time. His story, like many others, offers a kind of hope that demands patience.

It is difficult to maintain your optimism through a relentless cycle of false hopes and crushing disappointments. During my long bout of fever, I tested several antibiotics. Each time I was sent home from the hospital fever-free, I mustered hope and will and faith and counted on that awesome combination to hold my body temperature at 98.6. It failed over and over again. Soon it looked like nothing short of divine intervention would save me, but I had lost faith in that. Then one day, right at my hospital bedside, the infections specialist who had been called in on my case admitted to the fallibility of medical science. Striking his fist against his forehead, he cried, "Oh, I get so frustrated with this empirical method." That's all it is, I thought. No miracles, no magic, just the empirical method. I realized that we would have to continue testing antibiotics one by one, and sooner or later we would hit on one that worked. Eventually we did, and I enjoyed three years of good health. In the meantime, I, like Bill Gordon, found ways to compensate for medicine's shortcomings. He learned relaxation techniques and tried to build diversions into his daily schedule. I paced myself with my temperature cycle, working every morning before it began its climb, and sleeping in the afternoon when it peaked.

By demystifying the treatment process, the infections specialist alleviated my feeling of helplessness. There is much to be said for demystification as a means of restoring order and control. Seeing your illness for what it is physiologically and learning that it usually conforms to a limited, predictable pattern can at least allay your fears of the unknown. The American Heart Association, the Celiac Sprue Association, and other such groups know that lesson well and devote much of their effort to patient education. Some people take their diagnoses to the nearest medical library or search the World Wide Web for information on new treatment methods. Others at least learn the vocabulary needed to ask intelligent questions. Yet, given the complexity of an incurable illness and the range of variables that can affect its course, most of us still need skilled interpretation to help us apply this new knowledge to our own situations. Though the patients' rights movement has effectively challenged the old practice of "What you don't know can't hurt you," not every physician is a willing or able interpreter. How the diagnosis is reported can be a clue to how likely the doctor is to follow through and help you adapt to this new feature of your life. Three good examples from Ruth Sands, Delores Garlid, and Susan Alm will suffice:

> My first reaction was to burst into tears hysterically. The nurse and the doctor were very understanding. They didn't make me feel like a fool while I was crying. Then when I quieted down, they told me what the disease was. The doctor told me it was not the fast-progressing type, which was encouraging, of course, although I didn't really listen to what they were saying. I was too wrapped up in feeling sorry for myself. They certainly have faced this situation many times, and I thought they handled it very well. They made me feel like I was the only one they ever had to tell this to. I liked not just being another statistic.

> The neurologist came to visit me one evening and he had me get up out of bed and walk across the floor and touch my toes, and he said, "Where's the pain?" I said, "There isn't any pain in my leg. There's just this numbness in my toes." Then he asked me about the problems I had had with my vision when I was younger. Then he said, "Delores, I don't know for sure what's the matter, but what I suspect is that you have multiple sclerosis. What do you know about multiple sclerosis?" And I said, "The only thing I know about it is that people are in wheelchairs." He said, "Delores, what did you just

do when I first came into this room?" And I said, "Well, I walked across the floor and touched my toes." He said, "Never forget that you walked across the floor and are not in a wheelchair. Never forget that." So even to this day, I have not forgotten that.

——————

I happened to have a sensitive physician who was always there once the diagnosis was made. If I needed him, or if I had some crisis come up, he was available, and he was sensitive enough to schedule appointments very close together early on after the diagnosis. His role has been a facilitator in the sense that I am the one that indicates what the problems are, because lupus isn't a disease you can measure.

All three of these people feel that their doctors' handling of the bad news made it more bearable to live with, both initially and in the long run. Ruth was pleased to be trusted with the facts about her illness, even though her emotional state might have justified withholding them from her. Learning immediately that there is no single, inevitable outcome has helped Delores to be optimistic and take each new development for what it is, rather than as a sign of certain degeneration. For Susan, the assurance that someone is standing by to assist in times of crisis eases the terror of a disease that is prone to life-threatening complications. Knowing that her doctor will take the symptoms seriously even if they don't show up on laboratory tests encourages her to monitor the illness carefully and report changes before they reach crisis proportions.

While having a doctor who encourages optimism is no doubt of great help in coming to terms with illness, there is such a thing as errant optimism. Peggy Evans recalls:

When I became diabetic about 1960, the big thing in the medical world was that diabetics were not sick or handicapped.

They did not even like to call them diabetics. They were only people who happen to have diabetes, and they were no differ-ent than anybody else. They just had something that you could overcome. They talked about complications, but it was im-possible to find out what kind of complications there would be. I think that in their zeal to have a diabetic live a normal life, they weren't always realistic.

Consequently, when Peggy developed severe neuropathy twenty years later, she was taken by surprise and had to go through an entirely new adjustment process.

Grief over Lost Health

Peggy describes this process as corresponding to the stages of grief that Elisabeth Kübler-Ross outlined in her work on death and dying: denial and isolation, anger, bargaining, depression, and acceptance. While it would be overly simplistic to expect everyone's adjustment to follow this scheme, each of the emo-tions named is likely to manifest itself at some point over the long course of the illness. The emotions elicited by chronic illness do resemble grief in at least two basic ways: They are prompted by an experience of loss—loss of health, perhaps loss of the use of a part of the body, loss of hope for a long and unencumbered life, loss of peace of mind, and in some cases loss of a job or even of friends who find it awkward to stay around. Second, these emo-tions are preoccupying and make other matters in your life seem trivial by comparison. It becomes impossible to concentrate on anything but your immediate misfortune.

The boundary between an all-absorbing grief and a self-pitying egoism is rather vague. Fearing self-pity, some of us may try to reason ourselves out of grief prematurely. Yet, no matter how often you remind yourself that illness can afflict anyone and that your lot is no worse than anyone else's, the fact is that it is not just anyone who has been touched by it this time. It is you.

"Why me?" is, of course, an age-old question. While everyone asks it, many people claim to set it aside quickly in favor of "So it's me. Now what can I expect?" Much of the initial grief is, in fact, over *anticipated* losses. From her current vantage point as a teacher, wife, and mother whose health is fairly well stabilized, Carla Schultz remembers looking ahead after the onset of lupus to a life restricted to bare survival and thus devoid of meaning:

> When I was discharged from the hospital, I then had to go home and live. My friends were out working or in graduate school, and I had absolutely no purpose in life. By the time I got up in the morning and got dressed and had breakfast, I was exhausted. So the next syndrome I went through was a real—I don't know if it was grief or just depression, but I was very discouraged. What the disease did initially was put up all sorts of limits on my life: I'd probably never work feeling this lousy. I'd certainly never get married and I'd certainly never have children, and so that ruled out at least three options I could think of to do with my life.

Significantly, it was after discharge from the hospital and a striking improvement in her health that Carla began grieving. As she explains:

> The year in the hospital was to me less painful emotionally than the following year or two at home, because when I was in the hospital I was so sick I couldn't use my muscles. People had to feed me. I couldn't watch TV because I was so spacy. I can only remember clearly bits and pieces of that whole year.

After the Flowers Stop Coming

The urgency of staying alive day by day staves off the inclination for serious, extended mourning, as does the constant attention of doctors, nurses, and visitors. It is, to turn Gloria Murphy's phrase into a metaphor for this period, "after the flowers stop coming"— after everyone else's attention shifts away from your ill health and back to the daily routine—that grief is likely to set in. By the time you are ready to do the grieving that your family and friends expected you to do earlier, they may be impatient for you to get on with life again, especially if your health seems better. There is, of course, no correct schedule for mourning the loss of your health. People who report feeling detached and suspended in an air of unreality upon diagnosis also report having delayed grief. Two of the people I interviewed, Kathy Halvorson and Rachel Ryder, have lived in virtual secrecy with illnesses that came on in childhood. Both of them confided several months after their interviews that talking about their experience had unleashed profound feelings of anger and sadness.

Margie Rietsma, a single mother living on disability because of two mutually complicating illnesses, multiple sclerosis and rheumatoid arthritis, insists that people with chronic illnesses be allowed the right to grieve on their own schedules:

> When you lose your health with a chronic illness, you've lost part of you, just as if you'd lost a spouse. There should be facilities for people who've lost part of themselves to go and grieve. People were pushing me so hard: Accept, accept, accept. And they weren't giving me the time to mourn, to feel sorry for myself. People do not allow you to grieve for what you lose. They don't allow you to express it, to be angry, to be frightened, to feel a loss. It's just like going through the death of someone. You have to go through all the steps. You can't skip any of them. You have to go through the whole process, before you can come back and do or be whatever you can without that thing you've lost.

One of my most difficult experiences of grief followed a flare-up that occurred while I was visiting my parents over Christmas vacation. Still lacking a clear prognosis, I had been persuading myself that I was getting better on my own. This was the first time my parents witnessed one of these attacks, and it must have been frightening to see me writhing in pain and hallucinating from the high fever. They rushed me to the hospital emergency room where I was classified in critical condition. The family doctor did not expect me to pull through, yet I recovered in less than two weeks—surely cause for joy. My parents decided to celebrate my near resurrection by taking me out to eat. It was the worst choice they could have made. When the plate of food was set in front of me, I burst into tears. I couldn't touch it. One of the most frightening aspects of my illness is that my digestive system abruptly stops functioning. The disgusting heap of fried chicken and mashed potatoes was an all too graphic reminder that I could no longer trust my body. Nevertheless, I had to keep eating to sustain health and life. I had learned, once again, the distressing fact that life does not stop and allow you a reprieve while you get readjusted. My parents were chagrined. I tried to explain but could only stammer, "I'm going to die." They assured me that I was better now and ought not to worry about such things. But I wasn't thinking of the episode just passed. I was anticipating the next one. And I was grieving the death of that tentative hope that I might just plain get better on my own. This attack had reminded me that I would always be at risk. I could not even eat a chicken dinner without endangering my life. My parents treated my grief as self-pity and gave me a little talking-to, which made me snarl at them in anger. I remember that occasion as a moment of intense loneliness.

Misunderstandings like this reinforce the common belief that each case of illness is unique and private and inaccessible to everyone but the person inside the stricken body. While others can express sympathy, no one can truly empathize. Suffering, the saying goes, must ultimately be borne alone. As Phyllis Mueller puts it:

> I'm tired of people telling me what to do because they cannot tell my pain. They do not know where the pain is, they

don't know how it feels, they don't know how intense it is or how subtle it is. I have to decide that. I suppose it all boils down to mastery of my own life.

When the right to grieve is challenged, it feels as if your very integrity as a suffering human being is in question, and it is natural to burst into anger to defend yourself, as Margie Rietsma says she does:

> When my illnesses flare up and get really bad, I do grieve again. And I get real angry and real anxious and all the things I've felt before. And still people say to me, "You shouldn't feel like that." How dare you presume to tell me how to feel? You don't know what it's like at three in the morning to have this problem. Don't tell me I'm neurotic, that I have a lot of anxiety. Where are you at three in the morning when I can't sleep because the pain is so bad? When I can't sit, stand, lie, anything because the pain is so bad? When I've taken two sleeping pills and I still can't go to sleep?

Given time to run a natural course, the grief decreases, but because the illness persists, it is never really over. It surfaces again with each new physical complication. A life of chronic illness need not be bogged down by grief, though that can happen.

A Shift in Habits

Grief, a natural and healthy reaction, can nevertheless cloud your judgment at a time when some immediate and practical decisions have to be made: "Can I continue working at my job? Can I have a baby? Do I need to change my living habits?" Not everyone with a new diagnosis is forced into major adjustments in lifestyle. Most of us ease gradually into a way of life compatible with illness. Since few of us have a certain enough prognosis to begin making really decisive changes, it may be best to hang on to normal expectations as well as we can. I have never regretted sticking to my original plan to get a Ph.D., even though there were times when I doubted that I would live to complete it, let alone make use of it. Going to classes each day, reading assignments and writing papers, and measuring life one academic quarter at a time gave my otherwise chaotic existence a structure to undergird it. Getting involved in intellectual questions and the political issues of the day lifted me out of a melancholy preoccupation. If changes do need to be made, the need will make itself known. One day you stop to realize that you will probably fare much better if you discontinue one habit and adopt a new one. Robert O'Shea, ever looking on the bright side, found just the image for this gradual adjustment:

> I think chronic illness is a little bit like a receding hairline. It's very, very gradual. You learn how to part it. You learn how to wear a cap. You learn how to get a tan. And after a while you say, "Hey, this is me." After a while you begin to find an awful lot of handsome men who are bald.

Still, no matter how reconciled he may be to his bare pate, the bald man will surely admit that he would rather have a full head of hair. To repeat Delores Garlid's assurance to her friends, "I don't like it, but I can't take it away, and I *know* that." There are, however, degrees of knowing; from acknowledgment that you are sick to realization that you probably always will be, to what is termed "acceptance"—the ability to regard the illness as your own normal state of being. The aftermath of diagnosis is only the first stage in a lifelong coming to terms.

Chapter
2

Naming Your Unhealthy Self

"I think of myself as a very healthy person—with a problem."

At a party many years ago, I was introduced to a man who worked as a staff physician in the division of a hospital where I had been a patient two years before. We tried to establish whether we had met there, but neither of us seemed familiar to the other. "If you had been his patient, he would probably remember your blood pressure better than your face," his wife teased, but he objected, claiming that doctors of his generation are concerned for the whole person. Having no more common ground to explore, we wandered off in search of more engaging conversations. I settled into a comfortable group of friends, while he made small talk with my husband, whose favorite topic for stand-around chitchat was the inadequacy of the medical profession. He must have started his diatribe on my case with this poor man, because suddenly the doctor spun around on his heels and yelled across the room, "I know you! You're the liver from Chicago!"

I felt like a secret agent whose cover had been blown. Moving away from Chicago, leaving the site of my most painful memories behind, had given me a chance to escape that identity. At the same time, I had dropped my married name. I was a new person—or, rather, a newly restored former self, healthier and more independent. And here I was, being unmasked in public—worse than unmasked: flayed open, with muscle tissue peeled back like a picture in an anatomy text. That enlarged, defective organ that already occupies more space in my body than nature entitles it to had grown to outrageous proportions, obscuring the rest of me.

In the eyes of the friends and strangers assembled in that living room, I had turned into a walking, talking liver.

Of course it's a funny story and a great joke on the impersonality of medical care. I laughed as hard as anybody, and I have told it over and over to enliven other parties. Yet, like the best humor, it has a poignant edge. It plays on one of the daily anxieties that accompany chronic illness: that your identity will be subsumed by your disease. Who you are will be determined by what is wrong with you. If you want to be forthright, your name tag should read: "Hello, I'm a diabetic."

As if private anguish, grief, and unwelcome changes in your habits of living aren't enough to contend with, a diagnosis of chronic illness also tosses you up against a whole new set of social expectations. It raises questions that can only be answered satisfactorily after much trial and error: "How do people expect me to behave now that I am sick? Will they treat me differently? Will they think less of me? Do I have to overcome the illness to prove myself? If I give in to it am I giving up? In short, what does it mean to be unhealthy in a health-conscious culture?" Chronic illness, by demanding that you focus your attention on your body, will almost certainly affect both your self-image and your public persona.

The One-Legged Marathon Runner

Every culture has preconceived, if not always clearly articulated, notions of how people confronted with serious illness ought to behave: Should they accept the illness as a given or doggedly pursue a cure? Are they allowed to moan and mourn, or must they practice stoicism? Should they claim special, protected status or be shunned and hidden away? Should they assume blame for their illness or are they innocent victims of external forces? In American and other Western cultures, there is a dual prescription that the sick person can't help but experience as a dilemma. A concise statement of it appears in an article by Anne Hawkins in the *Journal of Medicine and Philosophy*:

The expectation of our culture is not only that the sick will continue to function as best and as long as they can (modern pharmacology helps to make this possible), but that their illness will serve as an opportunity for bravery and heroism. While this is a harsh expectation to impose upon the ambulatory sick, hospitalization imposes equally harsh demands that the patient endure a radical depersonalization and an infantilizing passivity. Thus, we expect the chronically ill to be psychologically capable of both maximum activity while ambulatory and maximum passivity while hospitalized, and we expect this flexibility to take place during a time when the individual is often undergoing extreme fear and bodily pain.

This dual expectation is spelled out in a slightly different manner by sociologist Erving Goffman in his book *Stigma*, a theoretical formulation of the ways in which people who somehow differ from the norm behave and are perceived. On the one hand, a person with a stigma is expected to acknowledge that difference, not hide it or be ashamed of it, and to feel a common identity with others who have the same stigma. On the other hand, this "stigmatized individual," to use Goffman's term, "is advised to see himself as a fully human being like anyone else" and to engage in normal behavior as much as possible, not use the stigma as an excuse to be or do less than those who do not have it. In order for this to happen, the stigma has to be passed off as an insignificant happenstance. At the same time, the stigma must never be forgotten or denied. "And because normals have their troubles, too," Goffman observes, "the stigmatized individual should not feel bitter, resentful, or self-pitying."

Goffman's book was an eye-opener for me. At last I understood why I have such a strong impulse to trip the proverbial one-legged marathon runner every time I hear his virtues extolled. It's just not fair. People who are caught up short by illness should not have to scramble to prove their full human value to their healthy counterparts. What the marathon runner represents is a seldom-questioned assumption that illness is a test of character. If you assume that much, it doesn't take a great leap to believe that people afflicted by illness have been specially selected to undergo the test. One of the first questions the newly unhealthy ask is "Why me?," which poses yet another dilemma: Either you are special and have been given a unique opportunity to transcend ordinary human experience, or you are deficient and have been given a penance to pay to atone for your deficiency. Feeling exalted and feeling unworthy are really two sides of the same coin: a conviction that you must be different from everyone else or this wouldn't be happening to you. Whether you settle for one of these explanations or try both of them on at various times, it is easy to overlook the fundamental truth that who gets sick is a random, arbitrary matter with no moral implications.

Even enlightened, well-meaning people who accept the randomness of misfortune may still insist that you *respond* to illness as though it *were* a test of character. Let it be said again and again until the truth sinks in: Human beings afflicted with illness are no better and no worse, no more heroic and no more cowardly, no stronger and no weaker in spirit than those who live healthy, unencumbered lives. We all share a common human destiny: to live as fully as the circumstances of our lives allow—no more, no less. Next time someone offers me the one-legged marathon runner as a model to emulate, I will challenge that person to run alongside him.

Who Am I Now That I Am Sick?

Even if you know intellectually that illness is not a cosmic selection process, the sense of difference—the stigma—can be felt quite strongly at the time of diagnosis: Something is *wrong* with me, out of whack, *abnormal*. I am changed somehow. I am *different* from how I was before, and I must be different from the healthy people around me. In these new circumstances, you may feel pressed to forge a new identity that in some way encompasses the illness: Who am I now that I am sick? People who emerge from the hospital with visible handicaps have their new identities thrust upon them. We who have no easily recognizable wounds have more leeway. We can even try to keep our illnesses secret and our original identities intact. This does not spare us from confusion, however. After thirty-five years of very private suffering, Kathy Halvorson says, "I still have a hard time figuring out if I'm just a complainer, and other people put up with it and don't react to their bodies as I do to mine."

The option of "passing" as healthy is a dubious privilege. It means living always with the threat of disclosure. You learn to be circumspect in whatever you do so as not to reveal your illness in socially inappropriate circumstances. Keeping the illness secret is no guarantee that your identity will be left untouched. Both illness and its medical remedies alter moods, change facial expressions and tone of voice, limit mobility—in short, make you seem different from how you would be if you were healthy. Other people may see your shortcomings and make judgments about your character, without knowing that illness is the cause. There are social taboos that prohibit you from announcing at every turn, "I'm really sick, you know." Sometimes, it seems preferable to have a visible disability. At a conference I attended, a healthy-looking woman with ankylosing spondylitis stated the problem succinctly in response to a comment by a paraplegic woman using a wheelchair: "You want recognition that you're normal. I want recognition that I'm *not*." Susan Alm found that wearing a brace on her hand after surgery had some advantages:

> Some small part of me said, "You know, this is good because now people know that I can't do things. It's a symbol that there is something wrong and there is a reason you can't do things," whereas I've had people ask me questions like "Why aren't you out running your own business?"

Passing as healthy does have its rewards. When people find you out, they will probably admire you for pulling off the masquerade so successfully. More important, conforming to a social standard of health is a way of keeping up your own, private determination not to let illness reduce the quality of your life. Yet, there are times when the illness demands submission and passing becomes impossible. You should then be permitted to let up on yourself and nurse your discomforts without losing either your self-esteem or the respect of others.

Unfortunately, popular culture offers few good models of behavior in times of illness. Most of the people I talked with simply shook their heads when I asked if there was any one person they admired who dealt with illness in a manner worth imitating. Interestingly, some people just assumed I was searching for examples of stoicism. Rosemary McKuen praised the late Norman Cousins, author of *Anatomy of an Illness* and *The Healing Heart*, for taking charge of his medical care. Phyllis Mueller offered former First Lady Betty Ford, who bravely went public with her alcoholism and her breast cancer. Today they might mention celebrities like Naomi Judd, Annette Funicello, or Michael J. Fox, who put their fame to work to raise public awareness of hepatitis A, multiple sclerosis, and Parkinson's disease. Esther Green, worried about losing her vision and becoming housebound as a result of lupus and diabetes, watches blind people get on the bus without help and thinks, "If they can do it, I can do it." What they exemplify is an achieved independence, not a supernatural heroism.

Adjusting to the news of chronic illness is, of course, more complicated than simply outfitting yourself with a new persona. After all, illness is not just some abstract, metaphysical state of being to be incorporated into your identity. It really hurts. It is really frightening. How you see yourself and project yourself to others depends on how much you hurt and how frightened you are. It is not easy to adopt an ideal persona when your body is imposing a different one on you. For example, I am usually pleased when people say they see me as a strong and spirited person because of the way I manage in spite of illness. That is just who I would like to be. But to maintain that image when I am sick, especially when my physical appearance belies it, I have to rely on humor and intellect to cover the sorrow and fear that the illness arouses. The effort can be exhausting, precisely because my physical resources are weak. I will continue making the effort, though I am grateful for opportunities to let go and spill it all and be accepted just as I am.

Achieving your ideal image can even be a little dangerous. If you manage to behave in an admirable way in times of crisis, people may come to expect it of you. During my long fever, I took on a major editing assignment even though I could have excused myself on the grounds of illness. I attended editorial committee meetings faithfully, hanging my intravenous bag from a picture hook on the wall and dripping in my antibiotic while we talked. One of the people I worked with then never misses an opportunity to recall the impression I made and to tell others about my heroism. As good as that might be for the ego, it makes me uncomfortable. I don't know if I could do it again. I also feel duplicitous, because it was by no means an act of heroism. I did it for a selfish reason: to keep myself from succumbing to a deadly depression. My imagination was not working well enough to do my own writing, but I knew I had to do something besides just be sick. I clung to that editing job for dear life. Rosemary McKuen, too, continues to be rewarded for the cheerfulness she showed in the early stages of her illness, but she has found it difficult to maintain it over the long run:

> I had a reputation of being enormously cheerful. I always tried to be as cheerful as I could, even in the hospital. The only time I wasn't able to was when I was down in X ray. I felt it was my responsibility to always at least try to be gracious. It was the good patient syndrome, but it was the good person syndrome, too. People get mad at me when I'm not cheerful. Now what I do when somebody asks me what's the matter, I say, "I'm pensive." Pensive is okay. Crapola is not okay, because I'm such a cheerful person. Pensive will cover a host of sins.

Yes, Misery Loves Company

People who have the more common or better-researched illnesses, like diabetes or heart disease, or those associated with campaigns for government support, like HIV/AIDS or breast cancer, can find identity and companionship in the group they have unwittingly joined. Meeting others who have adjusted to the illness without losing sight of who they are is comforting. In the supportive atmosphere of a peer group, you can more easily acknowledge the illness as a new, permanent feature of your personality. Inspired by a co-worker with multiple sclerosis who sought him out when he heard about the diagnosis, Al Keski hung a cartoon on his office wall that said, "A week ago I couldn't spell it, and now I are one." It was a way of owning up to the change in his life without being undone by it.

There is a risk, of course, that too close an identification with the group will promote an excessive concern with the illness you share. A few people I interviewed stayed away from illness organizations to avoid being caught up in a subculture that they would never have joined by choice. This is a risk that the organizations themselves struggle with all the time. Internet Web sites may serve these tentative members well by preserving anonymity and distance while still providing the comfort of mutual understanding.

Me and/or My Illness

The identifying terms that illness groups apply to their members are problematic and often in dispute. Gloria Murphy, active in the National Multiple Sclerosis Society herself, objected to the use of the term "MSer" in its newsletter: "It's like a stereotype, a label. I'm a person first—a person with MS." This desire to keep the human in the forefront accounts for the recent trend from "the disabled" to "persons with disabilities." Ironically, an Internet mailing list on disability that I subscribe to consistently abbreviates this preferred term as "PWD's," hardly a humanizing move. "Disabled" was already a replacement for "handicapped," which replaced "crippled." This perpetual cycle of euphemisms is not really a problem of language, but one of attitude. A word takes on negative connotations only when the condition it describes is thought to be demeaning or shameful. Nancy Mairs in *Plaintext* boldly reclaims the straight-talking "crippled" to describe what multiple sclerosis has done to her body.

Gloria's "I'm a person first" illustrates a need that many of us feel to visualize the illness as smaller than ourselves. Rather than letting the illness overtake our identities, we try to find some confined space within ourselves or our lives to contain it, and then draw boundaries around it: "*Here* is the illness. I will only let it make *this* much difference." It is, of course, easiest to do this graphically when the physical defect is confined to one organ and the symptoms are clear. Encouraged by her doctor to look upon diabetes as a manageable problem, Peggy Evans tried to imagine what place she could allow the illness to assume in her life. She was, at the time, the mother of two small children, so she decided to regard her diabetes as a third child and give it just that much attention. A reader who checks in with me periodically likes to refer to his illnesses as his "DATE," an acronym for diabetes, arthritis, (hypo)thyroidism, and epilepsy. I have a totem onto which I can project my worries: a rock that looks uncannily like a heavy, oversized liver. A friend spotted it on the shore of Lake Superior and lugged it back for me.

Body Image

This new identity you acquire or create for yourself has its primary source in body image. How drastically your sense of self is affected by illness depends on several factors: Whether the illness alters your appearance. Whether you believe that your health is subject to your control. Whether you see the illness as a natural phenomenon or as an alien force that has invaded your body.

How much attention you paid to your body before getting sick. How much and how frequently you hurt. Whether the illness affects your sexual capacity.

Illness-induced changes in appearance make for a confused, ambivalent self-image that depends considerably on how others see you, or how you think they see you. If the illness causes weight loss or leaves you "pale and peaked," my mother's favorite phrase for my appearance, you may become subject to public scrutiny. At the height of AIDS-phobia, a friend who was skin-and-bones after a lengthy intestinal illness noticed unkind stares on the street. A ravaged look at the least prompts concerned whispers. People will measure your health by how you look, extending sympathy when the bags under your eyes turn blue and rewarding your presumed progress when you flesh out and your color returns.

As much as I hate being pale and peaked, I can put up with it when my illness is raging and people know of its presence. When I have no other choice, I can even glory in it, impressing people with what a vital spirit this fragile, frizzy-haired, walking ghost possesses. Or, when looking decent requires a Hollywood makeup artist, I can pretend that looks are trivial and even give up combing my hair. Nevertheless I feel embarrassed when people say, "You're looking so much healthier. Last time I saw you, you looked just awful." No matter how much sympathy I get for it, I don't *really* want people thinking I look awful, even in retrospect.

Many people experience not weight loss but weight gain as their illnesses are diagnosed and new remedies are tried. Of the people I talked with, those who puffed out on cortisone or retained fluids were far more self-conscious than those who looked pale and peaked. The signals that weight gain transmits are confusing ones, and the newly plump are as likely to be judged unkindly as to win sympathy. Bill Gordon gained forty pounds during his initial bout with manic-depression, partly because of the medication he was taking, but also because of "being at home, being close to the refrigerator, and not being active enough," he says. His changed body image compounded the depression by making him ashamed to be seen by people who knew he had been hospitalized for mental illness. He was afraid they would take his weight gain as evidence that he was no longer capable of self-control. His appearance was the outward sign of a more fundamental sense of failure:

> There's a whole self-image and self-confidence issue that comes about. I have a lot more self-doubt than I ever had before, and I don't know what I can tackle. I don't know what to commit to. I don't know what I can follow through on. I hate to make commitments now, because I'm afraid I'll have to drop the ball. I'd just like to have some stability. I keep telling myself that if I can have a year of stability and a year of productivity, then maybe that would bolster my confidence.

Because the physiological basis of mental illness is still not fully understood, Bill may be held more accountable for his condition than someone with diabetes, for example. He is not alone, however, in his diminished feeling of self-worth. The physical deterioration wrought by ulcerative colitis undermined what little self-esteem Rosemary McKuen had managed to foster after a difficult adolescence:

> I'd feel just debilitated. I looked like a concentration camp victim. I would feel weak mentally, too. I would feel like a weak person. At that point in my life, psychologically I was a weak person. I didn't have a real strong psychological foundation. That would just exacerbate that lack of self-esteem. It was just basically "dump on Rosie." There were always self-effacing, self-deprecating kinds of thoughts.

When your physical appearance fluctuates with weight gain and loss, your image of yourself may fade from consciousness altogether. Susan Alm finds buying clothes difficult because it forces her to think about how she looks. She finds herself heavier than she had imagined or looking "puffy and yucky" because her skin is broken out. Esther Green has had the unsettling experience of catching her reflection in a store window and seeing an unfamiliar "moon face." She even calls herself "The Face" and thinks, "Nobody should be on the street looking like this." Yet neither Susan nor Esther has the kind of face or physique that would draw cruel stares. They look quite normal—invisibly ill, after all. Only they and a few old friends who remember how they looked before are aware of any difference.

A Body Out of Control

Loss of bodily functions can also damage self-esteem. The inability to keep your body healthy and under control feels like a personal failing. As Susan Alm puts it:

> It's very frustrating when you can't pick up a spoon or stir a pot of soup. When you have to have someone come in and do the simplest, very basic things for you, it's a very difficult thing to deal with. And it's difficult not just because your life is disrupted by having another person there, but because it's admitting that you can't take care of yourself.

An illness that strikes in terroristic fashion, defying all attempts to contain it, is not exactly compatible with a strong sense of self. In addition to that terror, Rachel Ryder had to bear the shame of epilepsy at a time when it was barely understood and very stigmatizing. Between ages fifteen and twenty-two, she lost consciousness in a seizure at least once a month, sometimes as often as once a week:

> I never knew when. I would have them in school. I would have them on the bus. I would have them at movies. Anywhere, day or night. I was very scared. I was scared to

sleep alone. Oftentimes I would go to bed and wake up with different pajamas on, because I wet my bed when I had a seizure. My mother would change the bed, change my clothes, and I would never know it.

When I would start to shake, I would grab onto something solid like a tabletop, so my hands wouldn't shake. I would keep my mind focused on one thing, saying, "I'm not going to get sick." That's what I called it: "getting sick." "I'm not going to get sick." And sometimes it would just pass then. Other times it wouldn't work. But it would be a great relief if it did work. It would be a miracle.

Rachel's shame was certainly not eased by her family's silence about her illness. Even the doctor, she believes, refused to acknowledge what the illness was, for fear of offending her mother's sensibilities. It was only after leaving home and becoming independent that she received a correct diagnosis. Thanks to the effectiveness of Dilantin, she has not had a seizure since. Nevertheless, the weak self-image has followed her through adulthood. She is surprised when people think her competent or treat her as though they really like her. Once when she was attending a university class, there was a commotion in the back of the room. She turned around to see a classmate having a seizure. The woman was admitted to the hospital for tests, and Rachel summoned up the courage to visit her, to offer herself as evidence that people with epilepsy can live normal lives. The day the woman came back to class, however, Rachel was shocked into realizing that the terror and shame had not left her:

> I sat through that class and I got more and more upset to the point where I thought I was going to have a seizure, I was so nervous. I got worse and worse, and I was shaking constantly. I was scared to go to sleep at night. I was a real basket case.

After a few days of this, her husband called a therapist and she went in for counseling that focused to a great extent on identity questions. In the meantime, she learned that the woman in her class did not have epilepsy after all but only an adverse reaction to medication she was taking. Rachel was again ashamed that she had bared her soul inappropriately. Coming to terms with a changed identity has been a long, agonizing, and very private process for Rachel, aided, ironically, by her husband's alcoholism. Participating in his treatment convinced her that to see herself as something other than a "closet epileptic," she would have to make a public admission. A few months after our interview, she spoke about her life with epilepsy to an adult education class at her church and found it a transforming experience. Hearing herself praised afterward for her courage, stamina, and honesty greatly relieved her shame.

Even illnesses that do not carry the social stigma of manic-depression and epilepsy can generate shame. In a culture overrun by joggers in quest of complete physical mastery, a body that defies control is a source of humiliation. A "buff" physique is as exalted as a beautiful face, and it is bad enough to be out of shape, let alone malfunctioning. Much of the popular attention to "wellness" reinforces the notion that complete health is accessible to anyone, as long as you find the right diet or exercise program or have the right mental attitude. Too simplistic a cause-and-effect link between will and bodily function offers the healthy a false sense of security and results in a "blame the victim" approach to illness.

Sick and Sexy?

Americans' obsession with sex doesn't help much, either. As we worry about what the ongoing, day-to-day consequences of this illness will be, sex is usually high on the list. Loss of sexual function diminishes self-esteem and threatens our most intimate relationships. Robert O'Shea observes:

> Some people I know who have suffered heart attacks move into massive states of depression. Why? Because anytime

you become sick, if you're a man, somehow you're less a man. One of the first questions that's asked in the therapy groups is "Can my wife and I have sex?" Now, they may not even have had it with any regularity before, but it just seems to be the question.

Though not everyone experiences a real physical impairment, such as impotence, debilitating fatigue, or pain that prohibits intercourse, many people suffer at least a temporary psychological impairment. Constant attention to the body and its malfunctioning may leave you too self-conscious about your bodily responses to let them take a natural course. It may be difficult to get sexually aroused, especially if the sensations of sexual pleasure evoke the body's own memories of pain. Medication, too, may suppress sexual response. Disregard for hospital patients' privacy, combined with the intrusiveness of frequent physical examinations, may leave you feeling too vulnerable to submit to sexual touching. A major psychological inhibition for men is fear of impotence, while women fear that illness will make them sexually undesirable. Viagra has solved the problem of dysfunction for some men, but the pharmaceutical industry has yet to come up with a pill that makes women attractive. Rosemary McKuen faced the fear in a more concrete way than many of us do when her diseased intestine was removed and she was fitted with an appliance to catch her bodily waste:

> I had to go through a total reevaluation of my physical appearance. I couldn't ever imagine myself attracting somebody in a bikini or in any of those normal, stereotypical ways. I would eventually have to confront the reality that I was having this ostomy, and if I was to develop any kind of an intimate relationship with anybody, that was going to have to be dealt with. So I had to look deeper down beyond the flesh. It was like having someone say, "Okay, all your usual ways of relating to people have to be completely changed." I had always used my body and my appearance. That was

half of what I did. You wonder, "If something happened to my husband or if our relationship broke down completely, how would I tell somebody? What would I do? Would they want me? Would I be afraid to be sexually involved?"

Rosemary, like most of us, faced this fear alone, working it out cautiously with her husband. There is still a need for counseling in this area, and for doctors unembarrassed to talk about sexual functioning in their review of symptoms. Left to our own resources, many of us measure ourselves against Hollywood images and judge ourselves inadequate. It is not some universal standard of sexual attraction and prowess we should strive for, but a sense of entitlement to whatever degree of sexual pleasure our imperfect bodies are capable of.

Self-Love and Self-Hatred

Self-love is a prerequisite for healthy sexuality, but it is difficult to achieve when your body is out of whack. Hatred of your own body is certainly not conducive to good health, sexual or otherwise, but it is a common consequence of chronic illness. The onset of endometriosis in adolescence brought Kathy Halvorson into a conflict with her body that is still unresolved:

I hated my body. I never hated my body worse than when that pain came. I felt real separate from myself. I still feel very separate from my body. A lot of the time I feel trapped by it. I feel that I got a bad deal—until I see a film on people who are really sick. When I used to get those pains, I would really pound on my body, I would slug myself. I would hit my abdomen just over and over and over again, because I hated it. And I thought somehow if I could hit myself hard enough on the outside, the inside would stop hurting. Or somehow my body would get the message that I was not accepting of that at all. I still expect anything from my body. It's like it's out of control.

Some people maintain that a previous commitment to physical fitness has saved them from this bodily self-hatred. They have learned how to interpret the body's own signals that something is wrong and are skilled at asserting control. Duane Barber always excelled in athletics, but now that multiple sclerosis has limited his choice of sports, he has become passionate about bodybuilding:

> This is an extreme, but if I had to I would crawl to the gym for a workout. I work my legs because I don't want that strength to diminish. A lot of times those legs feel heavy as oak trees, but I do it. You see, I feel good. When you exercise, your body releases a hormone called endorphin, and it gives you a feeling of euphoria, and that's another reason to do it.

Duane says that keeping up this regimen makes him feel as though "I have the disease and the disease doesn't have me." Trying his hardest absolves him of responsibility for his bodily defects. Interestingly, Duane talked openly and without shame— yet with some grief—about becoming partially impotent. Louise Taylor is another lifelong athlete who pushes herself to her physical limit. This has not, however, spared her from feeling that "there's no end to my body just falling apart":

> I still like my body—when it's working. That's a top priority for me, to go to the athletic club and work out with the weights. I spend a lot of time working at it, and I feel better about things and about myself. But when people tell me, "Oh, you look great," I laugh, because I know I feel like this body isn't worth two cents. So there's this dichotomy going on. People will say, "You're attractive." I hear it and it's meaningless, because deep down I don't feel it's worth anything. It's like a game I'm playing to keep myself going. I get to the point where I start feeling good and I start taking an interest in my body and in outside activities. And then that's

all taken away from me, so that I have to start round one
again.

In moods like this, Louise tells her friends, "Take me to the nearest car lot and trade me in." The analogy with the run-down used
car is a familiar one. Indeed, high-tech medicine has made re-
placing the body piece by piece a more likely option in some cases
than keeping it in tune. Don Welke, a mechanic in his early thirties who has been diabetic since age eleven, had no sooner recovered from a kidney transplant than he began anticipating a
pancreatic transplant that he believes will restore him to health.

The Mind-Body Split

Whether we batter our bodies or appease them with daily
euphoria-producing exercise, it is hard to avoid that phenomenon known as the "mind-body split." When your body is defective and cannot be fixed, the idea that mind and spirit are of
greater value than mere matter has considerable appeal. Imprisoned in our malfunctioning bodies, we will nurture our intel-
lects and our spirits, like blind people who develop their senses of
hearing and touch. The mind-body split has been dismissed as an
unhealthy and destructive idiosyncrasy of Western culture, to be
replaced with a holistic approach to life that reconciles the two.
That wholeness is a wonderful ideal in the abstract, but difficult
to achieve if your healthy mind balks at reconciling with a recal-
citrant body. The easiest way out of that conflict is to ignore your
body altogether. An artist friend of mine once asked me if I had
ever considered modeling for life-drawing classes. She had noticed the unusual positions I sat in and how long I could hold
them, while I continued to look comfortable and relaxed. "You
must really be in touch with your body," she said, in the jargon of
the day. She couldn't have been further from the truth. How
could I be in touch with a body that wasn't there? I didn't know
what unusual positions I was sitting in or whether or not they

were comfortable. I had simply cast my body aside like a child playing statue, letting it land where it may.

Taking refuge in the mind-body split is a delusion, of course. You can't literally sever your mind from your body. When illness flares up, your body asserts its presence and claims a hold on your mind. This is a truth overlooked by those who believe that you can think yourself well. Cooperation between mind and body yields to conflict. Your body becomes not just a separate part of yourself, but an enemy to overcome. For the short term, this state of war might be tolerable, but when the condition is a chronic one, it can be self-destructive, leading to shame, self-hatred, and terror. One way to resolve that conflict is to see not the body but the illness as the enemy. The language that portrays illness as an invasive force reflects a desire to reclaim the body and restore it to health. Whenever my doctor looked at my hospital chart and said, "You're febrile again," I would insist on rephrasing that as "The fever is back." His sentence implies that the fever is my own state of being and emphasizes my body's failure to function properly. My sentence places the blame much more clearly on the bacteria reproducing in indecent proportion in my biliary system. His statement is probably more accurate. The distinguishing feature of Caroli's disease is that the liver produces stones that block the flow of bile and create stagnant pools where bacterial infections are easily produced. The liver does this itself. In other words, my own body—not some alien invader—is inflicting this pain on me. Distancing myself from the illness psychologically is as difficult as curing it physically. The same holds for people with autoimmune diseases like lupus and arthritis, unless they can track down the foreign agent that damaged their immune systems.

Apostles of Imperfection

Reconciling mind and body means, then, asking whether blame is necessary. The shame, self-hatred, and sense of failure that chronically ill people are subject to are not entirely natural responses. They are provoked by a tendency to equate "normal" with "perfect" when, in fact, imperfection is the rule. Those of us who are even more imperfect than average have to set new norms, and not only for ourselves. I like to think of the chronically ill as "Apostles of Imperfection," all set to free a stressed-out culture from the demands of perfectionism.

A question that I have learned to ask myself when my healthy identity is in question is "Am I mostly healthy or mostly sick?" Like the classic test with the half-full (or half-empty) glass of water, it is often simply a matter of perception. If I am feeling good enough to do what I have set out to do during the day, I ought to pronounce myself normal and healthy, even though my skin is pale and my hemoglobin low, even though I can't eat fats without severe indigestion, even though fatigue sometimes cuts my workday short, even though I am never really free of fear that my liver will stop working.

Achieving this new identity as a mostly but not completely healthy person is, of course, a mind game that neither requires nor brings about any change in your physical condition. It is a game that we play constantly and must be prepared to lose sometimes. Often, we have to steel ourselves with reminders that healthier people may well interpret as denial or rationalization, like this one from Gloria Murphy:

> Every now and then I think about myself in terms of not being the same as I was five years ago or ten years ago and not being able to do what I did then. I remember when I could go out and walk with the kids. I used to coach track. I remember when I would run with six-year-olds. But then I get over that. I think, "Well, I have my scooter now and I can go faster than them."

The need to forge a new healthy identity, even though you're sick, makes you alert to signs, images, aphorisms, and proverbs that aid or hinder that effort. For years, I refused to say the line in the Apostles' Creed, "I believe in the resurrection of the body." I was not about to commit myself to eternal life with this one. Then I happened across James B. Nelson's book *Embodiment: An Approach to Sexuality and Christian Theology*, which put a whole new slant on bodily resurrection:

> Salvation, in its original meaning, is healing. It is the reuniting of what has been torn apart and estranged. It is the recovery of a center and a wholeness in that which has been split asunder. It is the overcoming of alienation within the body-self, between the person and the world, between the person and God. . . .
>
> Thus, beyond the dualistic alienations, we experience the gracious resurrection of the body-self. I really am one person. Body and mind are one; my body is me as my mind is me.

"Resurrection of the body" has come to mean, for me, reclamation and revaluation of my body, which is as much me as my mind. This mental shift has brought about a change in behavior. When my body asserts its presence, I try to pay it some attention before it gets too demanding. That means exercise, naps, stress-relief measures, and a bit of makeup, not to mask the flaws, but to train myself to look in the mirror without cringing. This attention, to a reformed ascetic like myself, can feel lavish, but I justify it as an effort at self-love which is important to the maintenance of good health and the search for a healthy identity. As James Nelson writes, "To know who one is, the person must also be aware of his or her own facial expressions, body movements, postures, and body feelings." In the case of chronic illness, becoming familiar with our bodies is a prerequisite for ending the alienation—and sheer terror—we so often feel.

A diagnosis of chronic illness is almost certain to upset the applecart of identity, and it would be foolish to expect to set it right again very soon. Instead, personal identity is usually in flux, because of a continuing experience of change, sometimes for better, sometimes for worse. It takes time and care to achieve the balance that will hold it steady. "Who am I now that I am sick?" raises the questions "Well, how sick am I?" and "How much does that matter?"

To see how those questions get resolved, I asked each of the people I interviewed, "Do you think of yourself as chronically ill?" Some people said yes and some said no, and their answers were unpredictable. Here are some examples:

> Yes, it is part of my personal identity because the illness I have is a chronic illness. I go from thinking of myself as a recovering person to thinking of myself as a sick person. It's very hard for me to think of myself as a well person at this point. Hopefully I will have some good periods where I can psychologically think of myself as a well person who has a problem that arises from time to time.

> I don't think of myself as chronically ill, but when something flares up, man, I know that I have a chronic disease. But I don't wake up and think, "I'm going to be ill today." It's just that the diabetes has become so much a part of my life that I don't think about being chronically ill—only when I have the symptoms, like my kidney going bad and the problems with my eyes.

> I think I've been one mass of illnesses all my life, but I have never really thought of myself as chronically ill until I got labeled chronically ill. This was in the last six years, with the kidney disease, because it is a life-threatening disease. The others were all inconveniences.

I don't think so. I think that I don't have the mind-set of a handicapped or disabled person as a general kind of thing. Now, I have to rethink that almost every situation.

———◦———

Yes, I do. I guess to me that means the absence of a long, sustained period of good health, where you don't have to cancel anything, where you're free to make plans, where you can do anything you want, virtually. To me that's good health.

———◦———

That's kind of hard to answer. I realize I have an illness, but I don't think of myself as sick. I think . . . It's hard to answer. But I know . . . I think of myself as a very healthy person—with a problem. That is more what I think. I have no real health problems, except for the MS.

When I examined the answers more closely, I realized that they were more alike than different. Most of them were equivocal and many were temporal, determined by immediate circumstance. They could be rephrased as "Yes, but . . . " and "No, but . . . ," which really mean the same thing: "I know that I have a chronic illness, but that is not all there is to me." The last answer quoted certainly brought home to me that a healthy sense of self can be maintained without denying the fact of serious physical degeneration. It was spoken in somewhat slurred speech by JoAnn Berglund, who was moving around her living room with the help of a walker and wearing a wig because her medication had made her hair fall out. She had just crossed the boundary from invisibly ill to visibly disabled. In her spontaneous groping for an honest answer to that question, I saw what I would call acceptance: acceptance of yourself as healthy on your own terms, "problem" and all.

"The Liver from Chicago" who opened this chapter doesn't mind being "the Liver from Minneapolis" when the circumstances are appropriate. My now retired doctor used to carry my X rays to medical conventions, introducing me as the sideshow freak that I must be from a physician's perspective. But in his direct dealings with me, he clearly respected my integrity as a very healthy person—with a problem. When I need reassurance that I am something more than sickly, I remember a pronouncement he once made after a routine physical examination: "Except for a few hundred stones, you're in excellent health." Even when that is no longer true, I want to keep my identity intact. What all of us need to work toward is an authentic sense of self that can hold its own even in the worst of times, so that we can admit being sick without any loss of self-esteem.

Chapter
3

The Etiquette of Chronic Illness

"How aaaaare you, really?"

I was attending a meeting one night when I felt the first stirrings of pain in my liver. Since I sometimes have trouble distinguishing, at first, between indigestion, nervousness, and incipient liver malfunction, I make myself assume that it is something transitory and benign. I work my psyche very hard to quiet the nervousness or to wait out the indigestion. If it is "real" pain, it will assert itself regardless. As I concentrated harder and harder on the business of the meeting, pulling my focus away from my midsection, I thought I could feel it subside. Then we took a break. I tried not to show my distress, though I passed up the coffee and cookies. A very kind, friendly woman who knew I had been sick recently came up to me and said, "How are you feeling now? Are you getting better?" I heard the "now" through an amplifier. Her question, a common courtesy, became a demand to know my state of being at that precise moment. Though I managed to back off a bit, I still could not say "fine." I responded that I never know from one moment to the next how I am going to feel, that the illness is ever present and threatening, and that I can only hope for the best. Then I started over on my attempt at mind control. Luckily, the pain did eventually go away, but I felt as though I had committed a serious breach of etiquette in exposing my terror to someone who simply wanted to wish me well.

The standard greeting "How are you?" is a usually innocuous social ritual. It does not call for a recitation of horrors, but only for assurance that all is well enough for conversation to proceed. But when the answer is not, in truth, the formulaic "fine," the question becomes an awkward reminder of our culture's ambivalence about illness: Where do you draw the boundary between a collective concern for each other's health and respect for an individual's privacy? How much do others need or want to know? How much do you need or want to tell? Keeping these claims in balance is a matter of etiquette that is also fraught with emotion. Invisible chronic illness can turn this seemingly trivial greeting into a fearsome moment of decision, and there are no clear rules to follow. What a relief it would be to know that all of us, healthy and sick, had similar intentions and expectations, so that no one had to feel either affronted or embarrassed.

Nearly everyone I interviewed expressed discomfort or even annoyance with the "How are you?" greeting. In good times, conversational habits are hardly a major issue, and most of us adhere to the forms. Yet when serious illness is an immediate worry, the question can seem coldly dishonest. It tantalizes you with an opportunity to reveal your suffering, yet reminds you that physical complaints are not suitable for polite conversation. Instead of answering the question with painful truths, most of us give in to custom. There is a more pointed variant, however, that seems to call for an honest response: "How aaaaare you?" or "How are you feeling?" People who know you have been sick imbue the question with meaning by rephrasing it this way. Their concern about your health is so evident that you may even feel obliged to answer correctly: "Both legs are numb and I've had double vision for two weeks, but now I'm starting on steroids." If these details have been weighing on your mind, "How are you feeling?" can be a welcome invitation to share the burden. On the other hand, it can feel like an invasion of privacy. Your illness becomes the topic of conversation whether you want it to be or not.

Choosing an answer means assessing, very quickly, your state of health and the benefits and hazards of revealing it, as well as the likely intentions of the person asking the question: Do they sincerely want to know or are they just showing concern? Few of the people I talked with had come up with satisfying answers.

After a lifetime of frequent pain, Phyllis Mueller has decided she wants to spare other people and preserve her image as a mostly healthy person:

> When I was twenty, feeling like I do today, if you said to me, "How do you feel today?" I'd have said, "Oh, not very good." At the advanced age of forty-two, if you met me on the street and said, "How do you feel?" I'd say, "Oh, good." I don't really feel good. This is good compared to last week. I don't want you to have to carry that around. I don't want you to carry that image of me as always being sick.

In her own mind, Phyllis reinterprets her answer so that it will be truthful: "good compared to last week." Carla Schultz, too, has devised a code to protect her privacy without lying:

> Well, I feel crummy again today, thank you. I don't want to impose that on people all the time. If people ask me how I am, I'm going to say, "All right," and that means "crummy." If I'm feeling really well, I will say, "I am terrific." It took me several years to get to "terrific," but I've said a lot of "all rights."

It is curious that both Phyllis and Carla rationalize their way around the hard truth. Even though "fine" will do just fine, they cannot say it without feeling a little dishonest.

No matter what you choose to say, "How are you?" evokes the unspoken "Well, how am I?" It requires you to take the measure of your aches and pains when that may be the last thing you care to think about. If physical recovery is unattainable, you can at least try to preserve your sanity by taking your mind off the illness. Frequent requests for progress reports impede that effort. If you rely on mental diversion to ease pain, innocent questions can even be harmful.

Though illness is ever present in our lives, still a worry in times of remission, we do not always want to think about it. For one thing, it gets very tedious. People who have been acutely ill for short, intense periods may remember deriving comfort from other people's interest in their health. They want to give us that same comfort. But when you know that the illness will not go away, constant attention to it is not comforting. It makes your ill health loom larger in your life than you want it to. Even in the midst of a debilitating setback, it is important to claim the privilege of thinking and talking about other things: the state of the economy, a movie you have just seen, the trials of your children's adolescence. We who live always with illness want to maintain the pretense that we are healthy enough for our present needs. After all, a successful pretense may be the closest we ever come to feeling really fine.

When you know that the sight of your waxen face in a crowd alerts others to be sure to ask how you are, you feel like a conversation stopper. Once you have given your own sorry account, asking "And how about you?" of a healthier person seems absurd. Friendships, too, are thrown off balance by this obligatory attention to illness. During my longest bout of illness, I tried to keep up with a group of friends who were getting together every week or two. My presence always depended on my state of health, though they even accommodated me by meeting at the hospital. It is not surprising that illness became the dominant feature of my life in their eyes. When we got together, they talked and asked each other about a variety of things, but I was expected to report on how I was feeling. Because I was, indeed, preoccupied with my ill health, I often couldn't remember what was happening in their lives well enough to ask them about it. They seemed to have more common ground with each other than I shared with any of them, until my health improved and we could move on. In the meantime, I began to feel marginal to the group.

The "How are you?" greeting is especially troublesome for the chronically ill because it presumes the possibility of improvement. At worst, it sounds like a test of achievement: "Haven't you managed to shake this thing yet?" At best, its frequent reiteration shows how difficult it is for people to understand chronicity, that this illness will never be over but is, in fact, a constant feature of your life. To let her acquaintances know how tiresome the question was getting during one long flare-up, Gloria Murphy wore a T-shirt that said, "Just fine, thanks." Delores Garlid has a quick but firm way of responding to people who do not understand the nature of multiple sclerosis. It draws an important distinction between her physical health and her general state of being:

> Before they knew about the disablement, they never asked, "Well, how are you today?" I kind of bite my tongue. These aren't people that I am around socially. I don't spend the time with them that it would take to sit down and explain. So I try to be honest with them. "The disability is the same as it was yesterday, but I'm fine, thank you."

Equally troublesome is the formula many people use to avoid posing the question: "You're looking good. You must be feeling better." It anticipates an answer to "How are you?" that may well be incorrect. Appearances can be very deceiving. For example, the bloom on the cheeks may be nothing more than a side effect of medication. You can correct the misperception by saying, "No, I'm not," but that seems cruelly frank, because it overlooks the good wishes behind the greeting: Maybe if I say you look better, I will help you feel better. How can you disappoint this kind person who is so hopeful about your recovery? Phyllis Mueller has learned over the years to interpret it as a measure of her success at passing as healthy: "At least I was able not to drag all these other people down with me. I was able to enjoy that part of today. Wasn't that marvelous?" When you hear the statement once too often, however, it begins to sound like "I sure hope you're feeling better so that I don't have to hear all the gruesome details about your illness." Heard this way, it invalidates your suffering and precludes you from sharing your burden with others.

Acknowledge the Illness

So what's a kind and well-meaning but sometimes bumbling acquaintance to do? It is much easier to say what *not* to do. Though not everyone with a chronic illness recoils at the "How are you?" question and its more pointed variants, it is safest and kindest not to ask it so directly. Since the boundaries between a collective concern for each other's health and an individual's private experience of illness are so fuzzy, they need to be defined on each occasion. The person with the illness ought to have that prerogative. Most of the time, it is comforting to have the illness acknowledged, briefly and discreetly, without being put on the spot. A quietly spoken comment like "I've been thinking about you and hoping for the best" conveys a wish without demanding its fulfillment. It calls for nothing more than "Thank you." Yet it is open-ended enough to allow for further conversation, if that is desired. It respects personal privacy without turning it into isolation.

Acknowledgment, pure and simple, affirms us as fellow human beings by recognizing the significance of illness in our lives without calling us to account for it. It is certainly preferable to deadly silence and forced jocularity. Two different expressions of the same sense of embarrassment, they imply that illness is shameful, something to be ignored or masked over. It is difficult enough to come shuffling into a crowded room on limp legs or bent over in pain. Trying to make eye contact with averted eyes or feeling as though you have wandered into a convention of amateur comics only makes matters worse, especially if you know that they have been talking to each other about your misfortune. There is a happy medium between being turned into a public spectacle and being rendered invisible.

Acknowledgment, pure and simple, without an overlay of forced emotion, allows the person with the illness to set the tone for talking about it. Those of us who have come to some fairly livable terms with our illnesses have little appreciation for pity. The dictionary defines pity as "condescending sympathy, . . . a disposition to help but little emotional sharing of the distress." If you are despondent about being sick, it is tempting to lap up all the pity you can get, but in the long run, it is not helpful or satisfying. It stops short of true involvement. False optimism is no better. Many people think that offering an assurance of recovery lifts the spirits and makes illness more bearable. In fact, it does just the opposite when it is clearly not grounded in reality. A distant cousin's miraculous recovery from a vaguely similar illness is not a strong enough foundation to build hopes on.

Attempts to minimize the illness are not helpful either, especially if they rely on comparisons with people in worse circumstances: "Just be thankful you don't have terminal cancer like So-and-so." A single comment by a casual acquaintance seldom has the power to ease sorrow or anxiety that is, after all, a natural side effect of illness. When it *does* happen, it is usually because someone has recognized and acknowledged the validity of our own feelings. Asked what she would say to healthy people if she could give them one clear message about the experience of chronic illness, Carla Schultz, who has lupus, responded:

> *Acknowledge* that the person is not feeling well. Don't say, "Oh, you'll be better in a couple of weeks. You probably aren't taking good enough care of yourself. Have you gotten enough chicken soup?" Just say, "This is really a crummy place to be, isn't it?" As soon as somebody said that to me, it lifted the whole guilt right off my shoulders. I wouldn't be sad and maudlin. I'd be relieved and say, "You're one of the few people who understand."

No Easy Dos and Don'ts

It would be nice to provide a short and simple list of dos and don'ts, but such a list would presume unanimity. We do not in fact all agree with each other, nor does each of us have consistent feelings about any one situation. Some people do like to be asked frequently to talk about their health, and nearly all of us like it on occasion. Others insist on total privacy. In the absence of consensus, specific issues of etiquette can be considered in the light of good sense and sensitivity: If I ask, "How are you?" am I willing to listen to the real answer? Is this person's state of health of genuine interest to me? Am I ready to offer practical help or emotional support? Can I respect this person's privacy? Will I be offended if I get an answer that I know is not truthful? Can I acknowledge the illness as a fact of life without acting embarrassed, without expressing pity or shame, and without feeling obligated to offer a solution?

Responsible people that we are, we chronically ill, can, of course, ease these awkward situations by taking the initiative: answering briefly but confidently, assertively changing the subject, or showing an equivalent interest in the other person's well-being. At a time when your illness is raging and that is what everyone knows about you, the best bet may be to anticipate the questions and forestall them. I was walking down the street one day and met an acquaintance who had recently lost a child to sudden infant death syndrome. I immediately wondered what consolation I could possibly offer her. Of course, I felt awkward. But she put me at ease. Before I could say a word, she turned her attention to my little daughter and asked how old she was and whether she was walking yet. At first, I was amazed that she could do that without bursting into tears. Then I caught on: Her way of managing an otherwise all-consuming grief was to become an active participant in the "How are you?" ritual. She had simply beat me to it and precluded me from making yet another awkward, tiresome, pitying expression of sympathy. In the course of a short conversation, I did find a natural place where I could acknowledge her child's death without obligating her to talk about it. Later I realized that was the only consolation a passing acquaintance could really offer.

It would be wonderful if "How are you?" *were* an authentic question, given new and fresh import each time it was asked. A genuine mutual interest in everyone's well-being would be healthy, indeed. And there may be no better antidote to the preoccupying worry that accompanies a long-term illness than concern for the welfare of other people. It is our culture's many ambivalent notions about illness that make these moments so awkward. Imagine if illness were just a matter of fact, a shared practical problem with no overtones. "How are you?" could be the lead-in for "What do you need? Is there anything I or anyone else can do to help you live more comfortably?"

Company and Practical Help

I have lost count of my hospitalizations over the last thirty-five years, but in each instance, there has been no shortage of people willing to help. While offers of help are certainly appreciated, some are more helpful than others. In general, specific offers are more valuable than open-ended ones. "Be sure to let me know if there is anything I can do" may be said with sincere generosity, but it is not easy to act upon. Illness that saps the body's energy and preoccupies the mind leaves you in sorry shape to organize your life. Deciding what needs to be done and who to call can take more out of you than just muddling along on your own. How much easier daily living becomes when you have one list of people ready to bring dinner over, another list of those willing to take your children for a few hours, and another of those who can drive you to the doctor's office in the middle of the day. Impromptu calls from people who ask, "Is there anything you need or would like to do today that is hard to do yourself?" are also appreciated. If the call comes just as you are struggling with household tasks or deciding whether you have the energy to run an errand, it is like having a fairy godmother materialize in front of you.

Visiting the sick is a long-established social courtesy, but there is a difference of opinion about how helpful it is to the one being visited. Some people say they feel comforted when close friends turn up at the hospital, but uncomfortable when casual acquaintances or co-workers see them at their worst. Many people rely on the company of visitors to keep their spirits up, while others prefer privacy that allows them to focus totally on physical recovery. Advice columnists like Ann Landers and Dear Abby frequently publish letters arguing that the hospital is a place to rest, not to socialize. Every time I read one of those, I think, "Oh no, there goes another visitor." I certainly relish the diversion that talking with visitors provides, though there are times when I am not up to it. At those times, I prefer the close friends who can simply be present in a comforting way without expecting anything of me. Louise Taylor speaks for many of us when she says:

> I usually have to get a single room, because there are so many people. I'm lucky to have so many concerned people. It's been really nice. It almost makes me feel like nothing's wrong. Sometimes it seems like one big, continuous party. It helps me not to think about what's actually going on with me—now whether that's good or bad, I don't know. I'm very appreciative of my colleagues and close friends, but there was this one man I used to work for who came to visit me, and I was embarrassed. There I was in my pajamas. I felt stripped, totally stripped. It's like that front was taken away, whatever it was I was being. It's like now you've seen the bad side of me, the sickly side of me, and you won't appreciate me or like me. Otherwise it's been a relief to have people come in. But sometimes I've had so many visitors that I didn't have time to myself. There were times recently when I started to look at the situation and I just wanted time to write in my journal or to think about how I was going to cope and deal with my life. But I was being bombarded with all these other stimuli. There was a difference for me between what I was getting from my friends in the hospital versus what I got when I left. I felt like an invalid once I got out, because I was so dependent on other people.

It is hard to maintain the balance between company and solitude when visitors are governed by their own schedules and are most likely to drop in unannounced. The assumption is that you are just lying in bed anyway, always accessible and generally alone. Sick people, especially, are subject to daily rhythms and might like the option of asking visitors to come at times of peak energy. There may be a rhythm to flare-up and recovery as well, a larger pattern than the daily routine. I notice that most of the expressions of concern I receive come when I am first hospitalized. Though I am groggy with pain medication and would rather drift off to sleep, I try to stay alert enough to answer the telephone and assure callers that I will be all right. The calls and visits taper off as word gets around that I am doing better. Yet that's when I appreciate company the most, when I am well enough to be bothered by the isolation and monotony.

Like Louise, I feel a great difference—a loss even—between being visited in the hospital and being back at home. The one, big party image is an apt one, especially for the evening hours when visitors arrive in clusters. Lying in bed and joking about it all comes easily. But at home afterward, in the face of normal, daily life, you discover how weak you are and that you need not only good cheer and companionship but practical help. I often find myself longing for the attention that overwhelmed me the first day or two in the hospital.

Useless Advice

A common error that well-meaning acquaintances make is offering unsolicited advice. "You should take better care of yourself" carries a double message: You deserve better treatment than you are allowing yourself, which can be helpful if, for example, it comes from a co-worker who is encouraging you to slow your pace until your health improves. Knowing that you can take care of yourself without depriving others eliminates a major source of anxiety. But the statement can also be heard as a judgment: "If you took better care of yourself, you wouldn't be sick." It proposes a simplistic personal solution to a problem that is not subject to self-control. The guilt that Carla Schultz mentioned feeling is fed by this tendency to look for causes of illness, and solutions, in the sick person's behavior. It doesn't help that health care organizations are classifying more and more diseases as "behavioral." My daughter brought home a worksheet from her eleventh-grade health class that sorted diseases into "organic" and "lifestyle." Liver disease, I learned, is a lifestyle problem. Excessive drinking may lead to cirrhosis and the use of unsterilized heroin syringes to hepatitis C, but taking better care of myself will not straighten out my crazy bile ducts.

Pop psychology has unleashed some annoying forms of help. If only we think more positively, people advise us, or, conversely, if only we delve more deeply into what is *really* troubling us. One reader told me about a solicitous in-law who attributed her long-developing illness to her mother's recent death. The in-law offered herself as an amateur therapist to help her talk the grief out and "deal with it" so she could get well again. Again, the perception that we are not dealing properly with our illnesses opens us up to charges of "denial," a violation of the Truth-or-Consequences ethos of American popular culture. Again, it is important to say that what passes for denial is a legitimate choice, a strategy for keeping life in balance, for surviving the emotional ups and downs. As a friend of mine likes to say, "Denial is God's way of giving you a good night's sleep."

When illness persists, what you obviously need most is a remedy. And so the newspaper clippings about miracle cures and the referrals to specialists and the computer printouts about the healing power of herbs come spilling in upon you. With time, most of us learn to accept these things with a tolerant "thank you" that acknowledges the sender's motives without regard to the usefulness of the advice. When advice-giving becomes habitual, however, it is hard to be so forbearing. Gloria Murphy tells how depressed she felt when a man who keeps close watch on the newspaper sent her a clipping about a woman who could walk normally again as a result of a special diet. She already knew that this option was not available in her case. Shortly after that, she saw the opening she needed to let him know, gently, that his advice was not helpful. He had sent her a clipping about a man with multiple sclerosis who performed as a square dancer. Gloria wrote back, "I never wanted to square-dance anyway. Why should I care to now?" The clippings stopped coming.

Even though it is easy to say thank you and tune it out, unsolicited, and especially unwarranted, advice works as a steady reminder that few people really understand the nature of your illness or care deeply enough to be informed. One of my readers was deeply hurt when her friends tried to talk her out of taking prescription drugs. They were sure that treating the disease "naturally," with herbs, would be much better for her. She didn't want to have to tell them that without the medication, she would very likely die. There is a great deal of difference between advice offered out of a kindly ignorance and advice offered by someone who has learned enough about your illness to be watchful with you.

Useless advice is also an intrusion. I never really understood my resentment about newspaper clippings until a conversation with a friend who has a history of compulsive overeating. She told me how being overweight had turned her into an object of public scrutiny. People she barely knew felt free to monitor her choice of food, to recommend diets, to advise her about dress, and even to make jokes at her expense to motivate her to lose weight. The implication of even the well-meant advice is that her overeating, an addictive behavior pattern she is trying to change, is evidence of a moral failing: "Since you obviously can't control yourself, it is up to the rest of the world to keep you in line." As our society grows more and more health-conscious, good health, too, becomes a virtue, and its absence a vice. My friend and I agreed that we want to claim responsibility for ourselves and have our choices respected, even if they sometimes prove to be wrong. That doesn't preclude asking certain people who understand the problem to intervene and help us when things seem to be going badly.

In Control of Me

News of illness makes its way quickly around a circle of acquaintances, especially if they work together or live in the same neighborhood or belong to the same religious congregation. Some people are uneasy about this and prefer to control the spread of information they regard as highly personal. Some also want the chance to tell people themselves, to prevent misunderstanding and to show that the illness is not embarrassing. It helps me immensely, however, to be spared "How are you?" and to know that my friends are answering the question "How is she doing?" instead. I imagine a safety net being spun all around me by people willing to intervene in my life if needed.

Most of us don't mind people talking behind our backs as long as they have our best interests at heart and as long as they share our convictions about what our best interests are. The latter point is crucial. For example, others often misjudge our physical capacity. They limit their expectations of us and avoid asking us to do things they would not hesitate to ask if we were healthy. Susan Alm, who has lupus, tells of being passed up for committee work at her children's school because the other parents are afraid of endangering her health. When she is weak and in pain, she feels protected, but when she is functioning better, she feels deprived of the right to make the choice herself. On the other hand, friends eager to pick up our sagging spirits encourage us to take on more activity than we can handle or suggest typical morale boosters that are inappropriate to our conditions. An afternoon at the beach is hardly relaxing to someone who must avoid sunlight. Through long experience with illness, we get to know our physical limits. If we are reasonably cautious with ourselves, we can be trusted to stay within those limits. The best bet is for people to ask us to do things and then allow us the right of refusal, without explanation. It should suffice to say, "I would like to do that, but I'm sorry, I can't."

The right of refusal is worth safeguarding, no matter what. That includes the right to refuse offers of help that threaten to complicate rather than ease our lives. Those who need solitude to grieve over setbacks want to be able to turn down offers of help without offending the people who make them. In a crisis that takes both a physical and emotional toll, having to placate other people's sensitivities is just too exhausting. However, help that is misdirected can often be accepted with adaptations. Peggy Evans, who walks unsteadily as a result of diabetic neuropathy, has a concrete example of this that serves nicely as a metaphor:

> If someone wants to help me, they usually want to take my arm and guide me, and I don't like that. I don't feel secure. So I hold out my hand and take *their* arm. There's a big difference. Then I am in control, I feel, of me.

If acquaintances, who are governed by etiquette, are to become friends, who are motivated by empathy, then they need to internalize the basic rules of behavior toward people who are chronically ill: Respect the right to privacy, without turning it into a stigmatizing isolation. Allow opportunities for candor without imposing an obligation to tell all. Acknowledge suffering where you see it, without the delusion that you can ease it. Affirm the right to take responsibility, even if you disagree with the choices made. Realize that the goal of your involvement is to help restore a sense of normalcy, which sometimes means ignoring the illness altogether. Often the most welcome help is diversion: an absorbing book or audiotape, a scenic drive, or a lively conversation about anything but illness.

Public Exposure

We who are invisibly and interminably ill risk our own greatest breaches of etiquette in situations where our ill health is suddenly exposed. Most of us strive to pass as healthy, not necessarily by being deceptive, but by keeping the impact of the illness on our lives as understated as possible. Those moments in which the disguise is lifted are fraught with difficulty: How much explanation do I owe? How much can I offer without being boring, self-indulgent, or crude? How can I guard my privacy without being rude to people? How can I protect my health without imposing hardships on others?

There are three bits of evidence, besides the sudden, unexpected onset of pain, that force me to go public: (1) I occasionally have an intravenous tube taped into my arm. (2) I have two Asian daughters who obviously did not grow in my womb. (3) I have to turn down alcohol and restrict myself to a low-fat diet. All of these giveaways elicit questions like "Why?" or "What's wrong with you?" Growing up Danish American in a small Minnesota city, I was taught not to be "forward." Consequently, these nosy questions struck me as bizarre, and I saw no option at first but to be completely and tediously truthful. Now, I treat each of these three opportunities for disclosure in a somewhat different way.

When people spot my intravenous tube, I usually give a very brief but factual answer like, "I have an infection and the only treatment for it is an antibiotic that isn't available in oral form yet." While truthful, this is really only a partial answer. The infection itself is not the illness, but a single manifestation of my liver disease. There are other remedies, but I am allergic to them, and I need the rapid delivery of the intravenous antibiotic because letting the infection get out of hand would endanger my life. Luckily, I've had fewer IV tube encounters now that there are some stronger oral antibiotics on the market. Minimizing the illness in this way allows you to reveal only as much as you need in order to be polite and to protect yourself. Shaking hands is a painful ordeal for Margie Rietsma, who has rheumatoid arthritis. She simply demures and says, "I have arthritis in my hands." Actually, the arthritis affects her entire body, including internal organs, but, as long as strangers don't touch her elsewhere, they don't need to know where she hurts.

Wearing the intravenous tube is the closest I come to being disabled in the usual sense. Because my veins are tiny, full of scar tissue, and hard to locate, I avoid using my arm to keep from damaging the insertion site. I sometimes see questions about the tube as an opportunity to promote better understanding of disability. This is especially the case when I have to "drip" in public. I administer the antibiotic myself, on a regular schedule that sometimes interferes with other activities. Rather than decline those to maintain privacy, I take the IV bag along and tape it to a light fixture or a wall. Sometimes I break the ice by explaining, briefly, what I am about to do and assuring everyone that I can manage it myself. But other times, when the whole process is getting me down, I let them know that being one-armed is no treat. I got plenty of sympathy and admiration as a one-armed single mother with two squirmy preschoolers, but I often felt afterward as though I had been wallowing in martyrdom. How do you tell when you have broken unwritten rules?

All but the most secretive among us have felt the temptation to tell all at the slightest invitation. After a long bout of illness that has worn down your family and friends, confiding in a freshly sympathetic human being can be restorative. Spelling out the details is also a good way to convince yourself that you have a reasonable understanding of the illness, besides a shaky set of emotions about it. Educating others may even be necessary to your survival. This is especially true for people with insulin-dependent diabetes, uncontrolled seizures, or other illnesses subject to abrupt crises. The diabetics I talked to generally choose to understate the problem when confronted with questions, to avoid being labeled as sickly. Instead, they explain it selectively to people they might need to depend on if they go into coma or insulin shock. As one of them, Don Welke, puts it, "I'm not about to wear a sign across my chest that says 'I am a diabetic.' People don't really have to know that. The people who do know need to know for my own sake."

The second set of questions was far more troublesome. I soon lost patience with people who stared at my beautiful Korean-born daughters and demanded to know, "Where are they from? How long have you had them? Are they really sisters?" I was tempted to ask in return, "Where did your kids come from? How long did the labor last? Are you sure you're their father?" I usually managed to wheel my grocery cart into another aisle before the inquiry got to "Do you have any of your own?" If I couldn't get away, I would just say, "Yes, these two are my own." Adoption is a curiosity for which the ignorant demand a good excuse, but it was more critical to me to firm up my kids' family security. Are they really sisters? Of course. Just watch them fight over who gets to ride shotgun in the car.

Adoption was a perfectly satisfying way for me to build a family. I have honestly never felt regret or sorrow about not having biological offspring. Nevertheless, when my mother announced my daughter's impending arrival to the neighbors, she felt compelled to add, "Cheri has that liver problem, you know." Norma Bellisch, a new mother with multiple sclerosis, explained with regret:

> When we adopted our little girl, it was hard to tell people, "Well, you know, years ago I had this strange disease, and I never told you because I didn't know how you would react. But now in hindsight I have to tell you what I did have." I wish I would have told them the truth from the beginning.

"But why?" I wonder. Do other people really deserve apologies for your infertility or, as in my case, for your avoidance of the health risks that childbearing would entail? The fallacy is easy to slip into. When I was in my twenties and getting questions like "Do you have any children yet?" or "When are you going to start a family?" I would answer, "I'm working on my Ph.D.," as though graduate school were a form of contraception. But I knew I was camouflaging the true answer. Having my children has made the issue moot. Kind, considerate people are the ones who say, "What wonderful daughters you have," not the ones who want their presence in my life justified.

Were it not for our obvious racial differences, I might even choose to lie about my daughters' biological origins. There are occasions when lying is an appropriate response. A little fibbing, anyway, can save you from detection. People who swallow pills in the presence of others can easily give a false explanation that spares them a soul-baring account of their chronic illness. This protective strategy is especially common in the workplace. Kathy Halvorson, who loses her motor control without warning, has a reputation at work for clumsiness. She contributes to it herself, cracking jokes whenever she collides with a doorjamb. She would rather have her colleagues laugh at her than know how debilitating her illness is. Sometimes lying can help release resentment about the limitations the illness imposes. Faced with a surprisingly common experience—being called to task for parking in a space reserved for the disabled—Lily Washington, a healthy-looking woman with asthma, would rather be thought selfish and inconsiderate than be humbled into showing the sticker that does, indeed, entitle her to the space. She meets righteous anger with sheer orneriness.

Fussy Eating

Of all the instances in which an illness can suddenly come to light, having dietary habits that attract attention is probably the biggest nuisance. So much social etiquette applies to eating that people on health-related diets can hardly avoid showing bad manners. It is an insult to pass up food that is graciously offered to you. It is rude to ask about the ingredients of a dish before you taste it. It is disgusting to pick at your food and take out the bits that you don't like or to dab at it with a napkin. Yet when I eat out, I do all these things. I am, in short, a fussy eater, the scourge of the dinner table. To ease my self-consciousness, I remember the famous writer in Sylvia Plath's novel *The Bell Jar* who ate his salad with his fingers, leaf by leaf, with such aplomb that no one dared to let on that it was peculiar. The growth of vegetarianism and reports on the harmful effects of fat, sugar, alcohol, and caffeine have made fussy eating more acceptable, so I am called to account less often than I used to be. However, as a slender person who watches her fat intake, I am still encouraged to take generous helpings of pasta in cream sauce and chocolate cheesecake. "What have you got to worry about?" people ask. Well, let me tell you. . . . Spoiling appetites is another social no-no, so it is hardly the time to talk about sluggish bile flow or stones caught in the ductwork. I try to be brief and to the point: "I have a liver disease and I can keep it under better control by watching my diet."

If dinner conversation is lagging, there is a risk that my liver disease will be put on the agenda. Everybody has something to say about health and illness, and it promises a lively switch from the weather or the latest diplomatic impasse in the Middle East. My liver disease, like any natural catastrophe, is bizarre, out of the ordinary, a matter of general curiosity. I am given the spotlight and expected to offer testimony on what it is like when nature goes berserk: "What's wrong with your liver? What happens when you get sick? Do you take medication?" I acquiesce easily enough, wanting to be calm and matter-of-fact. And telling about my illness spares me, too, from the strains of making small talk. Maybe I am performing a valuable service: allowing people a vicarious experience of illness so they can "purge pity and fear with pity and fear," Aristotle's test of a good story. But I am never quite sure when to stop. When does anatomical detail become too graphic? When does candor begin to look like self-pity?

There are many ways to respond to an invitation to eat away from home. Peggy Evans, on a strict diabetic diet, tells the host that she will eat before she comes and saves her bread allowance so she can have a roll and coffee. Asked to explain, she says, "I'm on a medical diet," and stops there. Phyllis Mueller, with her unpredictable digestive system, finds that eating out produces more anxiety than enjoyment, so when friends invite her, she says, "I would really like to get together with you, but can we just sit and talk instead?" Kathy Halvorson eats a little of whatever is offered and bears the consequences later. "I don't like being a prima donna," she explains. As much as I enjoy being invited to people's homes, I find a restaurant menu easier to handle. Knowing how much energy and pride people invest in cooking for others, I am always hesitant to cause trouble with advance warnings about my diet. But I also know what trouble there will be if I arrive and find lavishly and lovingly prepared dishes that I dare not touch. So I usually do say something, hoping that it doesn't sound like a plea for special favors. I propose simple solutions, like setting aside a dish of salad with no dressing. I have learned, however, to be straightforward about what I can and can't eat. Once I told a woman who had not yet planned the meal that fish and vegetables were always safe. She served shrimp, the fattiest seafood, stuffed in an avocado, the only high-fat vegetable in existence! I ate mincingly and prayed fervently. People who invite guests for dinner obviously want to please them, so my requests are usually treated kindly. It is harder to ask for discretion—to say, "Please don't make a big deal out of this. Don't serve me my unbuttered vegetables with a flourish. Let me remain incognito."

Excuses

There are many, many other instances in which invisible illness is revealed: Sudden, frequent trips to the bathroom that draw notice. A mysterious gurgling from your hidden ostomy. Sitting in the shade while others work on their summer tans. Lagging behind a fast-walking group. Losing your train of thought during a conversation because of drug-induced spaciness. Being overcome by fatigue in the middle of a workday. Wheezing audibly. Meeting old acquaintances after a significant weight gain or loss. Among the most awkward are those in which you have to volunteer information to avoid misperceptions. If you look healthy, people expect you to behave in a healthy fashion, free of limitations. Sometimes you may have to offer the illness as an excuse in order to protect yourself from judgment. I was paying for my purchases in the neighborhood co-op grocery store one day, expecting, as always, to be asked whether I get the volunteer's discount. I said no, but the cashier didn't stop there. "Why don't you volunteer?" she asked. When I said that I had preschool children, she countered with, "So do I. I bring them along." I told her I was also working part-time. "So does everybody else," she persisted. Her presumptuousness made me angry. What if I couldn't carry boxes of produce around or stand on my feet at the cash register? Why should I have to tell her that? Why couldn't I just say no? I realized how resentful I can feel toward people who do not anticipate such problems—people so used to good health that they never even imagine what it would be like to be sick for a lifetime.

Disgrace about being different keeps many of us from using this excuse, however. The inconvenience some people will suffer to protect their privacy is well illustrated in this anecdote from Louise Taylor:

> I had gone down to Penney's to buy nylons. I knew I had to go to the bathroom, but I thought, I'll wait. I'll pay for these and then I'll go. I couldn't do that. I asked the woman where it was and she said it was on the second floor. You don't go running through Penney's—a black woman in a small Midwestern town—without someone suspecting that you've stolen something. I tried to be very cool about that, not drawing attention to myself. I got to the bathroom and there were about three women in front of me. I just about died. I was going to say, "Do you mind?" but they all had the look of urgency on their faces. I looked at the face bowl and I thought, "This is not going to be proper. These women will just about freak if I get on this face bowl." So, in essence, I wet my pants. Embarrassed! I was so pissed! Plus, it was

cold out. I've done that several times since then, and I just hate it. Each time it's the same anger, same embarrassment.

The end of good etiquette is to make social life run smoothly, without discomfort for anyone. The end of passing as healthy is to live life in as normal a fashion as illness allows. Both of these ends are met if, in revealing situations, you treat the illness as a condition of life that has become a personal norm and is no cause for embarrassment. Being direct and matter-of-fact conveys this, and brevity conveys it as well as exhaustive detail. Sometimes breaking the ice yourself, acknowledging the illness before it gets revealed, is the best way to retain control over how much you need to say about it. In the long run, avoiding disclosure at all costs can be more troublesome than having to tell repeatedly what is wrong with you.

Chapter
4

A Friend in Need

"I'm free to ask for help if they're free to say no."

"A friend in need is a friend indeed." Although quoted as a proverb, as if its meaning were commonly understood, this is, in fact, an ambiguous statement. Who is the friend? Is it the one who is in need? Or is it the one who is a friend to you in your time of need? It suggests two very different concepts of friendship. If the friend indeed is the one who is in need, then friendship entails dependence: No friend is more tenacious than a needy one. If the friend is the one who responds to that need, however, then friendship is a form of altruism.

Those of us who turn to friends for help and sustenance in living with chronic illness easily get caught up in this ambiguity. While we know that the standard interpretation of the proverb is the latter one, we worry that our friends will read it the first way, in all its bitter irony. Nearly everyone I talked to about the effect of illness on friendship fears slipping from a reasonable, short-term reliance to an abject, lifelong dependence. As one friend becomes increasingly needy, the mutuality of love and concern that friends presumably share is thrown off balance. Chronic illness, an ambiguous experience in itself, certainly tips the scales. It works as both bond and barrier. It is an opportunity for intimacy that also reminds us of our fundamental solitude. Illness reveals our deepest fears and longings, but also pulls them out of proportion. It offers a chance for friends to show that they care for us, but if that care is expected and not freely given, need becomes an imposition.

When Friends Stay Away

Now let's look at the usual reading of the proverb: A friend who responds to need is a friend indeed. A personal crisis that reduces your capacity to care for yourself works as a test, sorting the true, generous friends from the fair-weather acquaintances. Most of us are impressed and heartened at how well our friends pass this test, at least in the beginning. Old friends prove reliable and friends-in-the-making become more firmly bonded than they would be in the ordinary course of things. Seldom do friends drop out of sight entirely, but when it does happen, the absence is troubling. Gloria Murphy remembers:

> One of my good friends in the neighborhood didn't talk to me for months after she found out I had MS. She just could not handle it. She was also afraid she would catch it. There was a lot of ignorance involved. It was very hurtful, even though new friends sort of came out of the woodwork that were very caring people. I did not understand being avoided. Then another friend arranged a coffee. We were having coffee and things weren't going real well, and I decided that it was time to go home. This just wasn't going to work. I went to pick up my cup and plate and carry it to the sink, and I dropped it. The friend who hadn't spoken to me jumped up real quick, and the other one said, "Aw, let's see if she can pick it up herself." We all sat on the floor and laughed, and that broke the ice. It was okay that I broke the plate and that I could laugh about it. From then on, she was back at our old friendship.

Breaking the plate broke the ice because it showed that Gloria's ability to laugh at herself—one of the traits that wins her friends—had remained unchanged in spite of serious illness. There is a common assumption that tragedy changes your character in profound ways, giving you an insight into cosmic truth that puts clichéd expressions of sympathy to shame. This exalted aura is difficult to penetrate with the usual subtle displays of friendship. When I confessed to a friend who had lost her baby how ill at ease I felt coming to visit her, she reminded me, "But it's just us," meaning "We are the same people you knew before." Gloria's friend apparently expected some awesome transformation and could resume the friendship only when she saw her acting like the Gloria she knew.

Most often, when friends disappear, it is simply because they don't know how to respond. Given the confusion about proper etiquette, this is understandable. Yet, where close friends are involved, it is less a matter of propriety than of powerlessness. Friends want not only to be *correct* but also to be *helpful*, to contribute to your well-being, not upset it. After word got out that she had lupus, Esther Green watched a friend drive by her house frequently without stopping. She began to feel like she had "some kind of deadly disease like leprosy." So she called the friend on the telephone and asked why she hadn't come to visit. The friend answered, "Well, I wanted to stop by, but I didn't know what to say, and I didn't know if you wanted to talk about it. I would like to know more about it but I was afraid to ask." Esther assured her that asking questions would be fine, and she would answer them as she herself saw fit. In fact, she appreciated the opportunity to talk about the disease to someone who would care to listen. Initiating your friends into the mysteries of your illness by talking frankly about how it is likely to affect your health and life expectancy can relieve that initial awkwardness.

"Real" Friends

One of the "advantages" of chronic illness is that friends who shy away in the beginning have plenty of time to make up for it later on. Those of us who experience intermittent crises find that it is not always the same friends who respond each time. Our friends' availability varies, of course, with the conditions of their own lives. A mainstay in one crisis may only telephone to check in the next time around. Even if there are justifiable reasons, it can feel

as though the friend has pulled away. In the long run, such a reprieve helps sustain the friendship by sparing the friend an emotional burnout or an oppressive sense of obligation. Nevertheless,
we tend to think of our best friends as the ones who can be
counted on consistently, who take responsibility for seeing that
we are cared for even if they can't be there themselves.

Gloria Murphy's diagnosis brought new friends "out of the
woodwork." The idiom fits. People who are part of the structure
of your life—neighbors, co-workers, parents of your children's
friends, members of organizations you belong to—become more
visible and significant as they offer help in times of illness. But
not all of them will become fast friends. A friend indeed is one
who sticks around even when need ceases, as it at least appears to
do in times of remission. The recovery may be as good a test of
friendship as the crisis. The kind of friendship that lasts "in sickness and in health" is more than altruism. It requires genuine empathy, an ability to see you as an individual, not just a sick person.
Rather than merely giving, true friends give on terms that suit
your unique character. In short, they get to know you.

In talking about the kinds of help they have received, several
people I interviewed distinguished between kind gestures and especially valuable forms of support. This, too, is a sorting process,
a way of identifying "real" friends. Of all the people who call on
the telephone to show their concern, the friends are the ones who
take time for conversation about subjects other than illness. They
understand that illness is isolating and tedious as well as physically debilitating. When normal social activity becomes difficult,
friends adjust their habits to suit your capacity. Most of Susan
Alm's acquaintances do rather formal entertaining, inviting her
for dinners that she sometimes can't attend and can hardly reci-
procate. What she welcomes above all is friends who will drop by
just to enjoy her company, with no other expectations. I remember how elated I was when my friends began treating their visits
to the hospital as social occasions rather than good deeds. They
came not to check on my progress but just to be with me and

with each other—to talk and laugh as we do any other time we get together. Carla Schultz recalls with fondness two friends who came to the hospital directly after their wedding, still in bridal gown and tuxedo. Other friends put on slide shows in her hospital room. Friends, then, are the ones who can still see and affirm the healthy aspects of our personalities despite the overlay of illness, who recognize our need for diversion and normalcy and are not afraid of humor in the face of suffering. Yet they also respect our right to solitude, when that is what serves us best.

Gloria Murphy describes a special friend who "just by a sixth sense" seems to know when she is needed:

> One day I was lying on the couch. It was raining, and I was really feeling sorry for myself. I had just been out of the hospital a day or two. I looked out the window and here was this person standing in the rain with her hair drooping, holding dead mums that were about two feet long. She had on platform tennis shoes about six inches high—red plaid ones with red shoelaces. She was just standing there smiling. I laughed so hard and she came in and sat down and we laughed and laughed. That was part of my healing.

Gloria has a clear preference for fun: "I don't call on people often that are heavy-duty type people who really want to get into analysis. I would just as soon enjoy the sunshine as spend time wondering, Why? Just come and laugh with me."

Admitting that "my biggest resource is my friends," Louise Taylor describes them as "the kind that won't let me be down on myself, so I get a kick in the butt, which is good for me." Gloria Murphy appeals to her friends, "Love me enough to tell me when I need to be told a criticism, too. Don't treat me like I'm fragile, because I'm not." Margie Rietsma, on the other hand, especially values a friend who will let her "rant and rave" about her pain and anger without commenting. These examples seem mutually exclusive, but they are not. Different moments call for different degrees of frankness, and friends are the ones who can tell the difference. For example, one of my friends who sat by me through a painful episode, listening as I railed about my insufficiencies as a sickly human being, told me later that much of what I had said was ridiculous and that she had the urge to tell me to grow up. I appreciated her honesty, but had she actually said that in the midst of the pain, I would have felt abandoned to a solitary despair. Instead, she gave me a rare chance to explain what it is like to feel pain so severe that you become irrational.

Big Commitments and Small Gestures

Practical help is nearly always appreciated, but, again, certain kinds stand out for the empathy shown. Bill Gordon was touched when friends took the risk of offering him part-time flexible work, knowing that he needed structure and a sense of purpose to aid in his recovery. Gloria Murphy cited a neighbor willing not only to go out and buy the items on her Christmas shopping list, but to return them if she wasn't satisfied. When my children were young, a number of people volunteered to take them off my hands for a few hours when I was weak and feverish, but I was especially grateful for friends who spent time with the kids and me together, allowing me to enjoy their company without getting exhausted. Watching my children drive off for a good time in a higher-energy household sometimes made me feel more deprived than supported.

Small gestures that show genuine understanding and a willingness to share in our distress are just as welcome as major commitments of time and energy. What we appreciate from friends is their eagerness to contribute to our health according to their own capacity. Ironically, my most generous friends often question the value of their efforts in my behalf. After recovering from a fever of several months' duration, I had a party to thank all the people who had stood by me. I issued the invitations in part by word of mouth. One of my good friends just didn't show up. A few days later, I heard from another friend that she didn't think the invitation included her because she hadn't done very much. The friend who told me this admitted that she, too, had doubts about whether she deserved my gratitude. Yet I thought of them both as steady sources of support because they had, at least, kept in touch with me.

That Awful Specter of Dependence

So far, so good. Illness scares off just a few friends and usually only temporarily. It calls forth the generosity of the rest and brings new friends closer. The lengths to which friends will go to help is convincing evidence of the essential goodness of human nature, and we feel fortunate to see it so clearly demonstrated. But the initial feeling of buoyancy does not last forever. This is *interminable* illness, and *invisible* besides. The need never ends—it only subsides from time to time. When it recurs, the signs may be too subtle even for close friends to read, especially if you work hard at passing as healthy. And so there are times—many of them—when help does not come spontaneously but must be solicited. It is at these times that the awful specter of dependence intrudes. For me, the critical moment is when I find myself alone with pain so intense that I know I need immediate treatment. When I was still married, I could usually depend on my husband. Now I have no choice but to put my life in the hands of a friend familiar with my illness who will rush over immediately, pack up the belongings I need, take me to the hospital, comfort me, cancel my appointments, check on my kids' needs, and notify my family and other friends. The big question is *which* friend? I do a quick mental run-through of my friendships and imagine the strains my need might place on any one of them. My friends keep assuring me, "Don't think twice. Just call." I have a Chinese cookie fortune taped to my refrigerator that reads, "Feel free to ask for assistance. Friends are willing to help if they know your needs." Yet I hate like crazy to do it.

Asking for help is, first off, an admission of helplessness. People of less individualistic cultures may be less unnerved by the prospect of dependence, but it certainly seems un-American. Our language reflects our values. Words like "independent," "autonomous," and all those compounds with *self:* "self-reliant," "self-sufficient," "self-confident" carry moral weight. When illness reduces the self to helplessness, self-esteem is diminished. Some people bolster the self by avoiding reliance on others altogether. Duane Barber talks of his success at this with a bravado that seems characteristically masculine:

> Right now I'm my own best friend. I think I'm pretty independent. That's the way I perceive myself. It's just that I know what I do and I know what I think and that's just the way I am. I do for myself. I hate asking for things. Having to ask for favors would be a major issue with me, but it never crosses my mind.

Duane has been lucky enough to enjoy a long remission, but even men with more recent needs describe themselves as resourceful and independent: "the I'll-do-it-myself type," as Al Keski says. Wives are the chief source of support for married men. Married women, on the other hand, express a rather surprised gratitude if their husbands show empathy, but turn more readily to female friends for support. The relatively few women I talked with who avoid reliance on friends practice a self-censorship that seems rooted in self-doubt rather than confidence. Lily Washington, whose asthma attacks often occur in the middle of the night, confesses:

> Another reason I have suffered more here than not is because a lot of times I won't force myself to call someone. I don't want to bother anybody—certainly not in the middle of the night. If I'm not able to drive, I'll just sit here and wait and continue to pop pills. One thing I could do better is not give in when I do give in.

This reluctance to "bother" people is very common among the women I interviewed, even those who do go ahead and ask. It would be easy to interpret it as a characteristically female consideration for others. Yet, it may have as much to do with feeling unworthy of special attention. Whatever the source, both men and women dread being regarded as bothersome.

When you rely too heavily on other people for practical support and emotional sustenance, you run the risk of becoming burdensome. Friends who at first are gratified to be asked for help may begin to resent the intrusions. But what does "too heavily" mean? And when do you know you have hit the tolerance limit? Unless friends come right out and say how burdened they feel, you end up speculating about the sincerity of their help.

Sandra Stieglitz, virtually housebound by multiple allergies and a severe hormonal imbalance, senses that she has "used up" her friends. While they still come around faithfully to do the practical tasks, like take her to the doctor or buy her groceries, they seem to have withdrawn emotionally. She explains, "By the time people have done the things I need for the illness or made concessions to the illness, there's nothing left for *me*, so companionship and things like that get left out." Peggy Evans, another person whose need for practical assistance has increased with continuing physical degeneration, asks her friends to be forthright with her: "They say they want me to ask for help, that it's very, very important for me to ask. And I tell them that I'm free to ask if they're free to say no." Knowing that friends will decline rather than harbor secret resentments does relieve the worry, yet I must admit that anticipating that first promised "no" is what sometimes keeps me from calling. But that is an inhibition worth shedding. The policy itself is sound. Moreover, a true friend is not likely to refuse you at whim. The "no" would probably be said with genuine regret and a compelling excuse.

Common sense has it that sharing burdens lightens the load. The larger the circle of friends you have to draw on, the less you risk wearing any one of them out. People who belong to closely knit, easily identifiable groups of friends find extra solace in that. Quick access to friends makes the task of finding help easier, and being regarded as an integral part of a group boosts morale. For Peggy Evans, it is a quilting group that has been together for many years. Carla Schultz testifies to the value of her book club:

> I pace myself very carefully. There is very little I will push myself to do. One thing is to get my book done for book club. Book club has been my one salvation. There are six to eight women, and they have been wonderful. I started it just before I got sick, and sometimes the only thing I accomplished in a month was to read a book. I never did not finish a book for book club.

Bill Gordon found a new source of support in a men's weekly prayer breakfast. It was these friends, especially, who helped him restructure his life after illness forced him to quit his job. He also parcels out his requests for help by keeping a list of friends he can call and noting how frequently he has called each one so that he won't make a "nuisance" of himself, as he says. I certainly am grateful to a group of former teaching colleagues who for many years got together weekly to critique each other's writing, commiserate about our children's unruly behavior, complain about injustices, ease our stresses, and affirm each other's strengths. Even though we have gotten too busy to keep up that schedule, I know that if I call one of them, I will hear from the others in short order. If the one I call is not available to help, another will show up in her place. I can't imagine how I would have survived the illness this long, let alone write about it, without them.

The Traveling Bowl of Jell-O

When friends have borne your burdens through a long and unrelenting bout of illness, you begin to feel burdened yourself—by the debt of gratitude you owe them. "How will I ever repay them?" is a common refrain. "It is better to give than to receive," the adage goes, and here you are receiving in great measure, over and over again. Whether or not friends expect repayment, some equivalent service seems to be necessary to correct a threatening imbalance in the friendship. Unfortunately, a tit-for-tat exchange is often out of the question. What I admire most in my closest friends is a spontaneous readiness to drop everything and come running. I would love to emulate it, but illness has reduced my spontaneity. I want to rush right in at all costs, even if it means skipping meals or losing sleep, but instead I think it through: "Is this wise? Am I strong enough? If I do it today, will I be all right tomorrow?" Luckily, I do have some healthy reprieves in which I can respond as readily as they do, but because my friends are aware of my limitations, they are less inclined to ask me for the kind of help they give me. Growing up in a small town taught me, though, that mutual caring is not just a one-to-one matter. It is a communal activity. When the course of someone's life is drastically altered—by the birth of a child, an illness, a death in the family—the neighbors know just what to do. They bring food: hot dishes, cakes, fresh garden vegetables, or bowls of Jell-O. There is no obligation to refill the bowl, though some people do. It is simply understood that, over the years, everyone will give and receive their fair share. I have come to see the traveling bowl of Jell-O as a metaphor for keeping the balance, though it has been a struggle to appreciate Jell-O even metaphorically. I have endured far too much of it on the hospital's clear liquid diet.

The best way for those of us with physical limits to partake of this communal giving is to do what is within our capacity. Several people I talked with said that their experience had made them much less reticent about telling others how much they value their friendship, not just as thanks for favors, but spontaneously, anytime. The experience of chronic illness also makes many of us suitable listeners when friends get sick. A friend of mine who learned that she had a small and most likely benign brain tumor called me first because she knew I could be matter-of-fact about it and not "freak out," the reaction she expected from healthier friends. Phyllis Mueller has found that this form of giving also brings rewards:

> I have people call me and say, "I have another bladder infection. I knew I could call you because you would understand." I find that I can actually be helpful to other people. Often that's the first time I reap the benefits, because they'll say, "I had no idea what you went through until I had that. It's painful." And I'll say, "Yes, but you sort of get used to it." They'll say, "I'll never get used to this." And then you realize that you have adapted, you have grown.

It is often said that the experience of illness enhances your ability to empathize with other people's suffering. Robert O'Shea, drawing on his observations as a counselor, refutes that. He insists that if you don't have rapport with people before illness sets in, you won't have it afterward either. What *does* seem to change is the value of time and the priority people assign to comforting gestures like physical affection and conversation. Now that her work life is restricted, Gloria Murphy has come to see free time itself as a gift worth sharing with others. She has helped to organize a lay ministry group at her church that answers calls for individual and family counseling. Some days she spends several hours on the telephone with a stranger in crisis. When a neighbor was in the final stages of cancer, Gloria found that she could assist in a special way, simply by being available:

> I spent about four hours a day just sitting beside her while she was at home. Even though I could not do physical things for her, I could read to her. Sometimes we just held hands. We laughed a lot, and she was hallucinating a lot and I would just hallucinate with her. We watched little bunnies in top hats dance around the bedroom for a whole week before Easter and she thoroughly enjoyed herself. She needed somebody who had the time to sit there and watch them hop,

too. I decided after that—after she died—that there are many ways of repaying people, even if you don't repay the person that brought the casserole that day. It will come on down the way. So I don't worry about that anymore.

Such opportunities for repayment, especially when indirect, show us that the adage "It is better to give than to receive" is another ambiguous one. On the one hand, it is more honorable to give than to receive, an interpretation that leaves us frequent receivers feeling disreputable. On the other hand, we learn through giving that it can be more enjoyable to give than to receive. Giving to others strengthens bonds of friendship without the threat of dependence that receiving entails. People who give to us in times of illness actually *like* it, as much as we welcome the opportunity to give back. Those friends who assure us that they feel free to say no seldom, in fact, do. If it is so fulfilling to give, maybe the best act of generosity we who are chronically ill can offer is to allow our friends to help freely and not begrudge them that better part.

A Rare Intimacy

Avoiding an abject dependence by settling the debt of gratitude does not, however, right all the imbalances in a friendship beset by illness. The experience of illness is ultimately solitary. The most empathic person in the world cannot literally feel what you feel, at least not simultaneously and with equal intensity. Even knowing what it is like from memory is not the same as living the particular moment of suffering. When I am in pain and wondering which friend to call, I am not only measuring the practical hardships that a request for help will impose. I also wonder which friend I should admit into my worst moment of despair. Who do I want with me? Who can bear up the best under the strain? Who can give me the most comfort? Countless trips to the hospital emergency room have shown me the kind of friend who is useful there: One with the patience to stay by my side until the pain subsides or is deadened, with no anxiety about wasting time. One who can stay focused on my immediate need for comfort and not look to me for assurance that I will be all right. One who can live in the moment, difficult as it is, and not rush into the future with unfounded promises of recovery. One who listens to my rage and frustration without trying to soothe it or scold it away. One who will cry at the horror of the illness and laugh at the absurdity of it, preferably at the same time. One who understands that what I want from a friend is not a remedy but a tangible link to the world beyond my malfunctioning body, a sign that I have not been abandoned to the pain. If this seems like a lot to ask, just holding hands will do.

Another difficult question remains: "Which of my friends do I dare allow to see me in this shape?" When the pain is at its worst, I get up on all fours and moan like a wounded animal. It is a humiliating situation for an otherwise rational human being to be caught in. The many times that I have gotten sick among strangers have been embarrassing enough, but there was some relief in not having to face them again. While I have few qualms about letting people visit me in the hospital and see me with matted hair, caked teeth, and a tube up my nose, I do my best to act cheerful, to keep up my reputation. If they happen to catch me in a melancholy mood, I feel as though they've got the goods on me. They know my secret: I am not the strong, healthy, well-contained person they thought I was. The issue is no longer simply dependence but vulnerability. Illness exposes your hidden aspects: it lowers your inhibitions, ruins your physical appearance, strips your soul bare. Who can we trust to see us with all our protective barriers down?

Again, the experience of chronic illness is full of ambiguities. There is also something richly rewarding about exposing yourself to friends in this way. Illness offers a rare chance for intimacy, an opportunity to examine the essential human fate you share without the patina of social convention. A man interviewed in Lillian

Rubin's book *Just Friends* talked about how unusual this is for men, particularly:

> I've known Elliot for years, since the sixties, but in the early times it's not very clear to me what kind of relationship we had. I don't think either one of us thought about such things then. The turning point was when he went to the hospital for an operation. I didn't know what kind of operation it was going to be or how serious it was. But I remember being very struck, when I went to visit him the day before the surgery, with the possibility that something could happen to him. I remember having this conversation with him that felt very distant, almost strangulated. He never spoke about his fears; I never told him that I was concerned for him. It was such a male conversation. After I left, I realized that I had an enormous amount of feeling for him that wasn't expressed. I was taken by surprise. I never knew it until he was in this situation where he seemed at risk. He must have felt somewhat the same way because, after that, we both made an effort to get closer and to share more of what was going on inside ourselves.

People who see you in this raw way often do become better friends. They feel privileged to know you so well and they claim a greater stake in your well-being. Once such intimacy has been attained, it may be hard to let it go again when health returns. As the emotional intensity called forth by the illness fades, it may look as though the friendship itself is declining. One quite common, but hazardous, way that friends latch on is by perpetuating the sense of crisis. The sick friend becomes needier, just to invite an intimate response, while the healthy friend becomes overprotective, asking constantly about the illness, watching for symptoms, helping to enforce doctor's orders. Illness becomes the core of the friendship. Unfortunately, a crisis-based relationship is not the kind that lasts through thick and thin. Soon it takes artificial pathos to keep it going. If the sick person alone seeks this intensity, the friend may shy away from what looks like an oppressive dependence. If only the healthy friend persists, the sick friend may resent what seem like threats to privacy and independence.

There comes a time after every crisis when recovery must be acknowledged and normalcy restored. Therapists who work with people recovering from emotional trauma use the symbol of the open arms, which embrace and comfort but do not close completely, so that the one being embraced can back away at will and become self-sufficient again. When the open arms are those of friends we will continue to see, the object is not self-sufficiency but a comfortable, everyday mutuality. While the intimacy experienced in times of illness certainly can cement a friendship, the most solid friends are those we can also just chat with, without fear that the friendship is on the wane. We trust them to remember and cherish the confidences revealed in our times of crisis and do not need constant, heart-to-heart candor to prove it.

Strange as it may seem to look for benefits in chronic illness, this underlying intimacy with trustworthy friends is one that is frequently mentioned. Not all friendships can tolerate such self-exposure, however. I once got sick in the company of a college dorm-mate with whom I shared the cynical, joking relationship characteristic of immature people living in close quarters. Her behavior surprised me: She sat by my bedside, holding my hand and stroking my hair and crying. She would be my friend forever, I thought. But when I recovered, we both felt embarrassed and had trouble restoring the old cynicism. Sadly, we drifted apart, but I am still grateful that I got to see a compassionate side of her that she usually struggled to deny.

The women I interviewed talked more freely than the men about their fear of being too vulnerable. The men tend to practice an emotional stoicism that keeps the problem itself at bay. Even when illness shows them the value of emotional openness, it is not easy for men to put it into practice with their healthy male friends. Bill Gordon believes that his friendships with men are really no deeper than they were before he got sick, and he is readjusting his expectations:

> Men who hadn't had a lot of hospitalizations and a lot of therapy just weren't ready to get to the point about feelings and emotions and all that. Let's say I want "X" emotionally from somebody and they don't give it to me. I can say to myself, well, they haven't been through what I've been through. They don't even know that that's part of life in some cases.

Recovering in Solitude

Despite feeling uneasy about it, women do tend to risk the hazards of vulnerability and reap its rewards as well. Yet two of the women I talked with were distinctly guarded about exposing their suffering to friends. Interestingly, both of them—Phyllis Mueller and Kathy Halvorson—have illnesses that remain undiagnosed and thus lack the validity of a recognized name. Each of them feels that revealing her illness to others means having to justify it as well. Phyllis has constructed a system for managing her illness that allows her to have friends around for support without inflicting the illness upon them. Though her friends know about her health problems, she keeps them at a distance when the illness is most active. For one thing, she does not let them know when she is in the hospital:

> I don't want them to be a part of my pain. Maybe I don't want them to see me in pain. Yes, that's as close as I can come: I don't want them to see me in a weakened condition. I want them to have an image of me as different from that.

This is not just vanity, however. She also insists that her recovery goes more smoothly if she does not have to worry about maintaining relationships in the midst of the crisis:

Sometimes I get into anger when I don't feel good, and if I feel really bad, I withdraw. I want to wrap a little cocoon around me. I'm kind of like a dog when he gets hurt and he runs to his bed and pulls his paws in over his head. That's exactly what I want to do. I want to isolate myself. In the hospital, I want them to stick a sign on the door: No Visitors. I can't handle people yet on top of that. It seems to take everything in me to manage what I'm going through. Do you know that feeling? Like people are going to suck some energy out of me that I don't have to give to them because I have to stay on top of this for myself. I think it takes such tremendous amounts of energy to have pain.

I certainly do know that feeling, and I would like to see the last sentence here cast in neon lights: It takes such tremendous amounts of energy to have pain. Even though I seldom isolate myself, I do prefer the company of friends who do not expect me to show courage or to ease their anxieties, because I am simply not in shape to give them anything.

When the isolation lasts too long and Phyllis finds that she wants her friends again, she makes contact in novel ways that do not put her illness in the forefront. Describing an especially difficult time, when family problems and an injury aggravated her condition, she recalled:

A very wise clergyman once told me that people who were outer-directed rather than inner-directed fared better. When I found that the total focus was going on me and my problems, I would direct my energies toward other people. I baked bread. I baked coffee cakes. I gave them to people. Sometimes I don't think they even understood why. I'd just say, "I was in the mood to bake and I wanted to do something for you." I made a tremendous amount of friends during this period [laughter], which in turn helped me. I found that if I directed my focus to them and got out of myself, that

they could respond to me. They could not respond to my
pain.

When she needs someone to respond to the pain, Phyllis turns to
professional counselors. She sees counseling as "a release for the
pain," a safety valve that leaves her friendships undisturbed.
Others, too, rely on therapy to maintain their emotional health
at times when their physical health is in jeopardy, but Phyllis sees
counseling as a replacement for confiding in friends. Reliance on
therapists, chaplains, and others trained to hear bad news protects you from exposing your vulnerability to people who may
have trouble bearing it. But it also means missing the opportunity to make some friendships more intimate. Gloria Murphy
learned this lesson when she tried to isolate herself in the hospital. Problems with her heart, a new threat added to the usual
worry about multiple sclerosis, had undone her efforts at acceptance. This was shortly after the lay ministry project she works
with was started. The people involved saw each other as co-
counselors with a shared belief in the therapeutic value of confiding in others, but they had not yet become personal friends:

> I was having a bad day and I started to cry. It was the first
> time I had cried through any of this. One of my BeFriender
> friends called and I said, "Just tell her I don't want to talk to
> her." She asked the nurse if I needed somebody and this lit-
> tle nurse said, "Yes, she does." Well, fifteen minutes later this
> gal had gotten into town with her hair wet and brought an-
> other one, and they sat on my bed from about one-thirty
> until seven and taught me to cry. I had always smiled. I don't
> think when we were children we were programmed that cry-
> ing was okay. I cried at movies and books and the Miss
> America pageant. I cried at weddings, but never at funerals.
> I never really cried at crisis time—just sentimental crying, not
> good, gut crying. And now I'm a wonderful crier. I love those
> gals dearly for encouraging me, with the help of this nurse.

> We laughed for a while and then we'd cry. They told me
> things like they would never give me my underwear back un-
> less I finished my crying. I felt wonderful after that. That af-
> ternoon is really a beautiful memory to me. It was terrible at
> the time. It was kind of like deprogramming somebody, I
> think.

Gloria's uncharacteristic vulnerability yielded a stronger network
of friends precisely because the counselors who forced themselves
upon her were also her peers. The major shortcoming of professional counseling as a surrogate for intimate friendship is that,
by definition and professional ethics, the vulnerability can never
be reciprocated.

Kathy Halvorson is even more intent on protecting herself
from exposure than Phyllis Mueller is. By her own admission, she
"hides." Few people know that she has health problems. She covers her symptoms so that no one will notice, and she withdraws
completely when she can no longer pretend. Before her marriage,
she kept up a cautious lifestyle that both preserved her health
and saved her from discovery:

> In order to work full time, I had rules. I would sometimes
> come home and eat—always a balanced meal—and go to
> bed, and that's it. On Friday nights, I never could do any-
> thing. That's all there was to it. And I'd think of every excuse
> in the book not to accept invitations or anything. I would be
> terrified that somebody would come to my door and see me
> in my pajamas. The phone was a terrifying thing for me, and
> oftentimes I wouldn't answer it, because I'd have to make ex-
> cuses. I mean I really felt someone was going to find out.

On a few occasions, friends did find her in pain, take her to the
hospital, and notify her parents. Though their intervention was
critical to her health and she is grateful in retrospect, she did not
fully appreciate it at the time:

I was angry, because I felt real weak. I felt real vulnerable, that somebody could do that for me—could summon my parents—and I'm an adult. I had no intention of telling them, even though they give me great comfort in that situation. My friends didn't give me that comfort, and I guess it's because I didn't invite them. I didn't like making it real, I guess. When I could spend the time in the hospital alone, I could cover it up, like it never happened.

Marriage and family have made hiding more difficult, forcing Kathy to examine her motives for being so secretive. She attributes it both to shame about being deficient and to denial born of fear about losing control of her body. In the meantime, research into residual effects of polio, which Kathy had as a child, has given some medical validity to her problems and made her more willing to talk about them. But she is still reluctant to let people know how much she suffers:

I'm still working it out. Sometimes I feel that I really should be by myself. That's the only way I can manage. And I don't want anybody else to know me like this. I want to see them on my terms, when I feel good, and I want to have a life that is a quality that I can control with other people. I can't get rid of that feeling.

Though she still entertains the ideal of being healthy in the eyes of her friends, she realizes that there is a cost, and she does not recommend her habits of secrecy to other chronically ill people. The duplicity she lives with is not manageable in the long run:

I do keep up a big front. It's still very much me, but I try to hide having deficits physically. The price of that with friends and colleagues is that there are some things that are left to their guessing. There's an aura of mystery, when I might disappear for a while. I never share this with people. So there's a real price I pay: The energy that goes into keeping that distance—the gap in reality—being on my guard that something is going to slip.

The Gift of Giving

If you want your friendships to be thorough, genuine and firm, then you must trust your friends with the knowledge of this experience that is so formative of your personality, your habits, your outlook on life. Rather than anticipate their reactions, which is tantamount to controlling them, you must trust your friends to decide for themselves how fully they want to be involved in your fate. If they want in, let them in. If they prefer to back off a bit, let them. Unless you are honest with them and allow them to respond honestly, there is still a lack of trust at the heart of the friendship. Complete trust, on the other hand, relieves the fear of dependence and the humiliation of exposing your vulnerability. A friendship that can bear this much trust and intimacy as a consequence of illness can hardly be threatened by anything else. Wouldn't it be reassuring to know you have friendships that secure? Why not regard illness as a rare and wonderful opportunity to find out?

Then, a funny thing happened on the way to the word processor. I got sick—again. My abdomen felt inflamed, I got the chills, and my muscles ached. My car was at a body shop having a dent repaired, so I had to haul my children through snowdrifts in their slippery snowsuits to take them to nursery school on the bus. I couldn't keep them at home because I was yearning to go back to bed. I lost my appetite and cringed at the thought of cooking food for them. Help would have been greatly appreciated. *But I could not make myself call anyone.* Had the pain been an unmistakable sign of liver malfunction, I could not have avoided seeking help, but this pain was amorphous and tolerable. The truly critical test, I realized, is not the intense pain that signals immediate danger, but the lesser inconveniences that make daily life difficult. How do I decide when I am incapacitated enough to justify depending on my friends? As I ran through my mental list of friends to call on, I thought about the burdens in each of their own lives—the jobs that wore them out by five o'clock, the children they had to care for, the meetings they had to attend, the food they had to prepare, and the housecleaning they had to do for Thanksgiving dinner. Could I call them away from all that, in a subzero windchill besides, just to save me from strain and struggle? No, I did not want to be that burdensome. I would go it alone.

Going it alone was no fun. I began to feel sorry for myself and to rail at the injustice that had put me in this bind. I had been free of pain for six weeks after a six-month cycle of hospitalizations and false hopes. The week before, I had received a very uplifting bit of career news. I was sure my luck had changed, and I was euphoric. I shared my euphoria with friends, eager to offer them something different from the anxieties they had endured with me so long. I wanted to boost my own morale, to get myself back on a rational plane before I let them know what had happened. "Which of my friends deserves to watch me wallow in self-pity?" I asked myself. Not a one of them. As it turned out, my sister happened to call. She picked the kids up at school and took one of them home with her overnight. I could not help but spill my self-pity all over her, and I felt like I had regressed to childhood. As the big sister, she indulged my childish behavior.

But was it childish? Was it unduly self-pitying? Was I wise or foolish in not calling on friends? Telling my friends about it afterward, I heard my trust in them confirmed. "Don't think twice," they said. "Just call. We'll say no if we have to." And of course I learned a lesson that the experience of chronic illness teaches over and over again: No matter how sophisticated your intellectual acceptance of illness, your emotions always lag a bit behind.

History does repeat itself. As I began revising this chapter, thirteen years after I first wrote it, it happened: tenderness and quirky sensations in my liver and in the reflexology spot on my foot, a fever of 101, insatiable thirst, loss of energy. This time I started myself on the oral antibiotic regimen that my gastro-enterologist and infectious diseases specialist had worked out, and I settled down on the couch. My younger daughter, now six-teen and the only one left at home, is a comforting presence who knows the routine. I did alert one friend and my sister, just in case. No panic. No shame. But, to compound the irony, this time the muffler fell off my car.

Over the years, I've come to see myself as both giver and re-ceiver. It is not only my need for help that can throw a friendship off balance, but also a friend's reluctance to let me help. If we are to trust friends so completely that we risk being vulnerable and dependent, then they owe us an equivalent trust. All too often, they deny us this trust, thinking we have problems enough as it is. The rare intimacy evoked by serious illness is a gift that we who are chronically ill keep offering, again and again, to friends. They, too, have burdens of gratitude to relieve. I, for one, want to de-mand repayment in kind. If friends will expose their vulnerabil-ity to me and risk depending on me—if not for practical help, then for emotional support—I will not hesitate to let them give to me as much as they like.

The ambiguity of the proverb "A friend in need is a friend in-deed" is not so troubling, after all. It is most meaningful when left unresolved. True friendship requires *inter*dependence and *mu-tual* vulnerability. Unless the friend who is in need is also a friend in time of need, and vice versa, the proverb has—indeed—missed the crucial point of friendship.

Chapter
5

A Place of Usefulness

"What will I have to show for my life these last four years?"

When I had the laser treatments on my eyes, I was still working. Most people didn't know I was having eye treatments. I didn't tell anybody I was going in. I was having them done on Saturdays. I was working for a company that wanted to keep the real healthy employees around and get rid of the unhealthy ones, and I knew that the laser treatments would either cure it or I wouldn't work at all. So I didn't tell them what I was doing. My eyes would be dilated for eight days! I walked around with one pupil the size of a quarter and the other one normal size. Nobody noticed that! I had trouble reading papers. I'd have to close one eye to try to read them, but I worked through it. It never showed up in my work. It was funny. I was thinking, "Boy, if I can adapt to this, I can adapt to being blind, too. Gee, this is nothing." But a couple of times it did get real difficult and I thought, "I can't go on with work. I've got to tell them I can't even see the diagrams to fix the machines." But there was some way you could bluff your way through it, and I do a lot of things by feeling with my hands. And it worked out. They didn't find out about the laser treatments until I had an emergency one on a Friday and I had to skip work for it. Everybody was kind of shocked except my boss. He had had a treatment on his eye the day before and was dilated so bad he couldn't read. And I said, "I've been going through this the last two months." So he was very sympathetic.

The man who learned to repair machines with his dilated eye closed and the aid of sensitive hands is Don Welke, a young father of two who has had diabetes since childhood. Two years later, kidney failure put him on dialysis and in line for a transplant. The time required for treatments and the resulting physical weakness finally made it impossible for him to keep up with his job. He went on disability and his wife went back to work. Almost immediately after the kidney transplant, he sought vocational counseling and began weighing his options. Don's persistent devotion to work in spite of debilitating illness is remarkable, but not at all uncommon among the chronically ill. His example raises the question "Why not just take it easy?" After all, illness ought to be a legitimate excuse for not working.

The answer lies in the unsurpassed importance that industrial societies assign to work. First of all, each of us is expected to be financially self-supporting once we reach adulthood. If we do live on someone else's income, then we are expected to perform services that make us worthy of that support. People who have no recourse but public welfare are regarded with suspicion, if not outright contempt. Second, having useful work to do is so central to our lives that we have no identity and little human value without it. The question "What do you do?" is even more unsettling than "How are you?" to someone unemployed because of illness.

I learned very early that physical infirmity does not free you of your obligation to work. Both my mother and grandmother developed osteoarthritis at an early age. My mother sewed all our clothes with her gnarled fingers, washed dishes in water so hot that I couldn't touch it, and hung clothes on the line until the weather got cold enough to freeze them before they dried. Curiously, I never really thought of her arthritis as a chronic illness until I began interviewing people for this book. It was simply a feature of life—something to put up with, and I expected to have it myself when I grew up. (I made it to fifty before it turned up in my thumb joints.) In my case, the harsh expectation that you work yourself literally to the bone might be attributed to the

Protestant work ethic, which, through its cultural dominance, afflicts people of other religious faiths, as well.

Bluffing

For the chronically ill, the force of the work ethic is compounded by the stigma associated with being different. Until the passage of the Americans with Disabilities Act (ADA) in 1990, illness carried with it no entitlement to special consideration in the workplace. The ADA changed legal conditions but has not entirely changed attitudes. The praise is still reserved for those who *surpass* their physical limitations and prove that they can work as productively as their healthy counterparts. The standard against which we measure our performance is perfection, and any deviation from that norm is a source of embarrassment. Even though Don's work was good enough to keep his co-workers from discovering his problem, his own awareness of having to strain harder made him feel disreputable. Why else would he use the word "bluffing" to describe his ingenuity in compensating for his limited vision?

Chronic illness is considered a serious threat to good, productive work, and there is much concrete evidence—such as frequent or long absences—to support that assumption. Conversely, rigorous work is often seen as a major threat to good health. In the search for a diagnosis, doctors will often ask probing questions about work, especially of their male patients, to get at sources of stress or psychogenic causes of illness. If the illness is not totally disabling, they may recommend a break for recovery or some change in work habits or even a change in vocation. Quitting work altogether is usually only a last resort. Yet, because the structure of work allows little flexibility and values productivity and economic efficiency far more than human convenience, people whose capacity is only somewhat limited still perceive work as an all-or-nothing choice, and it may well be for their employers, too. Kathy Halvorson's neurologist insisted that she reduce her work week to three-quarter time or she would "just fade out." That sufficed for close to three years:

> Then my department head came to me and said I had to go on full time or lose my job. They couldn't justify three-quarter time anymore. He said, "Are you okay now?" Of course, I said, "Yes, I'm okay. I'll do it." In my heart, I really think it's self-destructive. It scares me to death to think about going public with something like I can't work full time. It scares me to death that somebody's going to say, "What are you talking about? Who do you think you are?" I don't know why, but I'm really afraid of that. I'd rather risk my own happiness and be exhausted every day and bitchy at night.

"I don't know why," Kathy puzzles, as if her fear were incomprehensible. Yet it is widely shared by others whose illnesses have intruded upon their work lives. Owning up to a reduced capacity to work threatens both loss of income and loss of worth. The fear of becoming indigent and useless runs second only to the fear of death for sheer, sleep-disturbing terror.

To avoid that awful consequence, many of us pass as healthy and then work extra hard to keep our illnesses from being revealed, just as Don Welke did. Regardless of how open we are with family and friends about our limitations, we seem to believe that the workplace requires a prudent secrecy. Even Phyllis Mueller, who is more secretive than most, can still claim, "I put on my best show in the work market." Lorraine Czerny, a teacher who began acknowledging her heart disease only when it forced her into retirement, explains, "When you're working, you don't advertise it. You have to lie to survive."

Lying, cheating, and bluffing are part of a common vocabulary that people with invisible illnesses use to describe their work experience. Secrecy is an understandable mode of self-protection, and it is not always as active and deliberate as these words imply. A physical examination for a job as a flight attendant posed no tests that would reveal Lily Washington's asthma, so she simply neglected to mention it. She offered a typical rationalization: "If he's a doctor and he can't even detect it, then it shouldn't stop me from flying." Three years later, she quit of her own accord because the changes in air pressure aggravated her illness, but she still felt justified in trying. None of these people relish lying. When Bill Gordon began his search for part-time work to replace the high-pressured career he had to surrender, he planned to be open and honest about his manic-depression, to confront the stigma of mental illness head on. It didn't work the way he had hoped, though he might get a better reception now that the ADA gives him the right to file a complaint with the Equal Employment Opportunity Commission:

> I learned early on, but not early enough, that I shouldn't talk about my illness as much as I did in job interviews. People wanted to know why I left my previous job, because, as one guy said, "Nobody leaves a firm like that one." I just started saying, "I was looking for a career change." Deep down, I would rather let people know. When I tell somebody about the problem in a job interview, it's sort of full and fair disclosure on my part: Look, if you hire me, you're getting this along with me. That might even take the pressure off me just in case something did happen. I'm worried about that. I also worry about the person who recommended me or got me the interview—whether they will be frowned upon later if something happens. I guess I was looking for the perfect situation where somebody would say, "We don't care. We'll support you." But, that just doesn't exist out there. I think now that it's best to keep it to yourself.

From the employer's standpoint, hiring or retaining an employee whose health is in question is an economic risk. While the ADA has made it happen, it is often still regarded as either a humanitarian gesture or a legally required nuisance rather than sound management practice. It is not only reduced efficiency that makes employers hesitate, but also the cost of health care benefits. Nevertheless, what happened to Margie Rietsma is less likely to happen now, at least not in such blatant fashion. She calls herself a victim of "constructive firing," in which the employer makes job demands that push the employee to the limit. Her boss gave her additional work to do, called her at home after hours, and said that she looked unprofessional when she wore leather bands around her wrists to keep them firm and ease the pain of arthritis. She blamed this sudden hostility on the rising cost of her health benefits and saw his behavior as harassment. Finally, after collapsing at work, she accepted her doctor's warning that the stress was detrimental to her health and quit.

Financial Crisis

Though lifelong unemployment is the exception, many of us do reach some point at which the work we are accustomed to doing becomes at least temporarily impossible. This dreaded moment comes soonest for people with physically rigorous jobs performed on a stringent schedule, meaning, usually, those with the fewest skills and economic resources to fall back on. Loss of work is felt immediately as a financial crisis. No one I talked to had been left destitute by unemployment, but that certainly does happen, as the many chronically ill among the homeless population could testify. Disability insurance, Social Security, and supplementary support for household assistance, transportation, vocational counseling, and so on are intended to keep the bottom from falling out. But these do not alleviate all your financial worries if you have children to educate or a home mortgage to pay off.

Unfortunately, there is great inconsistency in both private and public economic provisions for the chronically ill. Because Bill Gordon's disorder is defined as a mental illness, his disability coverage was limited to two years, with no allowance for its chronic, recurring nature. The second year, he worried so much about what he would live on when the insurance ran out that his depression grew worse, making the search for a job even more difficult. Having to live, through no fault of your own, at the mercy of the government or an insurance company on an income that bears no relation to your aspirations and skills is a poor replacement for real work. And, as Louise Taylor has found, this kind of life is a job in itself, one that requires special administrative talents. Louise has kept up her profession, but several lengthy hospitalizations have put her out of work temporarily. Each time she gets sick, she has to prove that she is entitled to the health benefits promised her, and she has to force her way through this tiresome process at a time when she can barely see straight:

> It's maddening. Luckily, I had a good disability plan at work, but they are always playing games so that they don't have to pay you. They will pay you as long as the doctor continues to verify that you are disabled. They send out a form every month. Once when I was hospitalized, they called me to "see how I was feeling." I thought, "Sure you are." I feel like there's a person in my tree out there watching my every move. One of their requirements is that you keep applying for any chance you have of getting Social Security. That means filling out thousands of forms and then waiting a month or two for their decision. I don't qualify under Social Security's definition of disabled, so every time now I have been denied. Each time, I send a copy of the denial to the insurance company, and they tell me that I must appeal the decision. Right off the bat I said to them, "This is your game, between Social Security and the insurance company. It's 'Who's Gonna Pay This Woman?' I shouldn't have to be in the middle." They suggested I get a lawyer and I said, "Who's going to pick up the tab on that?" You pay into these plans and once you need them, they don't want to be there. It's a constant fight to get what I feel is mine.

Part-time work would seem a logical solution for someone who is slowed, but not stopped, by illness. Phyllis Mueller, for example, strings together temporary secretarial jobs so that she can take time off as needed. But part-time jobs seldom offer insurance benefits, which, for someone with a chronic illness, are a necessity, not an option. Where do you earn a legitimate income that allows the luxury of paying for your own hospitalizations, frequent clinic visits, and daily medication? Self-employment, working on a freelance basis as I do, is more compatible with the ups and downs of chronic illness, but it usually means paying for your own health coverage, if you can get it. With the standard disqualification for high-risk or preexisting conditions, private insurers easily exclude the chronically ill. I have insurance only because the state of Minnesota has a risk pool, the Minnesota Comprehensive Health Association, in which all insurers take part. It offers policies to otherwise uninsurable people with premiums at 125 percent of the average for comparable coverage. The premiums take a large chunk of my income, but I would go broke on the bills my policy pays. Group policies and membership in health maintenance organizations are available almost exclusively to people with full-time, long-term jobs. Many people who have no other access to health care coverage will continue, then, to work full time even if the job leaves them "exhausted every day and bitchy at night."

The trend toward regularly paid work performed at home with computer links to the employer holds some promise for the chronically ill. Freedom to be casual and comfortable, to avoid a commute, and to take breaks as needed makes it easier to keep up a job, as long as the workload itself isn't exhausting. One reader who does public policy work at home finds that this not only keeps her solvent, but also shores up her professional identity: "Working in my home office is the best way to forget that I'm sick. When I'm speaking with a senator's office, I feel like a part of the real world. I imagine the people on the other end imagining me in a tailored suit and pumps behind a desk in a nice office, when really I'm in my pajamas and slippers in my basement. It makes me chuckle."

Predictably, financial worries loom largest for people who are the breadwinners in their households, whether single or married, male or female. Yet women whose husbands earn incomes adequate to support them are spared neither the discomfort of economic dependence nor the dread of poverty. "I'm not planning on getting divorced," Susan Alm laughs, acknowledging that her economic well-being hangs by the ever more fragile thread of marital security. Nor do adults whose parents can afford to maintain them relish living like dependent children again. The risk of abject poverty is not the crux of the matter: no longer being self-sufficient is horror enough in a society that prizes independence so highly.

Feeling Useless

Despite wide variation in financial resources and responsibilities, there is striking commonality in how people experience the loss or reduction of their capacity to work. Whether well paid, poorly paid, or unpaid, work itself—its performance and its product—has an intrinsic value that is not easily relinquished. Homemakers like JoAnn Berglund, who has to lie down and rest after making beds in the morning, feel as diminished by a change in their accustomed pattern of work as those who lose an income besides. When people talk about the prospect or the actuality of being unemployed, they talk less about the economic problems than about the many other losses that unemployment entails: loss of colleagues, loss of a familiar environment and a routine that gives structure to your life, loss of identity, loss of precious time to produce something worthwhile, loss of dreams left unfulfilled. Each one of these is sufficient cause for grief. Flashes of grief—or shame—strike on such simple occasions as being asked for a work phone number when you cash a check.

Retirement is a big enough adjustment for a person of sixty-five with a lifetime of labor to look back on and the gift of free-dom to enjoy. A forced retirement in the prime of life is seldom welcomed, especially if it is to be lived out in physical discomfort. People newly out of work may find themselves immobilized by grief, unable even to perform simple jobs around the house or to take part in activities that would provide some diversion. This just compounds what many identify as the greatest loss: loss of worth experienced as a profound feeling of uselessness.

Don Welke has, on his own testimony, done quite well at maintaining a sense of normality throughout the course of his illness. Even as an adolescent, he didn't feel that diabetes was so-cially limiting. Yet when it threatened his capacity to work, it threw him into the first bout of depression he remembers:

> I knew my job and I felt good about myself. It seems like the turning point of the whole mess was the eye thing. I reacted in such a depressed way like I never have done before. I was down so low. It was weird. My work went down. I'd feel like if I went blind, I wouldn't be worth anything. I had just lost it. Before that, I was good at what I did, and I had confi-dence. Confidence, I think, was the big thing. After the eye thing, I didn't have much confidence in what I was doing.

Likewise, Bill Gordon felt humiliated when he returned from a sick leave and found his office relocated and his assignments re-duced. Though no one spoke to him about it directly, he inter-preted the evidence to mean, Bill just can't handle stress. We'd better put him out to pasture. Ironically, only his depressive symp-toms aroused his business partners' concern. The manic aspect of his illness manifested itself in culturally appropriate ways: high energy, compulsive achievement, and a self-imposed fourteen-hour workday. Before the pendulum swung, he had been evalu-ated first in his category for job performance. This affirmation of his talents compounded the grief he experienced when he finally resigned from his position after a lengthy hospitalization. The knowledge that he may never fulfill his colleagues' expectations is a persistent source of shame.

Bill then began his hunt for "that perfect situation" in which an employer is willing to say, "We don't care. We'll support you." Whether moral support can fully restore a damaged sense of worth is open to question. Al Keski was surprised to learn how sympathetic his employer and co-workers could be when he came down with multiple sclerosis. Before his diagnosis, his job as a personnel recruiter had been in jeopardy because of cutbacks in hiring. Rather than use the illness as an excuse to let him go, his employer redefined the position to make it less demanding without cutting his salary. Despite the financial security this gives Al, he is embarrassed by it. He feels that he is not really pulling his weight but is being retained out of charity. Assenting to the belief that chronic illness does not entitle you to special privileges, he compensates by doing extra tasks around the office. When his co-workers step in to relieve him of responsibilities that might put a strain on his health, he feels at the same time personally favored and professionally threatened. Seeing his co-workers reap rewards that would ordinarily be his undermines his self-confidence, which is already reduced by the illness. Al's most troubling symptom is blurred vision, and, he explains, "It's difficult to be assertive when you can't look people in the eye. I miss facial expressions. When people disagree with me, I tend to back off."

For all three of these men—one a skilled laborer, one a young and up-and-coming business executive, and one a midlevel white-collar worker—personal identity hinges on the work they do, and each takes great pride in doing his particular sort of work well. In this culture, we measure our worth as human beings by the rewards we earn and the utility of the work we contribute to the common life. People who make no such contribution or whose work goes unpaid are hard put even to say who they are. Lucky coincidences have helped Louise Taylor retain her job despite several flare-ups of multiple sclerosis, yet each sick leave has felt like a job loss. Not knowing whether or when she can return to work casts doubt on her professional ability:

> When people would ask, "What do you do?" I very quietly and gently said, "I'm in public administration." But I wasn't. I didn't have an occupation any longer. It had been taken away from me. I just felt that I had nothing, that I wasn't anything. Then they would ask where I work. My second reaction was to think that they don't need to know this, that I don't want to explain my whole medical history. So I would say, "I'm on leave," and give them a look that would shut them up. I'm getting better at lying, but it still feels like there is a five-minute pause before I answer. I'm not consistent in every social situation. I don't know how I'm going to respond. And it always feels like I'm the only one having to go through this.

Deprived of a public identity, you can look for affirmation of your value in your private life. Illness can undermine the respect you enjoy there, too, however. Married men, especially, suffer a keenly felt loss of role and status when they cannot support their families in the traditional ways. Don Welke describes his discomfort with the reversal of roles that illness brought about in his family:

> I get nicknamed "Mr. Mom" now. I'm the one who stays home with the kids, cooks dinner, and tries to keep the place in a halfway decent living condition, and she's the one who works. Actually, we've done a 180-degree role shift. Before the kidney transplant, when I was on dialysis, I had a really rough time dealing with that. I was not doing anything around the house. I figured, I'm supposed to be out there working and I'm just laid up. After the transplant, I figured, if this is the way it's going to be, I've got to do something about it. I'm sure Vocational Rehabilitation will be contacting me to find out if I want to go back to school or if I can

find another job that I'd be suited for. I don't really know what will happen. I'm just the one at home now. I'm not making the money anymore—she is. I would like to get retrained in computer programming. I look forward to that. You've got to look forward to something. Otherwise, you'd go crazy.

Regardless of educational and income levels and social status, most of us have certain expectations of ourselves tailored to suit the people we believe we are. Learning that you do not have the physical wherewithal to meet those expectations is a personal crisis calling for a new self-evaluation. This may be more upsetting for the self-professed high achievers, who at least talk about it more readily. As Carla Schultz puts it, "One of my theories in life is that once you're a junior high school council chairman, you are always that person for the rest of your life. It was hard for me to break with that." As crucial as this reevaluation is, it is often difficult to accept a period of illness as a reprieve from work and an opportunity to rethink goals and talents. Even in its benign phases, chronic illness can make you frantic about using time purposefully. When you have less than the average allotment, you feel you have to do more with it. Rather than regard the break in his career as a valuable period of recovery and self-examination, Bill Gordon instead mourns the waste of time: "What will I have to show for my life these last four years?" Restored health is apparently not enough.

The Show Must Go On

Apart from economic necessity and the authority of cultural norms, there are sound motives to keep working, even at a much reduced capacity. *Doing* gives us a sense of meaning that mere existence cannot convey. When chronic illness intervenes in our lives, we keep working not only *in spite of* but also *because of* it. Some of us even work extra diligently, both to convince ourselves that we still can and to divert our attention from the illness. The routine of work and its tangible products provide a safety valve for the anxiety that illness arouses. The books and papers stacked at my hospital bedside always provoke comment, whether admiration or advice to stop and take it easy. As I see it, working with a vengeance is essential to my recovery. When my body is ailing and my emotional balance is precarious, work helps me to look beyond the illness and maintain my will to survive. I am lucky that my work requires a functioning brain rather than brawn. Ruth Sands, a telephone company employee with multiple sclerosis, puts it this way:

> If I didn't have my work, I would have a tendency to become almost a recluse, because I find it quite an effort to get up in the morning, get dressed, and go out. So I need that extra nudge. I come home sometimes so tired that I feel I can't make it from the bus line to the house, and yet I get up the next day and go back to work. Otherwise, I'm afraid I'd say to heck with it and let everything go and then sit around and feel sorry for myself.

Rather than impeding satisfactory work, chronic illness is often a spur to higher quality work, since the best protection against losing a job or being resented by co-workers is to do it exceptionally well. Having your capacity to work threatened also makes you take your commitment to work more seriously. You quickly learn to compensate for your shortcomings. If your pace is slowed, you work longer hours, if the job allows it, to keep up your output. For every responsibility you have to drop, you take on another that you can handle. If your symptoms are intermittent rather than constant, you work in a frenzy on the healthy days. Work that is transportable goes along to the sickbed. Call it bluffing, compensating, or just plain working hard, this approach does not always allay the fears. A friend who used to have memory lapses before she had brain surgery and went on medication still panics at gaps in her train of thought, even though her doctor assures her that they are normal. If she makes an error writing up a sales slip, for example, she attributes it to her illness, even though her healthy co-workers make similar errors. Only perfection will convince her that her work is unaffected.

There is no clear line of demarcation between working to maintain a reasonably normal and healthy life and the fairly common phenomenon of overcompensation, defying limits at some risk to your health. Lily Washington is one who takes great pride in not letting her illness stop her from doing what she has set out to do. A dancer by vocation, she will wheeze her way through a rehearsal rather than take a break. On more than one occasion, she has left a performance for emergency treatment and raced back in time for the curtain call. She offers herself as a model of endurance to young dance pupils:

> When they get to pissing and moaning in class, I say, "I'm three times your age, I have asthma, I have scoliosis. Do not tell me, 'Miss Washington, I'm tired. Miss Washington, it hurts.' I don't want to hear it." When they know about my problem, it gives them the incentive to get their acts together.

Lily's literal interpretation of "The show must go on" is courageous to some and foolhardy to others. Her doctor votes for foolhardy, warning her that she is constantly endangering her health and shortening her work life. Uncertainty about the course of the illness, plus a sense of injustice about having such a limitation, has, however, left her with a tendency to live for the moment.

Patching Together a Work Life

In contrast to Lily, Peggy Evans has become reconciled to the fact that she cannot do all that she had counted on, though she has certainly had her share of feelings of uselessness. The neuropathy that left her with permanent disabilities came on just as she was contemplating a new career after raising her children to adolescence. Bright and motivated, with her diabetes under daily control, she had lots of options. Then her vision weakened, her legs gave out, and "each day that I woke up there was something new I could not do." Gradually her condition improved again, and as the illness stabilized, she had to reconsider her career plans: "I thought that whatever I did for the rest of my life would have to be done sitting down." What she did was settle for a practical avocation, quilting and designing quilt patterns. She was privileged to do so because she has a husband who can support her. Peggy's special insight was to acknowledge, in a realistic yet affirmative way, that her options were limited. Her work could no longer measure up to a standard of perfection, but neither did she have to give it up entirely. Instead, she limited the range of choices to include only those that were within her diminished physical capacity.

Peggy Evans is, however, a marvel of serenity. It is by no means easy to surrender your desire for achievement. Susan Alm is one of those perennial junior high council chairs Carla Schultz talks about: a talented historian who planned to educate herself fully, have a productive career, and also raise a family. Lupus intervened, leaving her fatigued and with pain of some sort every day. She has put together a flexible career as a freelance teacher, lecturer, and research consultant, besides being a mother to three children. Her work is well enough respected that she is offered assignments without having to solicit them. She eagerly accepts what work she can, given serious obstacles:

> I can't hold a pencil. I can't type for more than a very, very short time. I can't sit and read for long because the joints in my neck bother me and I get headaches. It's very difficult for me to sort through slides for my lectures because of the pain in my hands. So it takes me a tremendous amount of time to get my work done.

Nevertheless, she continues that work, not by defying her illness, like Lily Washington dancing through her asthma, but by recognizing her limits and pacing herself. She works slowly and she saves the most difficult work for what she calls, with some irony, her "good" days. She has won the admiration of people who know what conditions she is working under, but she puzzles those who are ignorant of her illness and see her settling for lesser rewards than her talent warrants. She herself lives with a great deal of frustration, longing for the full professional attainment that she believes would be hers were it not for the illness:

> I grew up in a family where there were high expectations about what you would do, and you did it. I always expected myself to do great things. I was pushed ahead on a certain track toward a career that hasn't materialized. I feel cheated. There was something I should be doing that I can't do.

Some of the frustration comes from watching her husband pursue his vocation unencumbered by illness or by a primary commitment to parenting. At times, she sees her plight as nothing more than an exaggeration of what many women face: the conflict between the demands of work and family. "It's just more acute with chronic illness," she claims, "because you don't have the energy to do either one."

Given her circumstances, it is hard to imagine how Susan Alm could do any better in the realm of work than she is already doing. As real and painful as her disappointment is, she has managed quite well to adapt her career to suit her limits while still remaining faithful to her original interests and goals. Her sense of failure might be eased by having more of the rewards that a full-time job brings: a predictable workload, a steady income, colleagues, recognition, professional identity, and assistance with the technical aspects of her work that give her difficulty. What she herself wants right now is a position that makes full use of her talents yet allows her to set her own schedule to meet the demands of her illness—that ideal situation that Bill Gordon, too, is after.

My own somewhat checkered work history is a variation on Susan Alm's. Ironically, I think I have benefited from having a longer history of illness than hers. Some of the frustrations Susan expresses have subsided for me. For starters, I was worse than the junior high council chair: I was the kindergartner who was asked to read aloud to the rest of the class while the teacher went to the bathroom. I was a born achiever and compulsive to boot. Anything less than perfection was a fall from grace. Like Carla Schultz, Bill Gordon, Susan Alm, and countless others, I grew up with great expectations. My gradual liberation from grandiosity began when I got sick during my second year of college. I had all I could do to keep up with my course work, though I still did it well. But I stopped thinking about where it might lead and what I might become. The college adviser's standard question "Where do you want to be ten years from now?" had no relevance for me. I expected to be dead. Spared from making a life plan, I chose an impractical, esoteric major because I liked the subject matter. I followed it all the way to a Ph.D. because there was nowhere I would rather have been than in school.

I finished my degree the same year that the news of declining enrollments hit and academic institutions put freezes on hiring. I found a temporary, but annually renewable, position that was well suited to my teaching interests and my uncertain future. I worked very well for six years, but with little hope of the rewards that come with being on track for tenure and promotion. Then some administrative turmoil that damaged morale and increased stress levels in the department helped me to acknowledge that there might be something preferable to a dead-end, second-class academic job. Had I been healthy, I would have scouted the country for one of the few openings that offered status and security. Instead, I took time off to write, adopted a child, and got sick again: a nine-month ordeal that forced me to reconsider my capacity for work. Consciousness of mortality has lowered my ambition for a stellar career and altered my sense of worthwhile rewards. Rather than move around every few years in pursuit of the ultimate in academic deanships, I have chosen spotty employment and living among family and old friends, in sight of lakes, deciduous trees, and cumulus clouds. Like other writers and artists, I scrounge for a living: an essay published here, a course to teach there, a writing fellowship when I can get it, editing others' work when I need quick money. I get enough satisfaction from all I do that I am seldom any longer tripped up by the grand old expectations that used to come in the form of self-accusations like "At my age, the Brontë sisters had written their immortal literary works and were already dead, and what have I done with my life?"

The Empty Days

Lowering my ambitions has been easier than freeing myself from the other source of frustration that I share with Susan Alm and Bill Gordon: a compulsion about using time productively and not simply "wasting" it on feeling lousy. I'm no good to anybody like this, I think as I lie in bed and watch the clock advance. Here again, though, the long duration of my liver disease has been helpful. Given enough experience of illness and recovery, especially when recovery is accompanied by a new fervor and energy for work, as mine is, you can learn to ease up on yourself. I have gradually shifted my perspective with the help of good advice such as this passage from May Sarton's *Journal of a Solitude*:

> I always forget how important the empty days are, how important it may be sometimes not to expect to produce anything, even a few lines in a journal. I am still pursued by a neurosis about work inherited from my father. A day where one has not pushed oneself to the limit seems a damaged damaging day, a sinful day. Not so! The most valuable thing we can do for the psyche, occasionally, is to let it rest, wander, live in the changing light of a room, not try to be or do anything whatever.

Letting psyche and body rest together certainly seems like a healthy response to debilitating symptoms of illness, and I am practicing it more and more. I only wish that it didn't take pain or fever to force me to "stop and smell the roses," to quote a popular phrase that has, ironically, added to our obligations. Heaven forbid that we miss the roses! All too easily, I slip back into compulsion on the precious healthy days. Had my teenage daughters not gotten me hooked on a noon soap opera, I might not even take time out for lunch. Sarton recommends a careful balance: "Each day, and the living of it, has to be a conscious creation in which discipline and order are relieved with some play and some pure foolishness." It is wise advice, but not easy to follow when the accident of illness removes the living of a day from your conscious control.

The serenity that others admire in Peggy Evans is the hard-won result of a necessary easing of compulsions about work. She has difficulty standing and walking, and retinal hemorrhaging has, at times, obscured her vision and restricted her head movements. There is not much work you can do without moving your head. After nearly a decade of adjusting to new symptoms that come and go, she has learned a different response than frustration and depression:

> One thing I have gained in place of some of the losses is time—a very precious commodity. I sometimes think it's too bad I'm not doing something marvelous with it, like writing a book or painting pictures, but I'm not, and it doesn't really bother me. What do I do with all this time? I spend a lot of it looking out the windows, at that beautiful scenery. I enjoy the birds and the rabbits and the cats that come and drink from the birdbath and the people jogging. I feel very much a part of all the joggers. It makes me feel less inactive. I've gotten to know people that I wouldn't have known before. I have time to spend with other people who have more time, and some of them have been handicapped in a way. They have a lot to share and offer. I just delight in fooling around

with designs. I could do it all day and all night, and sometimes I do. I have pages and pages, and no one enjoys it at all but myself. It's so much fun to be able to do it without feeling guilty.

A New Vocation

The Presbyterian church I attend asks its new members to pledge not only a portion of their incomes to the work of the church, but also their time and talents, by finding their own unique "place of usefulness" in the congregation. Using this term in place of "job" has helped me to think more clearly about how to handle the dual fear of becoming indigent and useless. First, you have to disentangle the economic issues from the questions of identity and human worth. When illness makes it difficult to continue the work you have been doing, there are really two matters to resolve: "What must I do to keep this illness from impoverishing me?" and "What can I do now that I have physical limitations?" While chronic illness may deprive you of your job, it need not rob you of your right to occupy a place of usefulness in the world. The ideal, of course, is to have financial needs and the need for worthwhile occupation met simultaneously, through paid employment. But if illness rules that out, there must be other options.

I was surprised and very heartened to talk to several people to whom illness itself had offered a new sense of purpose. When Esther Green, for example, learned that lupus afflicts African American women in greater proportion than any other group, she saw a definite place of usefulness for herself as a black woman with lupus. Though she is disabled enough to qualify for Social Security, she commits what precious energy she has to the Lupus Foundation's efforts to inform African Americans about the disease. After quitting her job and giving up much of her housecleaning, Gloria Murphy took on two new, less strenuous tasks: speaking on behalf of the National Multiple Sclerosis Society and lending emotional support to people in crisis through the lay ministry program she helped start at her church. Both Esther and Gloria are unemployed, but neither is out of work.

Coming to terms with chronic illness is, in many ways, like a conversion experience. It alters your outlook on life, reorders your values, changes your behavior, and can leave you with a missionary zeal to aid others in a similar predicament. Rosemary McKuen's story illustrates this remarkably well. During the five years of her life in which ulcerative colitis was a constant worry, she struggled to piece together a career in publicity writing and fundraising, combining part-time and freelance work. In retrospect, she is amazed at how productive she was at a time when she was filling her private journal with lamentations about illness. Her self-esteem, however, was at an ebb. Following her ileostomy, the surgery that removed her inflamed bowel, she spent some time on what she calls "headscratching," reconsidering her original aspirations. In addition to taking a clerical job, she started doing volunteer work for the American Cancer Society and was soon asked to speak to other ostomy patients about her experience. Traveling around the state appearing before groups, she discovered skills that she did not realize she had and learned that she could be effective in helping other people come to terms with illness. The work required her to reflect on her life and to think about what had sustained her during her many crises. After five years of this, at age thirty-nine, she enrolled in a seminary to prepare for a ministry in pastoral care with the chronically ill.

In the end, this book may be the most concrete example I can offer of illness providing a vocation. Always on the alert for redeeming value in this otherwise dreadful experience, I have been quick to believe those who tell me that writing it is my destiny. If I can successfully convey the experience of chronic illness to readers, then I have found my place of usefulness and can feel satisfied with my achievement. *Wuthering Heights* or *Jane Eyre* it isn't, but I have managed to pass up the Brontë sisters in one very important respect: I have outlived all three of them.

Chapter
6

Growing Up Sickly

"So that was who I was: the kind of kid who'd get sick if she didn't wear a neckscarf."

I was seven when I got polio. I had been sick with what seemed like the flu for a couple of days, and all of a sudden I was just devastated. We went into the doctor's office. My father had been called down from work. The doctor took a spinal tap and read it and went into the next room and closed the door, but I could hear every word he said. It was a restrained panic on his part. He said, "I'm calling an ambulance right away. She has polio. I'm going to have to take her to Sister Kenny." Right away! I couldn't even go home. I remember there was a real critical thing about catching it. He said, "She has bulbar polio and it's in her spine." I remember my father saying, "No, no, no. We'll take her up." And the doctor said, "No, you can't do that. She's got to get up there right away in an ambulance." My father said, "We'll make a bed for her in the back seat." He was very insistent and very strong, which was uncharacteristic, I think, of my father, because usually he would bow to a doctor's authority. My mother was in on it, too: "We'll make a bed for her in the back seat."

So they went to get the car and they put the blanket down. I remember being put in the bed. I remember lying there. I couldn't raise my head, I was so weak. They brought me into Sister Kenny. I was not in the lobby, I don't think, for more than five minutes. A little Filipino woman came with a wheelchair and took me off, and I didn't see my parents again for a month. And I think that will teach you how to be *real tough* and unneedy and not to show it. I was put into an infant ward with white iron cribs all around me because they had no room in my ward. Those babies—*babies*—cried incessantly. I had already worn glasses since I was four, and when I was moved out of the infant ward shortly thereafter, they lost my glasses. I was moved into the hallway right between two iron lungs. On one side of me, I remember a neck and a head. That was all I saw of the child. I didn't understand what in the world was happening, but I remember a feeling like, "Hang on, kid." Nobody explained anything to me. I had no idea what was going on. I knew I was sick. That was all I knew. You see, I was so weak, but not so weak I wasn't scared. The nurses were very perfunctory. I don't remember one nice nurse. I'm sure there were nice nurses, but they were too busy. They just couldn't cope with all the people. It was an epidemic.

Finally, I was moved into the children's ward where it was bed-bed-bed-bed-bed-bed . . . many, many beds on both sides and windows at one end. There must have been ten kids on each side, all girls. That was such a relief, to be with kids, and we could talk across the way. I made real good friends with one of the girls across from me. But there was some real pathos in there—kids who were already crippled up.

The nurses would come in with wringer washing machines and they'd put army blankets in boiling water, and then they'd put them in the air a little bit and then slap them on your body. They would wrap your legs up in those blankets. Not a word did they say. I don't remember them talking to us. This happened many times a day. I remember one time one of them really burned my foot, and I would not say a word about it. I told Jeannie, my friend across the aisle, afterwards, but I would not say a word. So that toughness, you know, whatever it is with kids . . .

When they transferred me from bed to bed, they had always carried me. And we always used a bedpan. The doctor and the nurse came to my bed one day. I don't know how long I had been there, but it was before my parents had been up at all. They got me over to the side of the bed and propped me up, and they had a hold of my shoulders. Then they released me and said, "Okay now, stand up." And I stood up, fully expecting to stand, and my legs wouldn't support me, and I fell and they caught me. And it was a *complete surprise* to me. Now maybe the nurse stayed back with me and talked to me about it, but I don't remember it. I remember her putting me back down and going away. I can't explain to you the feeling.

I would get letters from my parents and I could read printing, so they would print, and they'd send me stuff almost every day. Oh, it was so good to get mail. I've still got those letters. I remember phrases like "my good little girl" and "my sweet little girl," which were not the feelings that were inside of me. There's no memory that I have of ever expressing those feelings in the hospital, of expressing my fear to anyone, or that anyone ever held me. I remember when my parents first came, and I wanted to be so good for them. I just needed their comfort. It was the feeling I can get from them now when they're around me and I'm ill: "Oh, thank God, somebody loves me. Thank God, somebody's there, somebody wants to come and see me. They're not doing it out of pity. They care, and I trust that they care." But I don't think I ever got to express my need. I mean, when you're swooped away from your folks like that and set in with a bunch of babies, what are you going to do? You have to survive, so you crawl into yourself.

Of course, I did survive. I had the worst kind of polio you can have, and look at me. Every time I'd go back to Sister Kenny for a checkup, the doctors would look at me and look at my mother and say, "She is such a lucky girl. What a lucky little girl." I didn't know what to do with that except to feel grateful, but I remember feeling angry: "So what's lucky about what happened to me?"

This is where Kathy Halvorson's experience of chronic illness begins. Is it any wonder that she goes into hiding when she gets sick, having learned so young that the way to survive is to crawl into yourself? Or that she endures pain alone at home rather than going to the hospital, having such vivid memories of a traumatic hospitalization? Or that she is reluctant to let her parents know when she is sick, having heard the worry in their voices and knowing how much it meant to them for her to be good? Is it any wonder that she downplays the seriousness of her symptoms and covers them up with joking, having been told how lucky she is not to be crippled? Or that she has no expectation of comfort from friends, having been deprived of it at an age when it is a primary need?

Kathy's story speaks eloquently for itself, as a childhood memoir. Placed in the context of the rest of her life, it shows how powerfully an early experience of illness can influence the way you react to illness in adulthood. Witness Kathy's first visit to a neurologist for numbness in her limbs:

> He did a lot of tests on me and was extremely serious and engaged me in dialogue and talked a lot. And I was pretty distant from him. I wasn't willing to be open at all. I gave him the information he wanted, but he wasn't going to see my emotions. I was real scared. I was a good patient, still. I didn't want anybody to see that this was a big deal for me. And so he did a spinal tap and he said, "You know, things are abnormal to a point where it could easily be multiple sclerosis." He was very concerned, and talked to me at length about what that meant. I wasn't hearing a lot of it. It was like, "So what else is new?"

The spinal tap evoked unpleasant memories: "I had to be real steely about it, because it was real scary for me when I was little." When the doctor had finished with her, she was ushered into a dark room to lie down for a few hours to recover. Instead, "I got up after about ten minutes when I was sure no nurses were guarding the door, and walked home, feeling kind of impervious in a real strange way. It wasn't long after I got home that I had the worst headache I've ever had in my life." A friend found her in this condition and called the doctor, who was alarmed enough to make a house call. She still remembers hearing the thump-thump of his crutches as he came up the stairs to her apartment. Ironically, he too had polio as a child. Kathy's friend also summoned her parents from out of town:

> Everybody was standing around my bed. I can't remember telling anybody that they suspected multiple sclerosis. I don't know what I told them. The headache did not leave me for about two solid days. He couldn't give me anything to take that pain away. I had no idea I was going to get a headache. I just thought maybe I might faint on the way home, but that was all right. I'd make it. It made me angry. I was angry that I had to go through with it. It made me angry that I had to go public with it like that.

This resembles the polio experience in some ways, but with a significant difference: The powerless child has grown into an adult determined to retain control over everything: her emotions, her medical treatment, her whereabouts, the knowledge of her illness, other people's reactions and perceptions of her. The influence of childhood illness is not always simply determinative: once a poor sickly kid, always a poor sickly kid. That poor sickly kid can as likely turn the experience on its head and emerge as a strong-willed adult intent on perfect health.

The sort of butterfly you become depends on the nature of the cocoon that childhood illness spins around you. As people tell their stories about growing up with illness, it is obvious that parents play the greatest role in forming that cocoon. I used to assume that my parents' extra protectiveness was the standard response. I have since learned that there are many variations, none of which assures that the child will grow up free of emotional scars to match the physical ones. As Arthur Kleinman points out, "Understanding the influence of illness on the family necessitates understanding the family itself, not just the illness." Some parents underplay the seriousness of the illness or at least strive to keep it private. Some type their children as fragile and put tight restrictions on them. Others resent their imperfect children and refuse to take the extra responsibility that illness imposes. Some become martyrs to the special needs of their sick children. Others doubt the veracity of their children's physical complaints. Finally, there are parents who recognize the seriousness of their children's illnesses and take the necessary measures to safeguard them, yet encourage them to behave as normally as possible. Interestingly, these parents are often ones who are chronically ill themselves.

Family Secrets

Rachel Ryder's epilepsy is a prime example of parental efforts to keep not only the illness itself, but also knowledge about it, in check. Having seizures was very stigmatizing in the 1950s, so Rachel's mother can hardly be blamed for wanting to protect her daughter from becoming a social outcast. Yet by not acknowledging the illness, she left Rachel at risk of physical injury. Rachel's feelings about her mother's behavior are quite ambivalent. On the one hand, she is grateful for the protection and for the fact that her mother's pretense that nothing was wrong meant that she was not barred from normal teenage activities. As a mother herself, she sympathizes with her mother's plight as a widow alone with an epileptic daughter, alert through the night to the rhythm of her breathing. Yet she is angry that her mother's fear of disapproval kept her from getting the medical attention she needed:

> My older sister said once that she told my mother epilepsy was what I had, but my mother wouldn't accept it or believe it. My sister married a fellow whose father was a country doctor and her husband would go out with his father on his rounds, so he was the only person who really knew what to do. One time when they were staying at our house, I had a seizure, and he came rushing in with a cold cloth and put it on my head. He was the first person who had done that, and it certainly felt good. He had the natural talent, whereas everybody else would just pretend nothing had happened.

Left with a faulty diagnosis of low blood sugar from a doctor whom Rachel suspects of wanting to preserve her family's good name, she had to sort things out for herself:

> The Dionne quintuplets were very popular then, and one of them died from having a seizure. She had smothered in her pillow. And when I read about that and how she had this seizure and nobody was with her, it just all of a sudden fell into place. So I knew that I had epilepsy. I didn't even talk about it to anybody. I just knew in my heart that I had that. Maybe I assumed there was nothing you could do. And I was very scared.

Besides scaring her, this unspeakable secret made her both distrustful and ashamed. When she saw teachers at school conferring in low voices, she was sure they were talking about her. Once a counselor invited her to talk about the problem and offered his support, but she could not open up. Her mother's reaction to the diagnosis she finally received at age twenty-two deepened her shame, as well as made her angry:

> The neurologist came in and said, "Well, the good news is that you don't have a brain tumor." I said, "Well, what *do* I

> have?" He said, "Oh, don't you know you have epilepsy?"
> When my mother came up to see me that night I told her this
> and she burst into tears. I don't know, but I have a feeling it
> was almost as if a brain tumor would have been more
> acceptable.

There are, of course, other ways to interpret Rachel's mother's
tears: Relief at finally knowing the answer or at least having it
out in the open. Guilt about keeping the truth from her daughter for so long. Genuine sorrow that would be a natural response
to either epilepsy or a brain tumor. But what matters here is the
message Rachel read in her mother's behavior: Her epilepsy was
a shameful secret. Rachel herself kept that secret, even from her
own children, for the next twenty years. She believes that this
childhood model of secrecy made her well suited for the role she
came to play in her marriage—covering for her husband's
alcoholism.

The preservation of family privacy figures very strongly in
Phyllis Mueller's childhood experience, as well. As far back as
Phyllis can remember, she had stomachaches and muscle spasms,
but they grew worse at age ten. The change in her condition occurred right after her mother suffered what Phyllis calls "an emotional breakdown." She describes her mother as quite unstable all
along, a woman who "just didn't have it together to parent." For
example, when five-year-old Phyllis and her older sister would not
stop fighting in the backseat of the car, her mother left Phyllis at
the side of a country road and drove off to do her shopping. After
the breakdown, she had no resources for coping with the illness
of her child. Phyllis remembers being punished on mornings
when she had trouble getting up for school after a sleepless night,
but she can recall no signs of compassion:

> At one point, I remember, I was very sick and I said to my
> mother, "Mom, I just don't understand why I keep having
> these stomachaches. I don't know what it is. Do you know

what it is?" And she said, "Well, maybe it's cancer." I said, "What is that?" And she said, "Well, it's pretty bad, and if you've got it you'll die from it." I'm not sure I ever recovered from hearing that. I can remember becoming markedly worse after that.

As young as she was, Phyllis suspected a relationship between her mother's emotional illness and her own digestive problems. But she knew better than to talk about these things with the doctor. Her mother's breakdown was a family secret. While her father was caring enough to be remembered as the only "anchor" she had at home, he was complicit in protecting her mother from exposure and judgment:

> The doctor would say, "Is there anything bothering you?" My father would be sitting right there and I would not be able to tell them. It was a tremendous time of frustration for me. I cried a lot by myself because I thought I could get help if I could tell them what was wrong, but I knew I couldn't tell them for fear of punishment. Even when I was alone with the doctor, it was sort of like what I read about in concentration camps: You can tell now but you pay at the other end.

Her mother even blamed Phyllis's illness for her breakdown, and the accusation took hold. Phyllis began feeling responsible enough for the family problems to deny the reality of her memories for many years. It took psychotherapy to get her to examine the link between her illness and her abusive family situation:

> I felt a tremendous sense of rejection in that home, a tremendous amount of disapproval, and of course at age ten I can't understand why this lady doesn't like me. I mean, even much earlier than that I had come to that conclusion. So, in essence, I had to survive there, and my physical body paid for it, in a lot of ways. I think it became sort of a learned response, so that everything that happened subsequent to

that, my body did the same thing that it did when I was a child.

As an adult, that rejected sickly child withdraws when she is sick and nurses herself back to health, not wanting to risk inflicting her pain on others. But this is by no means a tragic ending. The traits that come through clearly when Phyllis tells her story are strength of character and a tremendous will to live happily even in the midst of pain. "Do you think there's a payoff in this?" she asks.

The Indulged Child

Being cast as the family's sickly child can be a powerful impetus for developing your internal resources, whether you are rejected, like Phyllis, or indulged, as I was. Although my liver disease, as I know it now, was dormant in childhood, I was very susceptible to whatever was going around. The story of my life, as told by my family, is a series of bizarre illnesses and frightening brushes with death. Very early on, I was marked, like Beth in *Little Women,* as the sickly little sister, the one to be pampered and protected so that a cough wouldn't become pneumonia or a sore throat scarlet fever. I was happy in this role only when I could exploit it to get out of going to school: All I had to do was get up in the morning, hold my stomach and moan, "I don't feel good." "You do look a little pale and peaked," my mother would say. "Maybe you'd better stay home." I usually spent the day reading books of my own choosing that I would not have had time to read without this handy excuse. But when my parents narrowed my limits to guard my health, I rebelled, becoming obstinate and defiant. When I call up my own memories and compare them with other people's recollections to see what sort of character I was as a child, the traits that emerge are intellectual precocity, an inner conviction about what is right that often set me at odds with adult authority, physical fragility, and a heightened sense of mortal danger. The first two were matters of pride, and I exaggerated them to cover for the last two, which caused me great embarrassment. I severed my mind from my body and staked everything on my intellect. For me, as for Phyllis, there was a payoff: an emotional strength that has helped me through life's misfortunes. But pretending your body isn't there is still an unhealthy sacrifice, no matter what the reward.

A family's response to illness in its midst depends, too, on the family's configuration. I suspect that being seven to ten years younger than my healthier sisters made me even more suited for the role of sickly kid. My sisters enjoyed more freedom and were entrusted with far more responsibility than I was, including the care of their skinny little sister. When I felt most constrained by parental protection, I thought of myself as an only child with three mothers and had to show a triple measure of defiance. Kathy Halvorson formed her identity as one who was physically vulnerable and deficient by contrasting herself with her brother:

> My mother was always saying, "Kathy gets it so hard. Anything that comes, she gets, and anything she gets, she gets it real hard. John hardly ever gets anything, and he's up in two days. And Kathy just lies in bed and throws up in a pan." So that was who I was: the kind of kid who'd get sick if she didn't wear a neckscarf. And my brother would just run out the door and deliver papers and he would be fine. How much is that a self-fulfilling prophecy and how much is that I just had a deficient body?

When that role of sickly child is fully occupied, there may be little room to accommodate the illnesses of other family members. Susan Alm now believes that she showed early symptoms of lupus in adolescence, but they were never taken seriously:

> I can remember my mother telling me, "You're not sick, you just think you are." It's like you're making this illness happen because you're lazy or you're trying to escape something. You

could be better if you thought you would be. The power of positive thinking. That's been haunting me all my life. All it did for me was to make me feel guilty. I didn't want to be sick. I didn't want to feel this way. And yet I was not able to control it. The point at which I realized that my mother's view of it wasn't really true was years later, when I woke up and my first conscious thought was pain. It was there before I could think in the morning. It preceded any willful act.

Susan happens to have a sister with a visible disability, which *was* acknowledged. Susan explains, "I wasn't the sick one; she was the one that had a problem. And I don't think any of them ever thought I was sick because I always looked all right." In Phyllis Mueller's case, the sickly role was occupied by her mother, whose emotional illness contributed to a family pathology with some serious adverse effects.

My family's configuration around my illness was severely jolted in middle age when both of my sisters were diagnosed with cancer, within less than a year of each other. I was cast into the unfamiliar position of the healthy sibling, and I felt the powerlessness that person feels in the face of another's needs. It was hard for my dad to make the adjustment, and he still called more frequently to check on my health than on my sisters'. My mother has Alzheimer's disease and could not hang onto the fact that Nancy and Joey had cancer and were going through chemotherapy. One of my saddest memories is of the family get-together we had for Joey's sixtieth birthday, which turned out to be her last. In the middle of everything, I felt the pain likely to be a stone caught in a bile duct. I tried to imagine it away as indigestion, but the cold sweat and dizziness couldn't be denied. I wanted to go home, but Nancy, ever the protective big sister, wouldn't let me. So I took one of the pain pills I carry and lay down on the couch. This scene must have jarred an old, old memory loose in my mother's brain. Soon she was standing at my side, crying and saying, "I worry so much when she's sick like that." I felt for my mother, who had to live with that anxiety for my health, but I felt still more for Joey, who had to endure the worst and final illness of her life without the comforting indulgence that Mom had always shown me.

Resentment and Denial

When a child's illness is unusually preoccupying, all the family relationships can suffer strain. Such is the case in Sandra Stieglitz's family. Her problems began in very early childhood with flulike symptoms that may have been allergic reactions. She remembers being either hyperactive or fatigued all the time and never feeling well. Her parents consulted many different doctors, who tried many different remedies, some of which only made her feel worse. The doctors' inability to find a clear physical cause tried her parents' patience and strained their credulity. They found no way to manage the illness other than to try, at times, to deny its reality altogether. Once, when she lost her vision temporarily, her father took her to a movie to cheer her up. She describes their response as "not wanting to believe me, but believing the experts. It was so changeable. Loving, caring, wanting to do what's right, but pushing, trying to do what the doctors say. Whenever there was hope, they'd go looking for an answer." The answer kept eluding them and, by her early teens, Sandra had been, to use her words, "thrown into the wastebasket of psychosomatic medicine, which means I ended up with a psychiatrist." She was diagnosed as schizophrenic, and her life became a chilling story of hospitalizations, suicide attempts, and antisocial behavior that absorbed the family's time, money, and emotions. As a consequence, her siblings' childhoods were, Sandra says, "deprived." Though they feel sympathy for her, their relationships with her are clouded by resentment and fear of being burdened by her needs. Both of them have pulled away, explaining that they need to do so to restore their balance. This leaves Sandra feeling both guilty for the pain her illness has caused them and victimized because, without them, she has little emotional support. She still lives with her parents as a permanently dependent daughter, but they, too, are in danger of becoming emotionally depleted. All the family members are, in some sense, martyrs to her illness.

Sandra's case has subsequently been reevaluated by doctors who see a connection between certain severe allergies and hormonal deficiencies and emotional instability, but this new information comes too late to free Sandra from the stigma of mental illness. She describes herself with a tragic fatalism that now governs her life:

> I believe that I was born sick, and I believe it's hereditary, and I believe it's things outside me. But there's also something sad and broken and unhappy about me, and I don't know how much that contributes. I was such a sad child, and I don't know how much is the result of the illness and how much is the cause. I just wonder if at some point as a child I was so defeated, that wherever those choices were for my body, I headed more and more in a serious direction.

Just a Normal Kid

The risk that a child's illness may dominate the whole family is no doubt best known to parents who are chronically ill themselves. Don Welke and Lily Washington both inherited their diseases from their mothers, who were intent on reducing its impact on their children's psychological development. When Don contracted diabetes at age eleven, the only restriction he noticed was a new set of eating habits. He did make frequent trips to the hospital in the first year of the illness, while his insulin level was being adjusted, but after that he learned to maintain the balance himself. His mother, diabetic for the previous ten years, was determined to keep his life as normal as possible. His parents placed no extraordinary limits on his activities and even sent him off to Boy Scout camp with his insulin and syringes. Since they were so matter-of-fact, he saw no reason to be secretive in front of his friends:

When I had to go take a shot, I had every kid in the place coming around watching me. The Scoutmaster couldn't stand to look at needles. He always had to leave the tent, or else he'd pass out. They'd almost charge admission in the tent to come in and see the kid take a shot. I felt like a celebrity and I played it to the hilt. And yet, as soon as the shot was done, there was nothing more special about it. They'd say, "Oh, that's nice, and we'd go back to normal."

It was only when he visited his grandmother that he got a sense of being "the different kid in the family." She fixed him special desserts and offered privileges that he was not entitled to at home. For the most part, he claims, "I really didn't think about the disease much. I just treated it. It was just there."

Curiously, Don's mother did not treat her own diabetes as sensibly as she treated his. While he surely benefited from medical advances in the ten years between the onset of her illness and his, he also believes she let the disease get out of hand. When her vision failed, she became immobilized by depression and did not seek treatment in time. She stopped taking medicine that didn't immediately relieve her misery. She has become, in Don's mind, not only the source of encouragement who kept his childhood normal, but also a negative example of how to maintain the illness in the long run. At the time I talked with Don, she had been considering taking herself off kidney dialysis—in effect, letting herself die. He was the only one of the children not visibly upset by the prospect:

I felt relieved. I thought, finally she's going to get what she's been wanting for so many years—peace. Her life is about 90 percent miserable. There's nothing medical science can do for her. She's gone beyond that point. She just wants to call it quits, which is an option a lot of dialysis patients have to cope with. I thought, well, if she wants to do this, that's fine with me because I know how much she's suffered. My brothers and sisters got really upset about it, but they don't know what it's like. They're not going through it.

He was not entirely blasé about it, however. Grief over the anticipated loss of his mother and anxiety about suffering a similar fate found expression in ulcerlike symptoms. A few months later, Don's mother did choose to die, at age fifty-four. The legacy she left him was a determination to keep a positive outlook and to practice reasonable caution so that he can enjoy a normal adulthood.

Lily Washington never even ran the risk of being cast as the sickly child. Asthma is her family's normal condition. All seven of her brothers and sisters have it. Their mother taught them both by word and example that they need not give in to the disease. She gave them their medicine and whatever attention they required to get through an attack safely, but she refused to treat them as "babies," a word she still uses to scold them if they complain about being sick. Lily summarizes her mother's advice as "Okay, you've got it. There's nothing you can do about it. Don't let it slow you down. Whatever you want to do, do it." Lily herself sees this approach to illness as part of a broader outlook on life that she and her mother share as African American women. The asthma was just one more disadvantage to overcome, one more test of her will and her strength to survive.

Like Don, who understood his mother's desire to die, Lily is hardly ignorant of the seriousness of this illness she has inherited. While her mother encouraged the children to live as though they were healthy, she did not protect them from seeing how devastating asthma can be. When Lily was seven, she and the other children stood by her grandmother's hospital bed and watched her gasp for breath as she lay dying.

Evidently it left a lasting impression. The frightening thing as I get older is that I see it getting worse with age. I have dreams sometimes about my grandmother's death. It's a slow, drawn-out, suffering kind of death. It was only a few years ago that this brought home to me that, well, I can die from this.

Don and Lily came out of their childhood experiences with mixed, but realistic, messages about their illnesses: You can live normally with them, or they can kill you. As adults, they behave quite differently from each other. Don exercises a practical caution. Lily does as she pleases and treats the consequences. Thanks to their parents' deliberate efforts to treat them like normal children, they both feel entitled to manage their illnesses as they see fit.

Among Friends

Whatever a family does to help or hinder a child's adjustment to illness, the outcome is repeatedly tested in the child's interaction with peers. The conformist tendency natural in childhood can be an oppressive force for a child made "different" by illness. Many of us have vivid and embarrassing recollections of when our playmates and classmates found us out. For Esther Green, it happened over and over. Asthmatic as a child, she was treated "almost like a glass doll." She lived under strict rules of behavior, and whenever she had a bad attack of wheezing, her parents managed to find some rule she had disobeyed to hold her accountable for bringing the attack on. Summer was the worst time.

> I remember the kids would come by and they would knock and want to know if I could come out. And my mother would say, "No, she can't come out and play. She has asthma." Well, this made me angry, because they said "asthma" and the kids didn't know what that was. They said, "the huffs." I could hear in the house, how they would run around and say, "Esther's got the huffs. Esther's got the huffs. She can't come out and play." And I said, "Oh, why did you have to tell them that?"

Besides embarrassment, Esther felt keen disappointment at not being able to take part in activities that children normally enjoy. She couldn't help but break her parents' rules. Sitting still on the steps while her sisters jumped rope was too much to expect of a child. That sense of injustice has stuck with her.

When Kathy Halvorson returned home from the Sister Kenny Institute, she had to do physical therapy exercises several times a day. What she remembers most about them is that no one outside the family ever watched. Her parents would send her playmates home when it was time for her exercises. "That was hard. It was kind of a funny feeling, like it had to be done in private." She assumed that her experience with polio was something to keep to herself:

> We had to take the Sabin vaccine, the sugar cubes, at school. I had a note from my parents saying I shouldn't take it. Somehow I was responsible enough to ask them, and they checked with the doctor, and he said I never had to take it because I am immune to polio. I was so embarrassed about that that I lined up anyway, and I got right up to the person who was giving out the vaccine, and I stepped out of line.

As soon as Kathy started menstruating, she began having the painful cramps and lengthy periods later diagnosed as endometriosis. Again, her family's sense of privacy set the tone. Her mother let her understand that she could stay home in bed if she needed, but she was much too reticent to discuss the pain and bleeding as a problem to be resolved. Kathy got the message, reinforced by the culture around her, that this was indeed "The Curse" and simply must be endured. Her feelings of shame at being so severely afflicted kept her stoical enough that even her closest friends weren't aware of how much pain she was in:

> I was even afraid to take Midol for the pain, because it made me seem like a baby. See, there was this dichotomy: Other girls went to school and didn't get down with their periods,

yet I would stay home in pain. It was something I had to plan my entire social life around, every month. And another thing I was angry about: They talk about this cycle, this twenty-eight-day cycle? Mine was twenty-one days. I would secure all my own stuff, like sanitary napkins. But I still couldn't buy it. I had a friend who would get it for me. I'd be so happy, like a smoker who's just gotten a carton of cigarettes. I would go shopping with my mother on Friday nights, and I would dread getting to that aisle. I would attempt to pull it off the shelf. Often I couldn't do it. When I succeeded, she would scoot ahead with the cart, so I'd have to run after her with this purple package. It was a really shameful thing.

Rachel Ryder's shame about being different was intense enough that she uses the word "paranoid" to describe herself as an adolescent. Even though she had a group of friends with whom she went to movies and parties, she worried constantly that they would resent having to take care of her if she had a seizure. Once they were planning to drive to a ski hill about thirty miles away, where they had gone before by bus. As Rachel was getting ready that morning, her best friend called to tell her there wasn't enough room for her in the car:

I was really, really upset about that, because I thought it was because of my seizures that they had chosen to leave me out. They probably didn't want to be responsible. They would have to bring me home early. So I remember standing at a window in our house where I could see my girlfriend's house and see them pick her up. I was standing there crying and my sister was kind of hovering around. I think my sister and my mother really felt very bad, too. But they never came to pick my friend up, and about half an hour later she called me and said, "Well, I decided not to go either." I never figured that one out, but anyway she didn't go and so I didn't feel quite so bad.

It may well have been because of the seizures that Rachel was considered the most dispensable person in the group. If so, her best friend was expressing solidarity with Rachel by choosing to stay home. Considering how important it is to most teenagers to be in favor with a group, that was a bold decision, as well as an empathic one.

Despite being different, Lorraine Czerny managed to grow up without that lingering sense of shame. Lorraine's heart was permanently weakened after she had scarlet fever at age four. She was left with chorea, or Saint Vitus' dance, which she outgrew after a few years, but her identity as the little girl who twitched had already been established. Her parents protected her by taking her only to church or to family gatherings where she would not likely encounter strangers. Surprisingly, she did not think of herself as a sickly child, but attributed her sense of difference to the fact that she was the youngest in the family and a farm girl at school in town:

> I never thought of myself as sickly. I remember a cousin told me I couldn't throw a ball straight. I said, "Why not?" "Well, because you shake so." I was probably eight or nine, and I was so astounded because I never thought of myself that way. A friend of mine remembers how I used to sit in church and pleat my dress with my fingers. I don't remember that.

What Lorraine does remember is "getting nervous" when asked to do something in front of her classmates, and feeling that she could never live up to the expectations that others had for themselves. This, she believes, has kept her from setting very high goals.

A Special Glow

Whether we were indulged at home as our family's most fragile child, mistreated because of our physical defects, or encouraged to develop our strengths, most of us learned early on that passing as healthy is the safest choice among peers. The role of the sickly kid is not usually a rewarding one. When circumstances forced us into it, we found ways to keep ourselves from being rejected. Behaving as though exalted by illness is one way to adapt. Don Welke escaped social stigma by turning his insulin shots into a carnival performance and playing the hero of the moment. But he was pleased that everything returned to normal when the show was over. There is a special place reserved for the noble sufferer, but occupying it successfully takes other redeeming qualities, like toughness, in Don's case, or, for girls, angelic beauty and kindness.

When I was about nine or ten, I allied myself with a fragile-looking blonde in my class who was allergic to the most basic foods, like eggs and milk. She had lots of friends who made a group project out of protecting her from adults' innocent mistakes. Several kids in the class could recite her list of allergies. It gave her a special glow, and I stayed close in the hope that it might reflect on me. I remember sitting on the steps of the school with her one day after a mass immunization. Both of us—but only us two—had gotten woozy from the serum. It was a privilege to be allowed fresh air on class time, and I remember thinking that she was much more entitled to it than I was. She, after all, had allergies and I was just sickly for no good reason. When I developed a spastic colon in junior high school, I finally had something concrete to go on. It was a malady that fit well with my identity as a high achiever, and my lopsided walk when the cramps were bad became a subject of friendly joking among my classmates. In more serious moments, I was congratulated for my perseverance, and there was some reward in that. Nevertheless, this wretched physical weakness was not what I would have chosen for myself. Because I couldn't hide it completely, I made light of it by flaunting my ineptitude at sports, on the mistaken assumption that athletic skill and intelligence were incompatible. Now, when I watch girls' basketball tournaments on television, I remember so well how I truly longed to shoot baskets.

In recounting her memories of a childhood beset by whooping cough, pneumonia, and a string of common illnesses that kept her back a grade in school, Donna Schneider concludes, "I was very shy and always felt like I was on the outside looking in." She follows that with an image of herself literally on the inside looking out: the poor, sick child left watching out the window as her father takes a visiting cousin to the zoo. The image should feel familiar to many of us who were ill as children.

Did It Really Happen That Way?

In talking about our early experiences of illness, each of us is, in effect, reconstructing childhood around a particular theme, selecting images that have some relevance to it and bypassing memories in which the matter of health is not of consequence. This is tricky business indeed. Events in our lives change their proportions as time intervenes, and some fade from memory altogether. Kathy Halvorson's recollection of the Sister Kenny Institute is almost surrealistic in its vivid detail: the white iron cribs and the windows at the end of the long row of beds. So critical was her entrance into the building that she remembers the face of a woman she saw for only a few minutes. Yet she has forgotten whether the nurses talked to her or whether anyone explained why she couldn't stand up. The horror of this memory is, of course, a reflection of a seven-year-old girl's profound fears. It is not a totally accurate and documentable portrayal, and Kathy knows that herself. "How do I know it really happened this way?" she wonders.

As we recall these childhood experiences, we focus, sometimes less than consciously, on features that serve our present needs. Still angry about having to suffer and yet feel grateful, Kathy found a rare outlet for her anger in the telling of her horror story. For years, Rachel Ryder believed that her grand mal seizures started after her father was killed in an accident. When her older sister told her there were several before that, she could no longer explain it away as the result of emotional trauma, but had to consider that the disease originated in her body. Once she had reconciled herself to that, she could look back and see that the seizures were not the whole story. She did have fun with friends. She did get good grades in school. Lorraine Czerny's ignorance of her sickly demeanor probably helped to make her the spunky, vital, white-haired woman she is now.

Telling a coherent story that explains how you came to deal with illness the way you do requires some consistency of character. But consistency is not a fact of life. Once you have had the catharsis of telling what it was like, the next step is to go back and correct for malproportions. I said, for instance, that I rebelled against my parents' protectiveness. I have plenty of nostalgic memories, however, of being confined at home and having my mother's full, solicitous attention. Getting sick was even a way to get attention when I wanted it. I also said that I was embarrassed about my physical frailty and tried to cover it over, but at other times I felt exalted by it, especially when I was under the influence of sentimental novels about children not meant for this world who had already been transformed into angels. Getting sick was a way to avoid discipline. In my house, unlike Phyllis Mueller's, a sick child was a good child.

Who's at Fault?

Those of us whose families are still around have an ongoing check on the accuracy of our stories, because the patterns established in childhood have a way of continuing. Illness can be like an extended childhood, by serving as an excuse for parents to prolong their authority over their children. The most troublesome way my parents did this was by offering me advice on how to stay healthy. This was once the cause of a rare confrontation with them. When I called to tell them I was sick again, they immediately began looking for explanations and found them in my behavior: If only I had stayed in out of the cold, if only I hadn't been working so hard, if only I had used a vaporizer in my bedroom at night . . . In other words, if only I had done as I was told, this wouldn't have happened. I answered curtly and followed the conversation up with what I thought was a reasonable and heartfelt letter asking for their respect. I explained that the first priority of any healthy-minded person with a chronic illness is to stay healthy in body, as well. They could trust me to take whatever measures were necessary. I asked them to accept my illness as I had and stop looking either for miracle cures or for a cause to blame. I hoped, especially, that they would stop blaming me. The letter's effect was not at all what I intended. They found it accusatory and offensive. My efforts to clarify how I felt had only confounded the problem. When my mother told my sister about it, she used one of her favorite pejorative terms to describe my behavior: "I don't know why she has to be so independent," she said. The choice of words was an eye-opener. I saw that we had a conflict of interests: She wanted to keep mothering the sickly child, while I wanted to break my cocoon and emerge as an adult for whom independence is a virtue.

Since then, I have come to understand why my parents might want to perpetuate the old pattern, and why it confounds them when I refuse to play my assigned role. For one thing, we are an upwardly mobile working-class family. My father has a rural background, and my mother's parents are immigrants. Each generation has departed in some significant way from the previous one. My life, too, has taken a different course from my parents' and, as a result, our habits and values are not entirely compatible. They are typical Depression survivors who save empty Band-Aid boxes and would feel profligate if they hired someone to do household repairs. I am a first-wave baby boomer who came of age in an era of prosperity, college scholarships, social activism, and feminist consciousness. The firmest common ground we have may be the shared history of my illness. In any such family, perpetuating the child's vulnerability is a way of ensuring that the parents will always be necessary.

Becoming a parent has helped me see what great responsibility they must have felt raising a child whose health was precarious. Parents' influence over how their children turn out has recently been called into debate. Some insist that parents can't compete with television and peer pressure, while others believe—or at least fear—that for every mistake a parent makes, there is a certain deleterious consequence. How powerless my parents must have felt when they could not save me from illness. Setting up rules of behavior with predictable consequences—"If you don't put those mittens on, you'll catch pneumonia!"—was as close as they could come to exerting control over an irrational force that defies even medical science. Then, like Esther Green's parents, they could blame the illness on my misbehavior and absolve themselves of guilt.

Feeling responsible and powerless at the same time surely must leave many parents feeling guilty, as well, for whatever suffering their children endure. Not long before Alzheimer's set in, my mother had gall bladder surgery that included a liver biopsy, and the report mentioned a couple of tiny cysts in her liver. "So it was my fault, after all," she said, as though we had all been waiting for someone to take the blame. I want to reassure my parents that I neither hold them accountable for my illness nor expect them to fix it, though I think I understand their impulse to try. When Bill Gordon told me how unnerving it is to hear his mother say, "Buck up," or "Just pretend it isn't there," in the midst of his depression, I understood both his anger and her frustration at having nothing more efficacious to offer.

Everybody's Illness

It has also dawned on me that this illness of mine is not my exclusive property. It touched the lives of my parents and sisters in very crucial ways. Having a child or a sibling whose health and life are at risk is an experience in itself that poses different problems than the experience of being sick. Doctors are becoming wiser about including parents and siblings in the treatment plan for the child and seeing that their needs, too, get some attention. Don Welke saw how his diabetes affected the whole family when he had to turn to them to ask for the extravagant gift of a kidney to replace his diseased ones. His brothers and sisters resumed their old places. The brother who is repulsed by illness was not a likely candidate, he knew. While the rest all had themselves tested for matching, only the usually supportive sister was willing to go ahead. "I didn't think she was going to do it, but she had a big deal about being the one to do it. It was her job to donate that kidney, no matter what anybody said." Don does not hold any grudges against the others. It worked out fine in the end, and he would not have expected anything different.

There are other things—short of donating an organ—that parents and siblings may need to do both to convince themselves that they are doing justice to the family's sickly child and to relieve their own worries. Most of us appreciate these gestures as long as they do not limit us to a childlike dependence. During one long bout of illness, my oldest sister made herself more available than the circumstances of her life had ever permitted before. She came to the hospital every day and took me out on passes when I was well enough. After I got home, she took me grocery shopping every few days and made sure I got out of the house for some diversion. Even after I began feeling strong enough to manage on my own, she kept coming, and I couldn't help wondering why. I realized finally that being closely involved in my recovery was a way of easing her deeply embedded fear of losing her sister. She was helping herself as well as helping me.

Flashbacks

Childhood illness leaves other forms of residue as well, much of it lodged in regions of the brain that lie out of reach of rationality. Children caught in life-threatening situations that are far beyond their comprehension and control develop fears that are hard to dispel later in life. Phyllis Mueller, for instance, panics and breaks out in a cold, shivering sweat whenever she has to have anesthesia. She thinks she knows why. When her mother took her as a very small child to the hospital for a tonsillectomy, she told her they were going to church. She suspected a lie, but still didn't know what was happening when the anesthetist slapped the ether over her face. She can recall vividly the sensation of being smothered and screaming in fear. When Kathy Halvorson sees someone her age on crutches, she has a flashback to the Sister Kenny Institute and sees the many children with shriveled legs lying in the beds in her ward.

These reactions need not be permanent. All the anxiety about my health that I witnessed as a child left me feeling extremely vulnerable and terrified of anything that reminded me of death. I couldn't even watch the sun set without feeling melancholy. I was more afraid of the dark than any of my friends, or so I believed. Well beyond the age of reason, I insisted that my mother stay in my room until I fell asleep at night, for fear the Grim Reaper would come and spirit me away. This was terribly embarrassing and I could not admit it to anybody. Today, one of my favorite means of calming myself when I am feeling anxious is to walk around my house in the dark, looking out at the night sky through my deliberately uncurtained windows and then back at my familiar objects in the light of the moon. It is consoling precisely because it reminds me that I am not afraid anymore. I don't know if I overcame this fear or if it just subsided on its own, but the fact that it is gone gives me hope. Being a sickly kid may be a powerful determinant of how you behave in adulthood, but it is not Fate itself.

Chapter
7

For Better and for Worse

"Sometimes I wonder why my husband stays."

"What can you say about a twenty-five-year-old girl who died?" That was the opening line of Erich Segal's novel *Love Story*, a best-seller that was made into a hit movie when I, too, was twenty-five and in fragile health. The answer is "plenty." Well before Segal's Jenny succumbed, the fatally ill young heroine was a familiar literary type. Alexandre Dumas's novel and play about the life and death of a courtesan, *La Dame aux camélias*, inspired many variations on the lovely lost Camille. Sarah Bernhardt on stage and Greta Garbo on film made audiences weep over her translucent, consumptive beauty. In Verdi's opera *La Traviata*, Violetta expires in a poignant soprano, leaving Alfredo filled with remorse at having distrusted her. Likewise, Mimi in Puccini's *La Bohème* sings herself to death ... from a respiratory disease. The Broadway musical *Rent*, based on *La Bohème*, offers a twist on the theme. Its Mimi survives, but another character, Angel, a gay man who dresses in drag, replaces her in the pantheon of dying beauties. Thus the glow of tragic romance is cast over the young men who have died in the AIDS pandemic.

From artful literature to melodrama, these stories appeal because they speak to our fear of losing loved ones before we have loved them enough. When death cuts love short, as my daughter learned the six times she watched the movie *Titanic*, the heart just goes on and on. Of course, there is nothing mawkish about the grief felt when death really does come too early, as it did when Jonathan Larson, the author and composer of *Rent*, died at thirty-six of an aortic aneurysm, just nineteen days before the show's premiere. Yet the sentimentality associated with dying young and beloved can cause conflict for those who are young and chronically ill: It can incite you to wishful thinking or scare you out of your wits. And, as young readers have reminded me, it's best to be loved *before* you get sick. Looking for a companion when you are fatigued or throwing up every day is not especially romantic.

In the early years of my marriage, I was well steeped in the fairy tale of illness-afflicted romance, and I knew that *Love Story*'s was the happy ending. I had my own fantasy version of it, which I called forth whenever pain or a drop in energy level made me behave in unromantic ways: My husband, remarried to a practical, motherly woman, would fold back the T-shirts she had stacked so neatly in his underwear drawer and gently lift out a framed portrait, which he would gaze at lovingly. It was a photograph of me, his fond memory, skin unwrinkled, eyes bright, smiling eternally.

That was not to be my fate. As I grew older and felt my marriage growing more strained, a question far more complicated than *Love Story*'s came to mind: What do you say about a forty-year-old who survives to spend long years with the worried lover, but never gets any better? There is no literary formula for that one. When movies do illness at all, it's a quickly terminal cancer. Diane Keaton and Meryl Streep become middle-aged versions of Camille. If I think back through literature, all I come up with is Edith Wharton's *Ethan Frome*, living much too long with those two hellishly resentful disabled women.

It is commonly believed that adversity endured brings couples closer together, and many people who have been restored to health after a threatening illness will attest to the truth of that. But when adversity comes and goes and comes again, it's a different love story. The tragically ill protagonist may even outlive the relationship. I remember precisely when my belief in the bonding power of shared suffering faltered. A student of mine, newly married, spent a year facing the daily possibility of her husband's death from cancer. A superwoman of the emotions, she coached him in positive thinking and read all she could find about his type of cancer so they could make informed decisions about treatment. When he went into remission, they felt confident enough to take jobs in another part of the country. I often thought of them joined together in a heroic struggle against death, and I imagined how she would survive his death, if it came, as a saintly young widow. About two years later, I heard that she had left him for another man. I was shocked. How could she be so callous after all they had been through together?

The Toll Illness Takes

In reality, chronic illness takes a toll on relationships. There is no census to measure that toll, but anecdotal information from illness associations and support groups sets the divorce rate at higher than average. My marriage would be included in that count. As the illness continued to disrupt our life together with no promise of relief, a new fantasy took shape. Whenever the thought of how much my illness had restricted him weighed too heavily on my conscience, I plotted an escape that would free him from bondage and me from shame. I imagined myself getting on a bus headed for northernmost Canada and simply disappearing from his life. I would leave behind a note that read: "You're free of me now. Find a new, beautiful, young wife who dresses well, has perfect posture, is gracious with strangers, cooks gourmet meals, keeps her elbows off the table, and can have lots of little children who look just like you. It's what I want for you. Don't worry about me. You deserve to live happily ever after." How I would survive was beyond the scope of the fantasy, but by this point it had usually served its purpose, which was to relieve my guilt. In our eighteenth year of marriage, the fantasy came true. He was the one who left, however, for a brand new life in another state. The divorce forced me to rethink everything. Did the illness drive us apart or bind us together in spite of other serious tensions? Ours fit the pattern of the many baby-boomer marriages that fall victim to "midlife crisis," whether the partners are healthy or sick.

Just how illness affects marriage is difficult to determine, because marriage itself is a precarious institution given to constant buffeting by many forces. It cannot be seen in clear, still focus, as an otherwise stable relationship simply knocked off kilter by illness. Neither is marriage the only relationship that suffers. Longterm lovers, whether straight or gay, do not escape the turmoil. Accounts of losing a partner to AIDS, such as Mark Doty's lyrical *Heaven's Coast*, are beginning to illumine the impact of illness on gay men's relationships. These tend to deal, however, with final illness and death, and don't satisfy the need for testimony from longtime survivors who have maintained or lost relationships.

Gender Matters

As a union of two people of different genders, raised to meet differing, and sometimes incompatible, expectations, marriage is already conflict-ridden. Illness highlights and compounds the differences that gender makes. The behavior customarily expected of men who are sick is not what is expected of women, and men and women tend to respond differently to the illness of someone close to them.

The configuration sick husband/healthy wife has a corresponding cultural ideal that, even though outmoded, can still loom large when illness sets in. Though the husband is an object of sympathy, cast out by misfortune from his accustomed place as breadwinner, he is also expected to wage an admirable struggle against his infirmity, never letting his anxieties show. The one safe repository for his complaints is his wife, who should bear them with patient understanding and even detect and respond to the feelings that he cannot express directly. The ideal wife will also assume the practical responsibilities of a private duty nurse. She will shave him when he is bedridden, keep track of his medications, and adapt her cooking to his dietary needs. Now that she is also likely to be employed, she will either work longer hours, take a second job, or learn to be frugal to make up for his lost income. He will reward her with a quick recovery and public praise.

The men I interviewed generally portrayed their marriages as a team effort with wives who automatically assumed the help-meet role. Don Welke, for example, tells how his wife sat with him for twelve hours at a time following his transplant surgery, watching him have pain contractions, and how she kept after the nurses to see that he got his medication on schedule. Bill Gordon's wife has accompanied him to out-of-town hospitals to try out new remedies for manic-depression. From the beginning, she even assumed responsibility for keeping him alive. She and Bill agreed with his doctor that Bill would tell her whenever he began to feel suicidal, so that she could keep close watch:

> I never would have made it through this thing without her, because she's the one I went to when I had suicidal thoughts, and she would get up in the middle of the night and follow me downstairs to see if I was taking pills. Once she caught me down in the basement just kind of contemplating this rope. But still she's carried on with the house and the kids and tried to make things normal.

Al Keski even uses the pronoun "we" much of the time in talking about his experience with multiple sclerosis, as though he and his wife share the illness. In contrast, Duane Barber kept his symptoms of multiple sclerosis to himself and withdrew from his wife emotionally to keep from revealing his fears. He believes that his failure to confide in her is what destroyed their marriage.

These men do seem to have the persevering husband/ supportive wife ideal in mind as they describe how illness has affected their marriages, yet they do not claim that the course has been easy. Their inability to provide for their families financially or to be fully involved as fathers is keenly felt. They regret making their wives bear extra burdens without the support that a healthy husband ought to provide. Don Welke believes that the recent complications of his diabetes have actually been harder on his wife than on himself, not only because she has had to go back to work, but because she is the one who bears the emotional strains:

> Every surgical operation I've gone through—and I've been through a lot in the last year and a half—has really been more trying emotionally on her than it has been on me. I don't get emotional about things like that. I just figure, well, if it's got to be done, it's got to be done, and I'll live through it. But it really bothers her. I'm dealing with the physical aspects of it. I haven't got the time for the emotional ones. She's just thinking, "What can go wrong now?"

His wife, too, seems to accept that division of responsibilities and to count on his stoicism. When his vision started to fail and his feelings gave way, the marriage almost succumbed, too:

> I was depressed for months on end, because if the laser didn't work I was going to be walking with a white cane. It really affected the life around me. If I started showing that things were going down the tubes or that this was the end, my wife would feel it and double that emotion. She would really go low. I would just totally withdraw from the human race. I wouldn't see any of my friends. I wouldn't talk. I stared at the TV. I would close her out and she would be so lonely she'd go out with the kids and do something and leave me alone to my depression. She wanted to know, was this the end of the marriage?

When Don's eyes finally responded to the laser treatments and his vision was saved, his marriage recovered, too. In the meantime, his wife sought counseling for herself. He believes this crisis actually strengthened their marriage by forcing her to become more self-reliant:

> She was so totally dependent on me, which was a mistake she made years ago, for everything—for moral support.

I could maneuver her any way I wanted. I could do anything—guilt-trip her or anything I felt like, and it would destroy her. She needed help probably just as much as I did, only in a different area. She needed to be able to stand on her own two feet, I guess the term would be.

Al Keski imagines his wife feeling as though she has a grown child on her hands, "more of a detriment than a help," because he insists on being involved in everything and on doing his usual tasks despite his limited vision. One task he has been forced to give up is driving the car. Climbing in on the passenger's side embarrasses him, and depending on his wife for rides makes him feel burdensome. Al is well aware of the resentment his stubbornness can cause, and he and his wife try to keep ahead of the problems by talking about them:

> I know she's very mad—upset—and yet understanding. We've talked a lot about it. This last time I was in the hospital was probably a good one for us, because we were without any other distractions. We had the opportunity to sit down and talk about various things, which was good. I think it does put an undue amount of burden on the spouse—perhaps a woman more than a man, depending on the ages of the children. It seems so often that divorce is a result. Now, that's one thing that you don't want to happen, but I can see very well how the individual who is ill could instigate it, even out of love for the spouse, to take a burden off them. It is a very trying situation to be in. You do test out a lot of your marital vows, and how much love there really is. I've been blessed with a wonderful wife.

When I first talked with Bill Gordon, he had recovered from one serious bout of depression but showed signs of slipping into another. He was understandably preoccupied with his health and not particularly reflective about its impact on his marriage. He was not aware of any tension, but thought I might get a slightly different story if I talked to his wife. Two years later, a new drug gave him the hope of holding the depression at bay. Ironically, this apparent return to health allowed hidden problems to emerge:

> During the illness, my wife and I, I thought, were getting along very well. She was having to work a lot harder with two children, because I wasn't around to help her out. Then when I got well, there was a problem with whose role is it to do this or that. You might even say it was a kind of power struggle within the family. She had been used to doing everything herself. She'd complain about that from time to time, and I know her real feeling was that she didn't like it at all. But, at the same time, when I came back and tried to reassert myself in the family, she had some problems with that. And I had a problem with that: that I couldn't take over my previous part in the family. I remember the time I took the checkbook back—not away from her, but to pay the bills and balance it. The first opportunity she got, she was doing it again. Some things she was happy that I took over, but then I wasn't doing them exactly the same way she was.

While Bill was too depressed to manage even ordinary affairs, his wife had restructured the marriage and the household to compensate, much in the way that women whose husbands are in the military function in their absence. This undoubtedly gave her some sense of control in a very uncertain situation, and she was not eager to relinquish that. Bill and his wife have gone into marriage counseling to ease the transition to a more balanced division of responsibilities.

> I guess the thing I'm worried about the most is the marriage. Look at it from Sandy's point of view: Here I was, pretty nonfunctional for four and a half years. She was trying to run the household. She had a baby in the midst of all this. Her mother died in the midst of all this. She had to admit me to

the hospital five times. We have a very large house. There's a lot of space that needs to be taken care of. We had financial problems during the whole time. It was just a mess.

What is curious in these accounts is that the men describe the impact of illness on their marriages from what they assume to be their wives' points of view. Seldom do they mention their own needs and desires and disappointments. They take for granted, first of all, that their wives will stand by them, and they seem to be satisfied with the support they get. Their major regret is that their wives have to assume this extra responsibility, and they clearly feel some shame about being the cause. On the other hand, they are pleased to see how these new demands bolster their wives' self-confidence. In general, the men I talked with measure the stability and success of their marriages against a social ideal, and they see the difficulties involved in meeting it, but they do not question the ideal itself. It serves them as well as can be expected.

What Married Women Say

Married women with chronic illnesses tell quite a different story. First of all, the ideal roles that govern the behavior of sick men and their healthy wives are not easily reversed. There is no good model to follow when it is the woman who is sick. There is a prominent one to avoid, however: the hysterical hypochondriac who exaggerates her symptoms in order to manipulate her long-suffering husband. Fear of degenerating into this type can make a woman very stoical. The usual assumption is that a husband has unavoidable obligations at work and may even need to work longer and harder to pay his wife's medical expenses. He should, of course, be with her in times of crisis, playing the solid oak tree to her withering vine. If he does actually participate in her care, he might be either the gentle nurturer or a goading Pygmalion restoring a listless Galatea to life. When actress Patricia Neal was paralyzed by a stroke, for example, her husband, author Roald Dahl, put her on a demanding program of physical and mental therapy that helped her function normally again. A television drama based on their experience portrayed him as the exemplary husband of an ill wife. After all they've been through, I caught myself sighing when I read about their divorce.

Chronically ill women do seem to know what kind of relationship they want: one that provides the aid and support they believe they would give if their situations were reversed. Yet, as much as they want this, many married women do not really expect to get it. And while they are dissatisfied, even angry, when their husbands fail to offer emotional support, they seem delighted with minimal empathic gestures. Kathy Halvorson cites this example:

> My husband doesn't always meet my expectations for taking care of me, but when we went on vacation to Mexico, it was over 100 degrees and very humid. He insisted the minute we got off the plane that I buy a big hat for the sun, and it was wonderful. He was just on me all the time to get it, and then he was on me all the time to have it on my head. I hate hats. But he was right: It made all the difference in the world.

Women whose husbands consistently take care of them in that way express surprise at their level of compassion. Describing her husband as "my best buddy," an understanding companion who often joins her in educating others about multiple sclerosis, Gloria Murphy adds, "He sticks by me. I can't understand that sometimes." JoAnn Berglund, too, considers herself lucky to have a supportive husband, even though he is reluctant to talk about her illness:

> I get so frustrated when I can't do things. I can't climb up on a chair and get something in a cupboard. I have to plan ahead and have my husband get something down and leave it down for me ahead of time. Whenever he goes downstairs,

I have something sitting right there to go downstairs. He has this dry sense of humor. He says, "Never waste a step. Never go up and down the stairs without something in your hand." I think, How come he doesn't leave? You hear of so many people getting divorced. I said, "Why do you stay? Are you going to leave me?" He said, "No, I don't think so." That's the way he always is. He isn't one to say, "Oh, how could you think that?" Then you'd question, why is he being so effervescent about this? He must be going to do something. My husband never, ever lies. He'll say, yes, I get on his nerves after he has to watch me struggle. It would be easier for him if he didn't have to see that. If you love somebody you don't want to see them hurting. Maybe two times a year, things will build up and I'll say to my husband, "Do something. Can't you just do something?" And I cry and cry hard. And he pats me and holds me and he doesn't say, "I'll do something." He doesn't give me a bunch of flim-flam. Afterwards, I'll apologize, not that I cried, but because I put it on him. He can't do anything. If there were a cure in Germany, he'd fly me over there. He would. He'd do it.

Peggy Evans is pleased that her husband's response to her needs has improved over the years she has been diabetic. At first, having to remind him of her health regimen made her resentful:

The big problem we had was when we took a driving vacation and I would want him to start at eleven in the morning looking for a restaurant for noon lunch, and he didn't want to do that, because you lost a lot of time that way. And so it would be noon and we wouldn't have a restaurant right there, and I would get upset, and he would start to say, "Now how long can you wait for lunch?" which isn't something you ask a diabetic. You just know when they have to eat and see that the food is there, and he didn't do that. Oh, we had a terrible time. That's the closest we've come to divorce.

By attending classes on diabetes and discussing problems openly with the family, Peggy's husband learned to be more understanding. When she fell and broke her hip, he was on his way out of town on business, but headed back immediately when he got the news. Peggy was surprised to see him. He had another two-week trip planned about the time she was scheduled for surgery to repair the hip, and he wondered whether he should go. She assured him that she could manage on her own.

> But I got to the surgery and I thought, "I can't go through this without him." I told him that and he canceled his trip. I really was surprised. He has grown enough to realize that I need that emotional support. I don't know if he would need it in the same way I do, but he could understand that I did. And so he canceled all his trips. I was very grateful because it certainly helped me a lot.

The choice between keeping work commitments and being available to see family members through difficult times is a major point of contention. Several of the women I talked to complained that their husbands would not readily make sacrifices of the kind they felt they made as a matter of course. The problem was not that the men balked at doing so when asked, but that they did not see the importance of standing by to lend support. When Kathy Halvorson went into the hospital for a hysterectomy, her husband made just a few adjustments in his work schedule:

> He was there for the surgery, more or less, but he went ahead with his appointment schedule and thought he could fit it in during the operating time. Thank God the surgery was five hours, because then he could get back in time. I know that sounds cynical. He was there when I got back from the recovery room and he was there most of that day, and then he left and went out of town. I was lying there thinking, back and forth, back and forth, "You know, life has to go on," and "Oh God, I wish he was here. Why isn't he here?" It's only in

the last couple of years that I have been able to let that go. I don't know why. Maybe it's just getting so old that I don't want to keep bringing it up. And again, he doesn't see it that way at all. He says he had to do these things, that his heart was with me, but how could he stop what he was doing and be there? Be there for what? That's unresolved for us.

Be There for What?

"Be there for what?" was a question that went unresolved all through my marriage, too. My husband was ready to drop every thing and rush me to the hospital when I was in severe pain, but once my physical needs were attended to, he was on his way again. Hanging around the hospital was morbid and made him un-comfortable, he said, and there was nothing he could do for me anyway. I dismissed this reaction as a personal idiosyncrasy and usually said good-bye without complaining. Besides, it was a strain to try to cheer him up when I was exhausted and sore. He did come by every day for a short visit, and when I thought about it rationally, that seemed faithful enough. Nevertheless, I wanted him to want to be there, but for what? Kathy Halvorson expresses it as well as anyone:

> I'm talking about emotions. He's always hurt by the way I criticize him for somehow not caring for me the way I need to be cared for. He says, "I am there. I do care." For me, the evidence isn't enough. I don't know what exactly he's sup-posed to do, but he kind of spaces out. When there have been a couple of crises and we've talked about it later, he talks about what can he do? What is there to do? Well, sit with me, talk to me. I want a close emotional thing, but that's not how he sees it.

Kathy attributes this misunderstanding to a difference in their upbringing. While she has fond memories of being held and consoled by her parents when she was sick as a child, her husband was never cared for in that way and thus never learned how to do it. But the problem has even deeper roots. This "close emotional thing" that the women I interviewed want, but can't describe any more precisely than that, is an elusive quality in male-female relationships. Training girls to show emotions and boys to hide them results in what Lillian Rubin, in her book *Intimate Strangers*, calls "the single most dispiriting dilemma of relations between women and men." The "what" that chronically ill women want their husbands to be there for is an intimacy and shared vulnerability that is difficult enough to achieve in times of good health. Illness compounds the need and may, unfortunately, increase the distance as well.

Kathy Halvorson admits that she actually feels ambivalent about where to draw the boundaries on intimacy. She wants her husband to care and to be there, but she also wants to retain her right to the privacy she has practiced so long. It was, in fact, marriage that brought her out of a self-protective isolation. "While living with someone I was no longer able to hide some things. It got too tiresome to hide it and I got more trusting," she explains. This increased trust has not, however, made revealing her pain and fear much easier. She is still searching for a mode of communication that doesn't require her to open up entirely, and she knows that some of her expectations are unreasonable. For example, she would like her husband to be tuned in enough simply to sense when she is not feeling well, so that she doesn't have to tell him. Yet if he finds out and then insists that she see a doctor, she resents this as an intrusion and an implied criticism of how she manages her illness. This is not easy for either of them, and she regrets that her husband "gets caught in the cross fire" of her conflicting feelings:

> It's nearly always a bad time, and if it starts out a good time I'll make it bad. I'll kind of throw it in and mention what's wrong in passing, like I'm talking about something as trivial

as what I'm having for breakfast. He'll pick it up and say, "What? How long has that been going on? Why didn't you tell me? Thanks a lot." What I want is understanding and comfort and now he's mad, so that puts distance between us. I've said to him that making the illness real is very difficult for me and that I try to block it out. I've told him that I try and hide my symptoms from him and he can help me by bringing it up. Then he gets angry often, because he thinks that I'm accusing him of not being a good mate. That's how it gets into a no-win situation.

An incident in my own marriage can be read as a paradigm of Rubin's "dispiriting dilemma." I had been on an intravenous antibiotic for about two months and my veins were showing signs of wear. As I dripped in a dose at 3:00 A.M., an eerie time of night to be sitting up alone with such compelling evidence of your mortality, the sharp plastic thread of the IV tube punctured the wall of my vein, sending solution flowing into the surrounding tissue. All I could do was wait until the seven o'clock shift of IV nurses came on at the hospital and go have the location of the tube changed. It took the nurse three attempts before she found a usable vein, and I went home with three tender, swollen bruises. At three o'clock that afternoon, it happened again. Fever, exhaustion, and fear got the best of me and I began to cry. I couldn't imagine how I would get through another month of antibiotics if my veins no longer worked. And if I couldn't take the medication, I might die. I cried and swore and called to my husband in the next room. He tried to reason with me a bit and get me to stop crying. When that didn't work, he blurted out, "I'm sorry, I can't handle this," and stomped off to play the organ, his usual stress relief. I felt devastated. I was in desperate need of consolation and my own husband would not provide it. I was much more hurt than angry. The shame I often felt about being a deficient partner made me sob harder, and the organ music grew louder.

A few weeks later, in a moment of better health, I looked back on this event and interpreted it quite differently. I decided that "I can't handle this" didn't mean "I can't stand this anymore" but something much more literal: "I can't do anything to solve this problem. I can't fix your veins." My husband was working in a mostly male environment with a traditionally masculine code of behavior in which control—of both the situation and his feelings about it—was of prime importance. My despair left him with a feeling of powerlessness that he simply could not "handle." He let it out in a burst of anger, one of the few emotions he had ever learned to express. Once I understood this, I could stop feeling hurt when he reacted this way—or so I thought. Then one day a very perceptive minister who had visited me in the hospital imposed a counseling session on us that neither of us had requested. I brought up this episode and offered my rational interpretation of it. My husband explained that what had set him off was seeing me lose my emotional balance. "You've always been able to keep your spirits up before," he said. "Why can't you do it this time?" The minister was not about to let it rest there: "What I hear you saying is that Cheri is not supposed to have any feelings, but you can be mad as hell." The standard we had been operating under was not the old double one: emotional woman/ rational man, but its opposite: upbeat, optimistic (rational) woman/angry (emotional) man. Neither one was fair.

When I related this incident to people I interviewed, several of the women recognized the pattern as their own. When they want simple consolation from their husbands, what they often get instead is a rational solution. When Peggy Evans, for example, was depressed about the worsening of her condition, her husband tried to reason her out of her feelings by pointing out where her perception was wrong. It didn't help. When Susan Alm wanted to talk through her feelings of hopelessness with her husband, he said, "I found you the best doctor around. What's the matter with you?" "I don't want a doctor," she cried, "I want a husband."

Sideways Anger

The angry response is also familiar, and often the anger "comes out sideways," as Phyllis Mueller says. Because a decent, loving person feels awful being angry at someone who cannot help being ill, the anger remains unfocused or gets projected elsewhere. Phyllis describes how this works:

> He will say something very snippy and I'll call him on it and say, "I don't understand that. You sound like you're angry about that." It's on a subject where I wouldn't expect anybody to be angry. After we talk it through it will start to come out, but it's around the bush, and I'm not sure it's just about my being sick. Sometimes I see him as just blatantly unfair, but I don't tolerate illness that well myself, so I don't think I really blame him. I just wish he'd say, "You're sick again today and it just pisses me off." Then it would be out there and I could say, "Okay, I'm sorry you're pissed off. Is there anything I can do?"

Of course, it is not only husbands who are angry about their fate. Wives of chronically ill men are no more reconciled to it, but may more successfully contain and even repress the anger, or convert it to the anxiety that Don Welke says his wife showed. Indirect anger rages on all sides. It is hard to avoid feeling resentful sometimes toward a partner who is healthy and oblivious to pain. It erupts in the form of a rhetorical question: "How would you like it . . .?" or "What do *you* know?" But that anger can quickly turn to shame. Esther Green, like Phyllis, assumes responsibility for her husband's anger:

> When he comes through the door in the evening, it seems like he's got an attitude just coming in the door. And sometimes I think, "Boy! Take that kind of attitude!" I think maybe it's me that's brought it on him. He's got to have this

hostility built up in him in order to withstand what he's got
to go through at home, you know.

Ending my marriage was more emotionally wrenching than anything I have ever experienced with my illness. In the days leading
up to the decision to divorce, my husband and I fought in bitterness, cried in sorrow, and laughed at our own absurdity. One of
the many events of our marriage we looked back on was the
angry organ-playing episode. He told me that that particular
bout of illness was the breaking point for him. Among the feelings it aroused was a vulnerability that he just could not tolerate.
In the three intervening years, we had degenerated into people
that neither of us would care to live with. He became cold and
withdrawn, and I grew frantic trying to break through his barriers. I recognized his behavior immediately in Lillian Rubin's sum-
mation of the difficulty men have fulfilling women's expectations
of intimacy:

> It should be understood: Commitment itself is not a prob-
> lem for a man; he's good at that. He can spend a lifetime liv-
> ing in the same family, working at the same job—even one he
> hates. And he's not without an inner emotional life. But
> when a relationship requires the sustained verbal expression
> of that inner life and the full range of feelings that accom-
> pany it, then it becomes burdensome for him. He can act out
> anger and frustration inside the family, it's true. But ask him
> to express his sadness, his fear, his dependency—all those
> feelings that would expose his vulnerability to himself or to
> another—and he's likely to close down as if under some com-
> pulsion to protect himself.

A long-term relationship marked by chronic illness requires exactly that kind of exposure. When my husband walked away in
anger, I was hurt. Later, I reasoned away that feeling and thought
I understood his motives. After the divorce, I had yet another re-

sponse. No longer having to maintain the relationship left me free to feel the anger I probably should have felt all along. I was angry at him for reacting in an uncompassionate way, but also angry about the gender differences—whether learned or innate—that made an intimate sharing of burdens so problematic at a time when it was of critical importance. Now I am hopeful that a generation of men encouraged to be more alert to their emotions and a generation of women raised to be more self-reliant will respond in new and less frustrating ways to each other's illnesses. One male reader wrote to assure me that there are more men around who are not "locked into stoicism." "But there are still problems," he added: "Knowing how and when to share feelings, and knowing how close is too close, and dealing with the feelings of vulnerability that come up when you do let yourself get close." And a female reader reminded me that changed circumstances simply pose different problems. When her husband of two years became ill and could no longer work full-time, she had trouble "breaking through my firm conviction that equality in marriage means people contribute the same things. Nearly a lifelong feminist, I had always assumed I would work for pay. I had no idea how strong was my assumption that men must, as well."

Off Balance

All the tensions that arise in heterosexual relationships cannot, of course, be blamed on an arrested capacity for feeling in the male of the species. Although trained to be more open emotionally, women, too, see risks in exposing themselves fully to their husbands or partners. Dependency, a danger in friendships, can be even more threatening in an intimate relationship, for lesbians and gay men as well as for male-female couples. For women who have struggled to preserve an identity apart from family roles, being tossed back under their partners' protection by illness can mean losing a sense of autonomy and equal worth. Some of the married women I talked with looked for symbolic ways, such as traveling alone, to show that illness had not put them at their husbands' mercy.

Both men and women worry about offering less to a relationship than the healthy partner does. This may be expressed in frequent apologies for being burdensome or in effusive praise and gratitude for support. Some people directly acknowledge feeling shame about being inadequate. Others project the feeling onto their partners and suspect them of harboring resentments. In a relationship thrown off balance, talking with mutual trust about these feelings is not easy. The greatest shame lies in the belief that you are depriving the one you love of a chance for basic human fulfillment. This shame bubbles to the surface when you cannot share in his or her favorite activities, when your illness drains the family finances, and, especially, when it limits your sexual relationship.

Intimate relationships are presumably built on a strong compatibility of interests, from agreeing on ethical values to having fun together. Spoiling your beloved's fun, even unintentionally, puts the relationship at risk. When illness keeps you from engaging in an activity you expected to be enjoying together, adjustments have to be made. There are several solutions. Al Keski and his wife belonged to a snowmobile club and rode in races and long-distance events. When his vision weakened and he could no longer do that safely, they sold *both* their snowmobiles. Susan Alm accompanies her husband on a sailing vacation each summer. Even though it wreaks havoc with her lupus, she does not want to begrudge him this pleasure. Yet his insistence on it also angers her:

> Sailing is exactly something I should never do, and yet it's important to him. I get seasick. Because I'm out in the sun I get this stuff all over my face two or three days later. I can't participate in any of the physical activity of it. I just sit there like a bump on a log. That's not what it's all about. Plus, we always take along our kids. So all I do is sit there and hold kids

who are throwing up. A real fun trip. But I will go once a year, and that's it.

Kathy Halvorson and her husband have reached a compromise: She will not object to his motorcycle trips if he will not expect her to come along:

> I finally admitted to myself and then to him that I didn't want to be on the back of a motorcycle. I was entertaining fantasies like, "Go out and get yourself some kind of Viking who can keep up with you." Of course you don't have to be huge and sturdy to do something like that. You just have to be normal. So that kind of anger was going through me. I was telling myself that he wouldn't get the other parts of me that are good if he got a recreational woman. I think we're both realistic about that now, and he goes off and does it by himself, and I can let that happen. It's still not real easy, but I can let it happen.

One of the most ingenious solutions is the one devised by Peggy Evans's husband. They enjoyed gardening in their backyard until neuropathy made it impossible for Peggy to stoop or bend without falling. He built a raised bed at wheelchair level where she now grows herbs.

Loss of income and exorbitant medical expenses can create rifts in an otherwise compatible relationship. Al Keski worries that he will become disabled and no longer be able to support his family. To prepare for that possibility, he practices a frugality learned in childhood that does not come as naturally to his wife and children. He is very reluctant to hire people to do repairs on the house and car, but when he tries to do them himself he gets frustrated. Consequently, things get left undone and become sore points. He thought he could alleviate the anxiety about becoming disabled by making financial contingency plans, but it took some arguing to persuade his wife. It was apparently more comfortable for her not to think about it. In the worst phase of Rosemary McKuen's ulcerative colitis, she and her husband were deeply in debt. Once he walked into the intensive care room and stammered, "How are we going to pay for this?" As insensitive as it seemed, she had to admit that it was a very real worry, and for many couples, it always will be.

What about Sex?

Sex is, of course, the most sensitive issue and the one that people are most reticent to discuss. Reason would suggest that a man whose potency is reduced by illness or a woman whose hip and knee joints ache would be excused for not being a frequent or fervent lover. But reason does not prevail in sexual matters. Another famous line from Erich Segal's *Love Story*, which served as a caption on the movie ads, is "Love means never having to say you're sorry." Yet, a great deal of apologizing goes on in the bedrooms of the chronically ill. If you have committed yourselves to monogamy, your illness limits not only your own sexual expression but your partner's, as well. Phyllis Mueller talks about the state of her sex life:

> My husband would like to express himself sexually more than I would. I'm not sure that he needs sex more, but I believe his way of alleviating anxiety, his way of feeling close, is pretty much in a sexual vein, whereas I have a lot of ways to take care of my sexuality. I don't necessarily need to have sex or intercourse to do that. I can get high just talking to a good friend, or I can feel close just cuddling or holding hands. To me that's as affirming, and to me sex is merely an affirmation of love. I'm not sure that he uses it in that sense.
>
> This fall I felt better than I have for a long time, but you don't just jump back into a sexual mode again. Sometimes it's like a forgotten part of my life. Pain supersedes my ability to express myself. I push myself to go to work, so one

could say, "Why don't you push yourself to have sex?" But it seems as though I have to keep going to keep a job, I have to keep going to be a good mother. It's like those are the have-to's. To me, sex is an elective. Maybe that's not a good way to look at it. Sometimes I miss being close, too, but what do you do when you have a vaginal infection recurring for three months, and then shoulder pains, and then a bladder infection? The infections don't make me want to have intercourse, because I'm afraid I'm going to get them back. I've built up a lot of fear and anxiety around getting those two repeat things. I find myself throwing up barriers and thinking, "Oh God, do I really want to do this? Will I get an infection? I can't deal with it anymore. I've got enough to deal with now. I've got this, this, and the other thing." I feel tired and stressed out a lot.

I don't think my husband's real happy about that. I think he tries to be "good" about it, but I think he's building a lot of resentment. We've had some stormy arguments about it. Right now I think he realizes it's close to impossible. We're kind of in a coast phase right now. We're there and we're together and we're not unhappy and we're not totally thrilled about it. We're just kind of waiting it out, because we've been through other periods of time like this, and this seems to work the best for us. If you push it, you both start getting a lot of pressure, and a lot of pressure makes you kind of crazy when you have sex. If it's not possible, then let's just leave it there for now.

"Just leaving it there for now" is a very typical approach, but it is not a solution to the problem. Resentments do build and do cause rifts in the relationship. What is needed are adaptations as creative as Peggy Evans's raised herb garden: New bedtime rituals that affirm the couple's love when sex is not possible. More frequent expressions of love and affection to make up for the infrequency of sexual intimacy. Alternative ways of being physically intimate that can satisfy without causing discomfort. It may take frequent, pleasurable practice of these to overcome the feeling that you are cheating your healthy partner out of a "normal" sexual relationship. But what chronically ill people often overlook is that, unless our partners offer us something other than a choice between perfection and "leaving it there," we too are being cheated out of the affirmation of love that sex ought to be.

Closely related to sexual inadequacy is the inability to beget or bear children. Infertility itself, if countered with extensive medical treatment and many vain attempts at pregnancy, takes on the character of a chronic illness. Like so many others of our generation, my husband and I were nonchalant about having children in the years we were getting educated and established in careers. We both knew that pregnancy was inadvisable in my case, but we seldom talked about it. Once into the now-or-never thirties, however, we thought we might be missing something. When I first raised the possibility of adoption, I learned that underneath his nonchalance was a sorrow about not reproducing that he had kept hidden out of concern for my feelings. How disappointing it must have been, then, to learn that I did not share that sorrow. What I wanted most was to raise children, and bearing them myself seemed inconsequential. Maybe I was just relieved to be spared that extra pain. Once again, he got angry, and I felt guilty.

No Mere Onlookers

If you feel shame and guilt about how your illness limits your partner's life, you are, consciously or not, assuming control over the way in which your partner reacts to your illness. I remember exactly when it dawned on me that my husband's experience of my illness was not simply vicarious. I was reading a first-person account of terminal cancer when I caught myself complaining aloud about the author's attitude. She tried to explain away the tensions in her marriage by saying, "I guess this is because I am unable somehow to involve him in the emotional struggles through which I am going." I read it to mean that she thought of her husband as a mere onlooker who had no feelings apart from hers. I wanted to know whether she had involved herself in the emotional struggles he was going through as a man about to lose his wife. These were real, too, and not just faint shadows of her own.

It struck me that I was equally oblivious. I had always been grateful to my husband for sharing my worries, as if he were only doing it for my sake. After all, he couldn't really know what it was like to be sick and in pain and apprehensive about getting worse. All he could do, I thought, was feel the reverberations of my suffering. I had forgotten that we seldom reacted in identical fashion to the same circumstances. We had different upbringings, different temperaments, different approaches to solving problems. Moreover, the circumstances we were reacting to were not identical. I knew what it was like to feel illness in my body, but he knew what it was like to live in a close relationship with someone whose health is unreliable. Realizing that the story of my illness had two versions, his and hers, gave me some respite from the shame I felt about ruining my husband's life. I saw, too, that the flipside of shame was arrogance: Believing we have the power to ruin our partners' lives is a grandiose notion. It is an illusion of power assumed by the powerless. We are a little like children who believe their own misbehavior is to blame if their parents drink to excess or get divorced. Adults who love their partners enough to stick around through a chronic illness are certainly capable of managing their own behavior. That simple observation is a liberating one: It means no longer having to figure out how to keep your partner from feeling angry or sad about your illness.

This lesson was reinforced when I recovered from the long fever that was the real breaking point in our relationship. I was ready to return to normal, but my husband was not. While I was euphoric about finally feeling good, he was still regretting his sojourn in what he described as "a year of hell." Like Don Welke, I could claim that the illness was harder on my partner than it

was on me. At first, I interpreted the many similar statements I
had heard as a ritualistic form of apology: "Of course I've suffered, but my partner has suffered even more just having to live
with me." Once you have surrendered control over your partner's
experience of illness, however, you can give it an entirely different
meaning: "Maybe I am better equipped to deal with hardship
than my partner is."

People who remain faithful and devoted to their incapacitated
partners' well-being are often described as "saints." I feel that
kind of awe sometimes watching my dad, in his sixty-fifth year of
marriage, washing and dressing my mother, cleaning up after her,
cooking her meals, counting out her pills, washing her clothes,
brushing off the nasty accusations that her Alzheimer's-addled
brain slings at him, and explaining over and over, when she wants
to go home, that she is already there. "It's a great life," he says, "if
you don't weaken." But sainthood should be neither a prerequisite for nor the expected outcome of such a relationship. Illness
itself falls on ordinary mortals, and each of us gropes for ways to
make life worth continuing. We should expect no more and no
less of healthy partners. Though I resist the idea that suffering is
ennobling, I do believe that it is an important dimension of a full
human life. The standard marriage vows, after all, acknowledge
the reality that a truly committed relationship will have to endure
hardship: "in sickness and in health; for richer, for poorer; for better and for worse." The challenge each couple faces is to make
that hardship not only bearable but mutually enriching.

What Is Love?

Had the heroine of Love Story survived, she would have learned in
time that love does not mean "never having to say you're sorry."
But neither does it mean making constant, shame-ridden apologies to your beleaguered partner. If Camille and her starry-eyed
lover were to make it over the long haul with a case of consump-

tion that just won't quit, they would have to learn new, real-life habits of loving, just as Phyllis and Tom Mueller have:

> My husband had an idea that people got married and were moderately happy and then they died, and this was a lifetime commitment, and marriage went along reasonably well. Once you were married, that was sort of the end of it. It was just there. You were just married. I think I looked at it quite differently. I had a lot of fears. I thought, "What if you don't care for this person after a certain period of time, and what if things don't go well?" I found out that that's not true from time to time. To me, love has to be very, very mature. It's not fantasy, it's not idealism, it's the very hard stuff.

So how, then, do we define this mature love, encumbered as it is by illness?

Love means feeling free to ask for emotional support and expecting to get it, because mutual support is inherent in your commitment to each other. It means that the range of emotions that illness draws out can be safely expressed, because you genuinely care for each other.

Love means talking openly about problems as they arise, rather than avoiding conflict and harboring resentments, and it means fighting it out if necessary to relieve the tension. It means acknowledging that anger is a natural human response to the limitations that illness imposes on a relationship, and that it needs to be expressed and channeled in constructive ways.

Love means demystifying sex by putting aside unrealistic expectations and deciding how the two of you can best achieve a physical intimacy that affirms your feelings for each other. It means talking very deliberately about how to do this and not waiting until you've failed at making love.

Love means taking the strain off this one intimate relationship by admitting that you cannot solve all your problems yourselves behind a screen of privacy. It means inviting family and friends to provide extra support when your own emotional resources run dry, and seeking professional help when illness puts the relationship in jeopardy.

Love means trading roles and responsibilities as each partner's state of health warrants without feeling freakish. It means finding self-esteem in your own adaptability and ingenuity rather than in how well you fit cultural norms.

Love means realizing that chronic illness will, indeed, disturb the smooth course of your relationship, no matter how noble your intentions toward each other. It means reaffirming your original commitment from time to time and finding hope in your bumpy history together while you wait for the current crisis to pass.

Love may even mean acknowledging that what binds you together is nothing more than inertia fed by a guilty gratitude or disdainful pity. It means, then, either repairing the damage or ending a relationship that no longer promotes good health.

Above all, love encumbered by chronic illness must be reflective and self-aware. It means keeping the illness in its proper perspective as only one of many factors that complicate an intimate relationship between two different people. Again, Phyllis Mueller offers wisdom derived from twenty-five years in a marriage that has enjoyed only brief periods of good health:

> If we got divorced a year from now and somebody said, "What do you think caused the divorce?" I couldn't, with any degree of honesty, say, "The fact that I have been sick so much." I really don't believe that in my gut. I think it would be a factor, together with his being brought up to push everything under the rug and never bring it out to look at it, so that he had to learn how to have feelings in his forties. It would have to do with my feeling abandoned all the time and having been raised in sort of an abusive environment. We've overcome so much of that, but it's been difficult, because we carried a lot of bad baggage into that relation-

ship. But I don't think illness would have done it alone. My husband said something the other day that just really shocked me. He said, "Well, you know, if we were really honest about this, your illness has probably not caused any more problems in the relationship than my crazy behavior." I clapped and I cheered and I did all the inappropriate things, and I said, "Thank you. That's one of the nicest things you've ever said to me."

Chapter 8

Parenthood with Limitations

"What will my kids remember about Mom?"

Becoming a mother through adoption at age thirty-five was the ultimate in planned parenthood. The adoption agency put us through a series of orientations, group discussions, home studies, and child care classes that gave us plenty of time and opportunity to examine our motives, our expectations for our children, our family patterns, and our lifestyle. We were assured that we could stop the process at any time, without blame, if we had qualms about going ahead. I sought and got my doctor's opinion on the matter: There was no evidence to suggest that I would not live to raise my children to adulthood. I knew exactly what kind of parent I wanted to be, and I was going to be very deliberate about it. For one thing, I would avoid the feature of my own upbringing that plagued me the most: a fearful overprotectiveness.

When my beautiful and brilliant daughter arrived from Korea at ten months, I was all set to be Mellow Mom. I resolved to take illnesses and injuries in stride, to reward adventurousness, and to correct her misbehavior calmly but firmly. For six weeks, it worked beautifully. When she rolled off the bed, I scooped her up confidently, looked quickly for bumps, and swallowed my panic so I could relieve hers. When I told my mother that she had crawled up the stairs for the first time, her response was, "Oh no! Weren't you watching her?" Of course I was watching—and cheering her on. When she pulled the diapers off the shelf and tossed them on the floor, I decided that her motor coordination was more important than the orderliness of the bathroom. I certainly was a good mother.

Then my temperature rose to 105 degrees and my hemoglobin dropped to 8, and I learned that being easygoing does not come easily. To the housebound and bedridden, disorder is chaos, adventurousness is naughty behavior, and a little whining is a tantrum. When she climbed the stairs, I had to drag myself off the couch to spot her. Before long, we had put up a barricade. When I bent over to pick the diapers up off the floor, I got dizzy and couldn't straighten up again. To avoid mishaps, I had to keep her confined. I could rest on the couch or drip in my antibiotic only if she was safe behind bars in her playpen. At my weakest, I couldn't even lift her out of the crib in the morning. I could carry her only a few steps, and if she squirmed I had to let her go. Her father's participation, part-time day care, and helpful friends got us through the worst of it. When I could do nothing else, I sang her breathless lullabies to keep her assured of my presence.

I had not changed my ideal of motherhood, but physical weakness made it impossible to uphold. I became very short-tempered, and Mellow Mom degenerated into Mean Mom. I yelled more, to stop her from doing things I didn't have the strength to undo, and I had trouble containing my frustration when she did them nevertheless. Though I was intent on using diversion tactics rather than physical punishment, the day she went stiff as I tried to lift her into the car seat with my single IV-free arm, I saw no recourse but to use that good arm to spank her. She was, and still is eighteen years later, a basically good-natured person with a stubborn streak much like my own. Mellow Mom wanted to nurture that strong will, but, in moments of exhaustion, Mean Mom took over and tried to curb it. I began to understand how isolated, frenzied parents slip into child abuse.

Three times during our first year together, I disappeared from home. While I was in the hospital, she spent weekdays in day care. Her dad's work schedule was quite demanding, so many evenings and weekends were spent with friends and neighbors, some of them strangers to her. I wondered how this might affect her sense of security, as a child already displaced by adoption. And I worried about what my absence would do to that magical bonding that experts in child development take so seriously. Our bonds had sealed very quickly, the night of her arrival. She was still on Korean time, so my husband and I took turns sitting up with her, trying to ease her into sleep on a mattress on the floor. When that failed, I sat with her in front of the hallway mirror. I recognized her face in the mirror as the baby in the photographs we had studied for eight months. She looked at my mirror image, then at me, then at the mirror again, and said, "O-ma, O-ma," the Korean word for mother. If she had put her trust in me so readily, how did she feel now that I could seldom carry her and sometimes went away entirely? I suspected that she felt abandoned, and of course my suspicion was confirmed, like all suspicions aroused by anxiety. One Sunday afternoon, as we pulled up in front of the hospital after a few hours of relief in the outside world, I leaned over to kiss her good-bye. She punched me in the face and started to cry. Many times after that, as I lay daydreaming, I would see my daughter Grace as an adult lying on a psychoanalyst's couch and saying, "My mother was sick all through my childhood, you know."

Eventually, we did settle into a livable pattern. The nurses overlooked the age minimum for visitors and let her come to see me in my room. She pushed all the buttons on the bedside stand and inspected the intravenous tubing. She even pulled up her sleeve and found an imaginary "owie" to match mine. Once the worst was over, it was her cheerful, affectionate presence that sustained my recovery.

By her second birthday, I was healthy again, and I stayed that way until she turned five. It was my longest remission ever. After one year of good health, we went ahead with a second adoption. Those three years were not the idyllic interlude I had hoped for, however. Sleep deprivation—the new parent's greatest health hazard—and a degenerating marriage interfered with my plans to stay mellow. Our last meal together as an "intact" family was a one-and-a-half-year birthday celebration for our younger daughter, Maria. Over the next nine months, the girls adjusted to the practice of moving back and forth from Mom's house to Dad's, and even Mom and Dad didn't stay put. The week the girls and I moved into a house all our own, I got sick again and was in and out of the hospital and on and off the IV for the next six months. In the meantime, their father moved out of state, re-married, and had another family. If ever children had reason to be in emotional turmoil, mine certainly did. Yet, as young women, they are bright, kind, responsible, loving—all I could ever wish them to be.

Not Quite Up to the Task

In talking with other chronically ill parents, I learned that my worries were not unusual. We worry that the deprivation and disruption our illnesses cause will leave our children emotionally scarred. In addition, we fear that our ongoing relationships with them will be soured by memories of all the times we did not live up to their expectations. The nature and intensity of our worries depends on the roles we had anticipated playing in our children's lives. Not surprisingly, there is some difference in the way fathers and mothers talk about their limitations as parents. While fathers regret all the things they cannot *do* with their children, mothers' worries range more widely over all that they cannot *be* for their children.

A primal fear for many women is not being equal to the demands of a new infant's life. That is a major component of post-partum depression, which doesn't require a "partum" to set it off. Adoptive mothers, too, experience a version of it. Memories of sitting limp and sweaty in the rocking chair with my daughter heavy in my lap helped me read the horror in Susan Alm's account of her third daughter's infancy:

> It was a very traumatic sort of experience. I mean, here you are, this new mother, and you can't even hold your baby!

There's nothing stronger than that desire to hold and nurture your baby, and if you can't even pick her up, that's really
devastating.

The pregnancy had set off her first serious flare-up of lupus,
which was not diagnosed until two years later. Her joints hurt so
badly that she could not pick the baby up. Having dropped her
once, she was reluctant even to try. The gynecologist dismissed it
as a common problem that would end when she stopped breast-
feeding. So she stopped immediately, giving up yet another bond
with her child, but still the pain didn't go away. Her husband's
work kept him away much of the time so she turned for help to
her older daughters, who were then just five and seven. In nonin-
dustrial societies, children of seven commonly tend baby brothers and sisters while their parents do the rigorous work that
subsistence living requires. But in middle-class America, trusting
the care of an infant to a child so young borders on neglect, with
both children as victims.

   Peggy Evans's diabetes also came on during her childbearing
years, when her older son was five and her daughter just short of
two. Having planned a large family, she chose to risk a third pregnancy. It was difficult and had to be closely monitored, but her
son was born healthy. She, too, worried about being an inadequate mother:

   One difficult thing about being diabetic with small children
   is that if they had needs and I had needs, I had to attend to
   my own needs first. This is antimaternal, I think, because in-
   stinctively I would want to feed them or change them or do
   whatever they needed. And if I was having an insulin reaction, I had to have sugar for that and wait until it was cleared
   up or I could not attend to the children, and that was hard
   to handle. I would have insulin reactions with no warning
   sometimes, and they took the form of exploding emotionally
   with temper at the children, who had done nothing. They
   were quite tiny. This disturbed me a great deal. I wondered

what this would do to their little psyches and if it would affect their growing-up years.

Peggy safeguarded their little psyches by explaining what was happening in terms they could understand. As a result, they answered even well-deserved scoldings with "You need sugar, Mommy." She also strove to make their childhoods "normal" by baking cookies, cakes, and pies that she couldn't eat herself. As hard as she tried to limit the impact of the illness on the family, it was still a threatening presence that had to be faced. Even the baby learned to sit quietly in the high chair while Peggy measured and injected her insulin, and she taught her six-year-old son how to dial a neighbor's telephone number in case she went into a coma. Both Susan's and Peggy's children assumed responsibilities for themselves, their siblings, and their sick mothers that many adults would find awesome.

A father's job is generally regarded as a legitimate intrusion on family time. Absence due to illness, however, is at least experienced as a deprivation. For the first three years of his son's life, while he was building his career, Bill Gordon spent only weekends and rare evenings at home. For the next four years, manic-depression made him sometimes physically and often emotionally unavailable. Through the worst of it, he felt "a great deal of loss" about not doing "as much as a father should." While their second child was still a toddler, Bill underwent a course of treatment that may well keep him stable. The illness left him determined to be much more involved with his family, and he reasserted his presence with a fervor that he laughs at himself: He bought top-quality ice skates for everybody and got them out on the rink every winter afternoon so they could have some fun together. But the newly restored father was not instantly welcome:

> Jason will spill his milk on the table, and my wife will be upstairs, and he'll start screaming, "Mom! Mom!" and I'll be in the room. He won't even ask me. He's so used to depend-

ing on Mom. The other night he and I were talking about the whole situation when I was sick, and I asked him if he was mad. He said, yeah, he was mad that I couldn't play with him. He doesn't understand anything about the illness, other than that I was sick.

Jason doesn't understand, yet he is mad, and he is certainly not atypical. Assuaging the anger, the fear, and the burdensome sense of responsibility that an uncomprehending young child is likely to feel is no easy task. The competing demands that the illness poses make it even more difficult. You face the dilemma of having to care for your ailing body and your children's needs at the same time, with limited resources. If you define ideal parenthood as unflagging attention to your children's best interests, how can you help but fall short? In buying the extravagant ice skates, Bill was repaying his children what he felt he owed them: the time, attention, and financial benefits that his illness had deprived them of.

Confusion and Disappointment

This problem is, of course, beyond the comprehension of younger children. It is hard enough to explain what "sick" means to a child who has known nothing worse than a quickly passing fever and a drippy nose. If the illness is invisible, the parents' failure to respond to the child's needs may look willful. When I was seriously ill and obviously in pain, my children knew it and became very compliant. But when I was feeling the slight discomfort that might develop into pain if I didn't lie down and relax, it was very trying to have to convince them that I needed to be left alone. They were like emotional sponges who soaked up my anxiety about getting worse and squeezed it back on me in the form of whiny demands for attention. I wanted to still their anxiety, but my own was overpowering. Unless I could find a way to divert their attention, they sometimes got angry, and the only sure way to quell their anger was to let them know how serious this was—

in other words, to scare them. But neither anger nor fear are emotions you like to encourage in your children.

 Both anger and fear are very natural reactions, however. In younger children, whose desires are immediate and self-centered, the anger explodes when you say no to requests that you just can't fill. As the children grow and learn to respect the limitations of the illness, explosive anger may subside into disappointment, which shows just as clearly. The child's disappointment is matched by the parent's frustration at having to disappoint. Al Keski feels it keenly:

> We've tried to get out together as much as we can and do things as a family, but still the intentions are better than the actions. The kids try to understand, but it's difficult. We'd go to a movie and I couldn't see everything on the screen, so I'd ask them what was happening, and they'd get mad at me. They thought I was complaining because I couldn't see it. The last couple of years I haven't been able to play catch with Brent or go fishing. We tried fishing, but I'd cast out and I couldn't see the bobber out there. That got frustrating. I can't say that I did much with my dad. I grew up on a farm, and we didn't do many recreational things. The biggest thing was deer hunting with my dad, and all of us boys did that together. I guess I wanted more than that for my kids.

Wanting more for our kids than we can give them, many of us push ourselves anyway or at least compensate during our healthier periods for their disappointments.With fishing out of the question, Al is a faithful spectator at his son's soccer games. He cheers when the crowd does, because he can't see the plays for himself. His foremost concern right now, and a source of stress, is how he will finance his children's educations if he becomes disabled. People who knew my situation and saw me out and about with my two little ones used to ask, "Where do you get your energy?" I don't know that I had any. What I had was sheer will to avoid giving them cause for anger and disappointment. Even if we learn to accept the limits that the illness places on our own lives, few of us can feel complacent about its effects on our children's. As Phyllis Mueller, the last of whose three children is in high school, puts it, "To me, it wasn't fair for them to go through a whole childhood with me saying, 'Mommy can't.'" Yet, there are many times when such a refusal is necessary, and then the best way to meet the anger is to share it. Margie Rietsma says:

> We'll make plans to do something, and sometimes I get up and I'm sick and I can't. They'll get upset, and I say, "I know you're angry. If I were in your place, I'd be angry, too, and I don't want you to miss out on things because I'm sick. But just remember, there's nothing I can do about it. It happens, and we'll just have to postpone this till later, that's all."

When Children Feel Vulnerable

When my girls were seven and four, a film crew from the Menninger Clinic in Kansas came to interview us for a movie called *Chronic Illness: The Constant Companion*. To the interviewer's question, "How do you feel when your mommy gets sick?" four-year-old Maria replied, with no hesitation, and with body language to match her answer, "Scared." When parents leave their children to go to the hospital, they may worry that they will never come back. When illness makes us look ravaged and powerless to protect them, they may feel unusually vulnerable. Each time I got sick, I told my daughters not to worry because I would come back feeling better. The more evidence they saw of that, I thought, the less frightened they would be. Instead, I watched them fall into a pattern, as each girl coped with the situation in her own distinctive way. Grace shifted into practical gear, got me a glass of ice water, called my sister or a neighbor to get help, and kept herself busy picking up clutter or washing the dishes. Maria stood at my bedside, patting my head, tucking my blankets around me, and snuffling back her tears. Hard as I tried to reassure them, I could never completely convince myself, either.

  Children may also fear catching the disease, even if that is impossible. After Gloria Murphy learned she had multiple sclerosis, her kids refused to kiss her goodnight for fear of getting "Mom germs." My daughters, though adopted, wanted to know whether their livers were going to stop working right. Telling them that they would not inherit my illness did not entirely relieve the worry. They had learned the frightening truth that bodies can malfunction anytime. When illness is a major family concern, it should be no surprise if the children become hypochondriacs. Where there is genuine cause for worry, extra parental vigilance takes hold. As a juvenile diabetic himself, Don Welke has well-founded fears for his children's health:

> It's a fact of life to watch your kids all the time. I know the symptoms, so if they start drinking too much water I get shook up, and I have to watch them real close, check their urine, if we think it's something strange. We're always conscious to make sure the kids don't have it.

Because young children's emotions are so closely linked with their parents', we often expect them to be angry or frightened in situations where we are frustrated and fearful ourselves. Overly eager assurances that Mom or Dad will be all right may, in fact, instill fears rather than ease them. Sometimes the best approach is not to anticipate an emotional response at all but to treat the matter literally and give the child a simple, factual explanation of why things are the way they are. Carla Schultz's five-year-old daughter was unrelenting in her request for a baby sister. Because pregnancy had reactivated her lupus, Carla was hardly ready to grant the wish. Her own regret about not having another child got in the way when she tried to answer her daughter:

> You can imagine how we felt. My husband is better about that than I am. Maybe it's my guilt feeling. I basically think

that if I had another child I couldn't risk getting sick again. It's just a nightmare to think about it. At one time we told her, "You're so lucky you're an only child, because we can spend more time with you." Finally my neighbor, who has rheumatoid arthritis, said to her, "If your mother has a baby, she'll probably get sick again. Would you rather have your Mom well or have a baby?" I thought, how silly of me not to tell her that we love her very much and we'd love to have a baby but we just can't and why. It's a much more productive way of dealing with it.

Rather than guarding against such unsettling emotions as anger and fear, it is wiser to help your children find appropriate outlets for expressing them. Having other people around who can take the pressure off helps a great deal. The other parent is the obvious first choice. Gloria Murphy's husband, for example, took over the task of explaining multiple sclerosis to their sons, talking through their feelings about it, and anticipating what it might mean for them in the long run. Sole custody parents, such as I have been, need to rally others to the children's aid. Entrusting their care in times of illness to a small number of readily available relatives and friends provides them with a consistent source of emotional support, as well. If your resources are temporarily wrung dry, or if they choose not to confide their feelings in you, they can turn to these others whom they love and trust. When my nuclear family underwent the fission of divorce, I was amazed to see how rapidly my sense of family expanded. I had support to draw on that I was not aware of as a married, but nevertheless harried, mother. Many of the people I interviewed would be greatly relieved by such assistance, even though their spouses are present.

A Repository for Bad Feelings

Problems do arise that family and friends cannot easily handle, and then it is wise to seek out professional help. Often, all that is needed is a safe, impartial repository for "bad" feelings. When Don Welke went on kidney dialysis, his son started attending a discussion group at his elementary school for children facing problems at home. Margie Rietsma attests to the value of professional therapy. In part, too, because she is a single mother, her children have had to assume adult responsibilities at home, as well as forgo the standard forms of family recreation. She thinks they have reason to feel cheated and angry: "But they have a therapist to talk to—a person who's not involved that they can go to and tell anything they want to. They don't have to worry about hurting my feelings, because I'll never know."

That third party can also draw out feelings the parents may never have anticipated. On the Menninger film, Grace was asked what she would tell other children whose parents are sick. In her seven-year-old wisdom and her twelve-year-old vocabulary, she answered, "I'd tell them it's not their fault. They didn't get sick because of any specific thing you did." Clearly she had struggled with this matter herself.

Illness Is Not Abuse

In our eagerness to guard our children against emotional damage, we tend to overlook a couple of significant truths: They have the same inherent survival mechanisms that we have learned to rely on ourselves, and there is no such thing as a perfectly blissful childhood anyway. Left to their own devices, children will usually thrive on whatever is given them and, with love and encouragement, turn it to their advantage. With the newspapers full of the disastrous consequences of parental failure, it is sometimes hard to sustain optimism. You cannot deny that abused children often become dysfunctional adults; however, a child whose life is subject to limitations beyond the parent's control is not an abused child.

Illness does not diminish your capacity to love, and there are plenty of ways to show love besides taking your kids fishing. It didn't take much energy to recline beside my children's beds, hold their hands or scratch their backs, and sing lullabies. When my breath was short, I reminded myself that it was certainly not the quality of my voice that kept them listening. When I was spaced out on pain medication, I could still kiss them goodnight. When I was in the hospital, I sang over the phone. What really matters to children is frequent assurance that *they* matter very much. The payoff for me in this bedtime ritual is that both my girls still enjoy quiet, affectionate bedside conversation.

Though parental illness itself does not constitute abuse, there is plenty of room to use it in an abusive fashion. There are, of course, sick parents who tyrannize their children. Not feeling well makes you irritable, and children are handy targets for anger and frustration that can't be contained. Tyranny can even become a deliberate style of child-raising. It is tricky to maintain authority over your children or to get them to honor your special needs when you don't have the physical stamina to enforce the rules you lay down. When all else fails, you can commandeer your children with belittling language or manipulate them by playing on their feelings of guilt. Fear of making the parent's illness worse can keep an otherwise defiant child in line. The hysterical mother who flies into a fury with no warning and the brooding father who must be protected from childish noise and other ordinary unpleasantries are familiar types. The temptation to fall back on such behavior strikes even the most loving parent in moments of weakness. The best way around it is to have a supportive spouse or other nearby adults who will reinforce the rules. Another option is to lower your expectations of proper behavior to what you can realistically manage.

Lessons and Benefits

Many of the parents I spoke with were surprised and heartened at how well their children weather hardships and at the benefits they seem to derive from that. Seven years after the lupus flare-up that left her unable to care for her baby, Susan Alm talks with a mixture of regret and pride about the amount of responsibility that her oldest daughter has assumed in the family:

> Rita has got the brunt of it, she really has, and I feel bad about that, but there's nothing I can do about it. In a sense I had some of the same thing, as the oldest of five kids. I can remember taking care of my sisters from the time I was about ten on. A lot of people don't learn those lessons until they're quite a bit older. She's far more responsible than 99 percent of the other children, and I've had other mothers tell me that, too. If a group of kids are going somewhere, she's the one they'll give the money to or tell what time they have to be home, because she's the most responsible. And when she babysits, the people tell me how wonderful she is, but it's because she's had to do it. She's almost too responsible. She sometimes has a hard time dealing with kids her own age, because I think she is a lot older in some ways. Both girls are very strong participants in Jenny's care, and are very strongly bonded with her, which is very interesting. It just had to be that way. I didn't have a choice. Rita is very close to Jenny and really cares for her.

Susan's repeated emphasis on the necessity of this arrangement suggests a lingering compulsion to apologize, as though she could have offered Rita a much better childhood had she not been sick. She is making up for it now by entrusting more of the household and babysitting tasks to her second daughter, rather than habitually relying on Rita. The real risk that teenagers in the Alms' upscale neighborhood run, however, is not excess responsibility but a careless dependency. Maybe Rita will envy her friends, maybe she will feel resentful, maybe she will claim to have been deprived of a normal childhood. On the other hand, she knows something about how to make her own way in the world. Listening to Susan, I was reminded of Tillie Olsen's short story "I

Stand Here Ironing," in which a mother recounts all the obstacles
that necessity put in the way of her daughter's development. As
sorry as she is, she ends up reconciled: "Let her be. So all that is in
her will not bloom—but in how many does it? There is still
enough left to live by."

Entrusting children early on with responsibility for their own
care does have payoffs, as Gloria Murphy learned:

> One of the fears I went through was, "What will my children
> remember about Mom?" That was my biggie. They will grow
> up and all they will remember is that they had to iron their
> shirts when they were ten and nobody else did, and they
> washed dishes and nobody else did. Well, now when my old-
> est boy went away to his first year of college, he made money
> ironing girls' shirts. That helped.

As awesome as it seems to prepare a six-year-old to handle his
mother's diabetic coma, as Peggy Evans did, it is far kinder than
leaving the children ignorant of real dangers. Margie Rietsma
took the same approach and found that her children "can be real
little troopers when pushed to the test." In fact, her eleven-year-
old son's presence of mind saved her life:

> I was lying on the couch watching TV, and the next thing I
> knew, I woke up in intensive care. It seems that I stopped
> breathing. My son called the emergency number. I've given
> them instructions in what to do, because I don't know
> what's going to happen. My son knew I was not feeling well
> that night when I was lying on the couch, so he kept talking
> to me, and evidently I stopped answering.

This alertness is a habit that children of chronically ill parents develop very early. I was taking a five-minute rest on the couch one
evening while the supper finished cooking, and I had casually
dropped my hand across my upper abdomen. Maria, then just
three, imitated the gesture and asked, "Why this? Mommy sick?"

I had mixed feelings about that. I was proud of her quick perception, but I didn't want this innocent young soul to be on her guard all the time. A few weeks later, I did get sick. I felt the pain starting up just before the kids' bedtime, and I managed to stave it off until they were asleep. Then it came on with full force and I took a Demerol and got in bed. Maria woke up again before the medication had taken effect and found me moaning. She wanted to climb into bed with me, but I had to refuse her, because any movement beside me would aggravate the pain. She cried and I felt awful. When the pain finally eased up some, I had to get myself up to go to the bathroom. She took me by the hand, led me into the bathroom, shut the door, lifted the toilet lid, and helped me pull down my pants. The role reversal seemed to console her. It was not just fear that made her cry, I realized, but a compassion that some people never achieve in a full lifetime. Both my daughters have that quality.

Compassionate Protectors

The unconditional love and affection that small children show their parents is a great morale booster in times of illness. As these relationships mature, the compassionate child may become a confidante and protector. Several of the people I talked with claim that their children are among their closest and most reliable sources of support. They understand the illness, anticipate problems, and serve as interpreters to the rest of the world. Susan Alm's children help around the house without having to be asked and explain to their friends and schoolteachers that their mother is not often able to give rides or chaperone school events. Though having child-raising behind her will simplify her life in many ways, she does not look forward to seeing her children leave home. They, too, may find the leave-taking difficult if they believe that their mother's health depends on their presence. Each of us needs to have other sources of help ready in order to let our growing children off the hook.

Precocious though it may be, this concern for the parent's welfare is a sane adaptation to what is ultimately a family matter—as long as it doesn't become overly solicitous. There is a risk that compassionate children will keep their own needs under constraint. Esther Green has seen this in her grandchildren:

> They'll call up and say, "Grandma, how do you feel? Are you tired?" I'm afraid to say yes because maybe they want me to do something, and if I say yes, that's a letdown. So I say, "No, I'm not too tired." Once I had said I was tired and the little girl had wanted me to come to school for a play, and I felt bad about that. So I say, "No, I'm feeling okay," to feel them out and see if they were thinking to ask me to go someplace.

Phyllis Mueller has seen the same behavior in her children and has encouraged them to be straightforward about how much her participation matters:

> A lot of times when they wanted me to do something, they tried to be real considerate and say, "I know you don't feel good." They're kind of reluctant to ask me sometimes. I feel kind of bad about that. I think I would have participated a little more fully in their lives. Sometimes when they've wanted to do something, like go shopping, I don't have the energy to get out there and do it. I don't like to turn them down, because I would be there and I would do it, if I had enough energy. Other times I've pushed myself to do it. I would show up for their school things. I usually didn't beg off things like that. I tried to decide on a scale from one to ten, how important is this to the child? If it was a nine, I would try to get there. If it was a three, I'd say, "Would you really mind if Mom didn't come to school today?"

Children who learn to be honest about their own needs relieve their sick parents of the strain of constant guesswork and the guilt that results from guessing wrong. As parents, we can repay their trust by being equally honest. Both Gloria Murphy's and Peggy Evans's children have taken the initiative in determining just how much the illness is going to affect family life. They have intervened when their mothers' attempts to ignore new symptoms have clouded the atmosphere. "Don't you think it's time you called the doctor?" is a gentle prodding that Gloria has come to expect from her teenage sons. Peggy's children talked her into getting a wheelchair, which meant accepting the fact that she had become more disabled. They made the appeal on their own behalf: They didn't like leaving her behind when they went out to do things that required walking long distances. Rather than deferring to their mother's physical fragility, Peggy's children respect her emotional strength enough to hold their own in family disputes:

> My daughter and younger son were still living at home when I first experienced the neuropathy, and they did not let me feel sorry for myself. This is important, because I think we lose perspective when we are ill and have been ill for a long time. They also do not let me get too demanding. I have to depend on others, and first of all I depend on my family. There were things I wanted to do not at their convenience but rather when I wanted to do them. I had some plants I wanted to repot, and I needed help getting out the dirt and getting all the things together and carrying them, and I had waited and waited and waited until it would be a good time for one of them and it never was. Finally, I said, "I want to do it now." That did not go over well. They had a little mini-intervention, and we sat around and discussed that, and I was in tears. But it helped, because they began to see my frustrations and my point of view, and I began to put things in their perspective. I should have said, "This is something I would like to do. When can we do it?"

Watching her children grow up and leave home as "well-balanced and productive and basically happy individuals," Peggy has put aside her worries about the damage her diabetes might do to their psyches. She believes, now, that much of her effort to make their childhoods seem normal was unnecessary:

> For a long time I tried to accommodate the family. I didn't want the diabetes to interfere with family. That was wrong! It should have. I really think that it would not have been much interference, but I should have taught them earlier to respect the few demands that it has, and that this was something I just had to live with and had no choice. But I underplayed that.

Normal Is As Normal Does

In retrospect, Peggy has learned a lesson of great benefit to families affected by chronic illness: Normal is as normal does. Children come to expect what they are accustomed to getting and to define the world in terms of what they have experienced themselves. Familiarity with illness, disappointed hopes, sudden crises, and adults who cry or explode in anger is excellent preparation for life in an imperfect world. And such a childhood need not be cheerless, if the parent who is at the center of the crises seems to be thriving nevertheless. The best bet is for the parents to behave as though this is a normal way of life.

Demystifying the illness and making its trappings a routine part of the child's environment is a start. I often took my children with me when I went to have blood drawn or the location of my IV tube changed. When it was time for me to drip at home, they would get out the paper tape I needed and tear it into little strips for me. An irreverent humor can aid in the demystification. Gloria Murphy's sons decorate her wheelchair for special occasions and joke about putting mudflaps and rearview mirrors and horns on her scooter. Her twelve-year-old pushes her as fast as he can the length of an indoor shopping mall and clocks his time.

Treating the illness as a normal condition does not mean

hiding its dangers. Besides training children to take action in emergencies, it is a good idea to talk openly and realistically about all that can happen. Children's imaginations may conjure up even worse scenarios than the disease really presents. Susan Alm went to the hospital for surgery when her youngest daughter was five, and, even though she came home soon and recovered quickly, it had a profound impact:

> She went through a time period when she would not leave my side. She would not go visit her friends. She would have kids over, but she would not go play at anyone else's house. She wouldn't sleep overnight at Grandma's. She wouldn't go anywhere. Even when she got to school in the fall there was such a noticeable change in her behavior that her teacher called and talked to me about it. She was really a lot more fearful. She was often asking the teacher who was going to pick her up and when they were coming and that sort of thing. She was really afraid that she would be left alone and that her security blanket, her Mommy, would be gone. She really needed to know exactly what was happening and what was planned for the day. It wasn't for a long time that she finally said to me very casually, "You know, when you went to the hospital, Mommy, and you were going to die?" It just occurred to me then that she really believed that and it wasn't for months that she could verbalize it. It took a long time, but by the end of the school year she was fine.

"Are you going to die?" is the question that all children eventually pose, or at least ponder by themselves. Grace first phrased it as "Does everybody die?" but she, like Susan's daughter, always wanted to know precisely what was happening and what to expect. We never did sit down and have the one big discussion about death that I figured we would have—nor did we have the one big discussion about sex. Over the years, I answered questions as they came up, including whether I had a will and who I had chosen to take care of them. If our children are as normal as we hope, the really pressing question is, "If you die, what will happen to me?" They need realistic assurance that they will be cared for even in the worst event. And, before Grace left home for college halfway across the country, she needed assurance that others would take good care of me in her absence.

The Difference Age Makes

How children manage the knowledge of their parents' illnesses and the attendant worries does vary by age and developmental level. Tiny children who still see their parents as extensions of themselves will respond in kind to their parents' moods, at least on the surface. Teenagers undergoing a psychological separation from the family may avoid showing sympathy for fear it will draw them back into their parents' grip. Al Keski is watching his daughter's new independence with a cautious understanding, but at the same time he blames himself for the increasing distance between them:

> My daughter has definitely got her own interests at this point. I guess I don't want to deny her that, because you're only a kid so long. You do worry about them and about these things that are happening in the world, with sex and drugs and alcohol. They're going to be exposed to them and you hope you did your best. She's getting to be pretty much on her own now, and I think she has handled the illness quite well. She's quite close to her mother and they do share a lot. We were quite close, I think, before the illness. Sometimes when she would get into a disagreement with her mother, the two of us could sit down and just share. We lost that. It's because of the illness, I think. My personality changed, not to my wishes by any means. Lack of patience is the biggest thing. I try to understand, but I think I come to snap decisions. Too often I say no, which isn't really the right answer.

Adult children may be nervous about having to bear responsibility for prematurely helpless parents. Remembering how his mother's last years affected him and his siblings, Don Welke worries, each time he has a setback, about becoming a "living liability" to his children. The same child may respond to the illness differently at different stages of development. Susan Alm has watched her ultraresponsible first daughter experience new insecurities as she goes through her teenage years, including frequent nightmares that Susan associates, in part, with the uncertainty of her illness. The course of behavior is never set once and for all. There is no time when you can sit back and exhale and say, "Well, I've taken care of that problem, and my kids should do fine from now on."

In general, a child who has grown up with a parent's illness accepts its limitations more readily than one whose healthy parent is suddenly incapacitated. Esther Green's grandchildren take Grandma as she is, while their parents often seem impatient with her new infirmity. Only two of her six children have taken time to talk to her doctor or read literature from the Lupus Foundation. JoAnn Berglund tells this story about her son's difficulty adjusting to her new condition:

> My son Dave was about sixteen when they diagnosed the MS. When I came home from the hospital after a time lapse of three or four weeks, I remember him standing in the living room. He looked at me real crabby: "Are you going to die?" I said, "Probably not, unless I get hit by a car because I can't walk across the street fast enough." He said, "Oh." He was mad at me, that I would do this to him. Do you know, he never faced it until this August, when he was twenty-five. He's married and has a child. He'd say, "I don't want to talk about it." If you don't talk about it, it doesn't exist. And my daughters both told me, "We can't talk to him." The first thing I asked the doctors was, "Is it hereditary?" and they said no. But he was concerned that the baby would inherit it, and I think he was afraid—he never said it—that he might get it.

This time when I was in the hospital I had major chemo-therapy, the same as for cancer, and I was so sick when I came home. I really wanted to take a bath, and my son's wife is in the medical field and I figured, she's drawing blood and everything, so she'll be the one who can help me take a bath. I knew I would have trouble, because I was really weak. I thought, "She can help me." It won't bother her. I found out later that she thought, "Oh my God, giving my mother-in-law a bath?" It turned out okay. She's honest. But I was in the bath, and I couldn't get out of the tub. I couldn't get my leg up. My husband's got a bad back, so I didn't want to ask him. I thought, "Well, this is it. Dave's very strong. It's going to bother him that I don't have any clothes on, but that's too bad." Better that I should stay here and drown or freeze? So I said, "Barbara, get Dave in here. I'll throw a towel over me the best I can." So he took my arms and she took my feet, and he carried me out and he was holding me and he said, "Where do you want me to put you?" I said, "Set me on the toilet seat." Then he left the room. I came back out and sat in the chair and he sat on the floor. He said it was the first time he ever realized that I really was sick. I don't look sick, but I really had something. He wanted to talk. He's a very quiet, reserved type. He asked this strange ques-tion, "How does your marriage survive this?" I said, "Fine. Your father isn't thrilled about it, but we manage." As soon as they got in the car, Barbara told me, Dave said, "You know, I never realized it, but my mother is sick." Then he felt guilty: "Gee, I haven't done enough." His friend Bob came over not too many days after and told Barbara that Dave talked for a long time about me being sick. It was like he fi-nally had to face it.

Dave's capacity for denial bewilders his sisters, who were fifteen and thirteen when their mother's illness was diagnosed. The older girl is, according to JoAnn, the one who handles it best, with candor and good humor. The younger one, who is very organized, assumed the practical responsibilities like cooking and housework. JoAnn describes her: "I can still see her, when I came home. She was sitting in the rocking chair like someone's old maid aunt, just rocking. I don't know if she felt she had all the responsibility." While age, sex, and developmental level are all significant in predicting how a child will respond, the critical factor is one that cannot be measured: the distinctly individual character that observant parents identify in their children's first few months. Some children are simply more fearful or more given to resentment than their siblings, and some are more compassionate.

A Chance to Teach by Example

What most of us want from our children, anyway, is for them to idolize us in childhood, tolerate us in adolescence, communicate with us after they leave home, emulate us when they become parents, and bear with us in old age. Achieving this depends not only on our treating them reasonably well, but also on our showing them by example how a decent, respectable human being behaves. Chronic illness offers a special opportunity to demonstrate exemplary patience and discipline. Breaking down under the strains of illness damages the image of mature, adult control that we would like to convey. How awful if your kids only remember Mom or Dad as a whimpering, decrepit, impotent figure. Thinking about that can sometimes be an effective means of pain control.

Yet, while passing as healthy may serve you well in public, it is not really the wisest course to follow among intimates. Even the most secretive people I talked with have found it best to drop the pretense with their children. Duane Barber will not make the mistake of withdrawing emotionally from his teenage son, as he did with his wife. He sees the boy only on weekends and they usually go to a gym together, which gives him a natural opportunity to talk about and demonstrate his physical condition. Rachel

Ryder first told her four children she had epilepsy after the oldest had started college. They had watched her take Dilantin for years, but the only explanation she ever gave was that the pills were to make her feel better. "Boy, is that the wrong message to give to children!" she laughs. When she did tell them the story of her adolescence, they were very sympathetic. She found that breaking her silence allowed them to speak more freely, too:

> When I told my kids that my mother probably knew about the epilepsy but never let on, they were really speechless. We were having a little family meeting, and in that meeting, all hell broke loose, because they all started pouring it out like Peter in Gethsemane. Things came flowing out from these kids who were like a bunch of basket cases. And I think it was because I had shared this very painful moment with them and was crying a bit. All of a sudden it was okay to talk about your problems and worries. It was really interesting. I was a wreck after that, because I hadn't realized how much they do keep things to themselves and are scared to talk about them.

In fact, Rachel's new openness has changed the family dynamics in profound ways. As she herself suspected, not revealing the epilepsy had not protected her children from "catching" her feelings of shame and her habits of secrecy. Her daughter, it turned out, had been practicing bulimia, and Rachel's confession opened the door for her to talk to Rachel about it and to seek counseling.

When Kathy Halvorson underwent a hysterectomy at age thirty, her mother revealed that she herself had had a hysterectomy shortly after Kathy was born. Even though Kathy had asked for a baby brother or sister and had suffered miserably with endometriosis from the onset of menstruation, her mother had never told her about the surgery. Kathy regrets missing the understanding they might have found if she had known earlier. As private as she keeps her illness even among friends, Kathy has resolved not to hide it from her daughter, now seven, whom she adopted in infancy. Jane was tuned in to her mother's moods by age three. She notices new bruises that Kathy gets from stumbling into things, and she is extra affectionate when her mother is fatigued.

> I'm just grateful for Jane, because she's the one person in my life who is really seeing the whole picture. Maybe there's a way I could hide it from her, but I think it's such a tremendous opportunity that I have no desire to hide it from her, especially when she adores me! I wonder how it's going to be to have her growing up with me and seeing it from the inside like nobody's ever seen it. I look forward to sharing that with her. I really want to be honest with her, but I feel like I don't want to be a burden to her.

Not wanting to be a burden—the "living liability" that Don Wolfe fears becoming if he loses control of the diabetes the way his mother did—is a strong motivation for practicing stoicism in front of your children. However, when the discomfort of the illness is hard to disguise, the effort to seem unneedy can look more like martyrdom. Your children may see character flaws in place of the physical ones. As a teenager, I thought that my mother was a stick-in-the-mud because she was never willing to walk anywhere. If the family wanted to go hiking without her, she assured us she would be all right in a tone of voice that betrayed hurt feelings. Not wanting to be a burden, she became an aggravation. Had she just told me outright how much pain her arthritis caused her, I would have been more sympathetic, even though I was at a typically self-centered and rebellious age. I wish she had trusted me enough to talk to me honestly and let me react in my own way.

Phyllis Mueller has chosen an approach that spares her children from witnessing her pain without denying the reality of it. She pushes herself to maintain a full family life, and her children seem to know and appreciate the costs of that:

My children will often say, "Gosh, So-and-so's mother was in bed today because she has a headache. Can you imagine if Mom went to bed when she was sick? We'd never see her." They seem to have gained a pretty good perspective on my efforts to function here. That's a form of keeping going, too—the good reinforcement you get.

Yet there are times when she does choose to retreat, and then she tells the children what is happening. She does not need secrecy in order to have privacy:

I feel that they need to know that so they don't think it's something they did. At the risk of them leaving home just thinking I'm sick all the time, I would prefer that over feeling somehow they were deficient. I think you could create a whole houseful of neurotic children if mother just went to her woodbox and curled up and didn't say anything.

Best Wishes

Listening to Phyllis talk, I am struck by what a thoughtful, loving, conscientious parent she is—one who carefully balances the demands of her illness against her children's best interests and weighs the likely consequences of the choices she makes. Nevertheless, her experience as a parent has not been trouble-free. To her surprise and horror, one of her children went through a period of drug abuse, which may or may not have been a consequence of her illness. The point of her story is the message she hears reinforced again and again when she attends Al-Anon meetings as the parent of a chemically dependent child: Some things are simply beyond her control. Try as we might, we cannot protect our children's psyches from all possible harm. They, like our other family members, will bring to this shared experience of illness their own personality traits, their observations of the world outside their home, the experiences they undergo without us, and the influence of their peers. What they derive from living with their parents' illness will almost certainly be distinct and different from what we wish for them. What is important is that we wish them the best and do what we can to help them achieve it.

This realization is sobering, but also freeing. Once, in a conversation with some friends of my generation whose incomes keep them reasonably secure, someone began enumerating all of the things our parents wanted for us: higher education, good marriages, well-behaved children, higher incomes than theirs, nice houses. "And all we really want for our kids," she concluded, "is emotional well-being." It struck me that anxiety about the impact of my illness on my children's psyches was nothing more than an updated version of my parent's overprotectiveness, the feature of my upbringing that I most wanted to avoid. If I really wanted to be Mellow Mom, after all, I would have to let that worry go and be content with simply loving them as much as I can.

That image of my daughter lying on the psychoanalyst's couch has faded away altogether. When Grace was a sophomore in high school, she went through a depression that began to show in her schoolwork and in withdrawal from old friends. I took her to see a therapist and sat out in the waiting room filling out forms while they began their talk. After about forty-five minutes, I was invited in, and the therapist summarized for me what problems they had identified. There was only one surprise: The list did *not* include my illness. The therapist asked if I had anything to add, and I told her that I had a liver disease that often upset our family life. "Gee," Grace said, "I never thought of that."

At nineteen and sixteen, my daughters' personalities and talents are fairly well set, but there is always room for fine-tuning. One evening during Grace's final year of high school, I had to make a sudden trip to the emergency room. In the past, we had always scrambled to find a way to get me there, but this time there was no need: Grace would drive, and Maria would help me into the car. Though they had been in the emergency waiting room before, this was the first time they were in charge of admitting me and standing by me as I lay on a cot waiting to be examined. Both girls were very serious and self-contained at first, but once I had been given a shot and my pain began to subside, things took an unusual turn. Grace, the practical stoic, burst into sobs, and cried and cried, as though she were letting go of a lifetime of pent-up tears. I was relieved to see it happen. Maria, usually the tearful one, was fascinated with the medical procedures and asked questions and offered me her finger to squeeze as the lab technician drew blood cultures. Under the euphoric spell of the painkiller, I beamed with pride and told them what I've always wanted them to know, that despite all this pain and worry, I am truly happy with my life and with their presence in it.

I chose the name Grace for my first daughter because she is a gift of grace, having come to me through no effort of my own. Coincidentally, the name that a social worker gave Maria on the day of her birth, Eun Sook, means "grace" in Korean. It was a double measure of grace that brought the girls to me and enabled us to continue life as a family despite the upheavals we have been through. I have to trust that this grace will stay with us. Grace's Korean birth name, Keun Young, which means "root of a flower," is also a wonderfully appropriate symbol. In romance literature, the dying young heroine is likened to a frail blossom, and her memory is preserved like the petals pressed and dried between the pages of a book. How much better to be the root of a perennial flower that spends its dormancy in the frozen ground accumulating the energy to blossom again and again. I knew that if I could only get my children's roots planted deeply enough, they would thrive on sun and rain.

Chapter
9

Patience as a Way of Life

"I wake up in the morning and I test my parts."

Living with an ever-present illness is like being encased in a portable bubble made of fragile glass. The bubble may be transparent enough to be invisible, so that you can move it around under the optical illusion that you live in the open air, but its invisibility also compounds the danger. You must constantly protect it against impact, because its broken shards might be deadly. If anyone presses near enough to break it, or if you move too precipitously, the discomforts restrained inside will spill out amoeba-like, undoing your efforts to control them. While the roominess and heft of the bubble are determined by the nature of the illness, where you take the bubble and how fully you occupy its interior space is a matter of choice. The choices vary from time to time, depending on whether the bubble seems more like a protection or an encumbrance. Sometimes you want to flail against its walls in defiance; other times you feel content to huddle inside.

For all but the most stoic among us, what keeps the bubble intact is an earnest desire to avoid or at least reduce whatever physical suffering our illnesses impose. For me, that is life-threatening infection with high fever, and abdominal pain so severe as to be intolerable. Kathy Halvorson once tried to tell her gynecologist how endometriosis felt: like someone was pouring concrete into her uterus. He chuckled at her cleverness. I was grateful for the image, because it describes what I feel: concrete filling my liver until it bursts and spills into my abdominal cavity, hardening as it is poured so that its rough edges grate against my diaphragm and the muscles between my ribs. I can't breathe, I can't lie down, and I can't imagine anything worse, though someone else has probably experienced it. The knowledge that pain like this can come on at anytime never leaves me, though I have good stretches when I don't have to dwell on it. Thus, the threat of pain determines, to a great extent, how I live my life, even though nothing I do can prevent it.

Nevertheless, I consider myself lucky. While the threat is ever present, the pain itself is sporadic. I cannot say, like Susan Alm, "I never have a pain-free day," and only periodically do I have the heightened awareness Kathy Halvorson describes:

> I never expect to feel good. When I feel good, it's glorious. When I have a couple hours, I'm very aware of feeling good. And that means not feeling tired, mysteriously not feeling tired. It means not having some kind of pain or something in conjunction with whatever is going on with my body. Or not worrying about something happening or fixing something or taking medicine.

My illness is best described as terroristic. It allows periods of good health but can disrupt them at any time. Susan's lupus is constant and unrelenting. Kathy's symptoms intensify and recede but never give way entirely to good health. Other illnesses, such as diabetes, seem to offer daily good health as a reward for diligent self-discipline. In either case, to be alerted by the absence, rather than the presence, of symptoms is a pretty clear indication that illness has become the norm.

Acceptance

The word "acceptance" is widely used to denote an optimistic attitude toward illness that gets past the initial horror of it and enables you to proceed with life. No matter how philosophical you are, however, pain is never really acceptable. Practice does not make perfect. Phyllis Mueller is adamant about that: "The more pain I have, the more surgeries I have, the more scared I get. I don't seem to condition myself to it very well. Having more pain does not make me accept it any better." Nevertheless, she finds that some of it is manageable and can be set aside temporarily: "There are days when I refuse to recognize my pain. I just go on as though it's not there." Some pain can be eased by relaxation techniques, mild medication, acupuncture, or chiropractic treatments. With self-hypnosis, Margie Rietsma can make herself relax enough to tolerate some of the pain of arthritis. When pain keeps her awake at night, she diverts her attention by composing poems.

Weakness may be easier to negotiate than pain. I have learned that there is a point at which fever is clearly perceptible, about 99.5 degrees Fahrenheit, and another point, 102 degrees, at which it becomes debilitating. I can adjust to living at 100 or even 101, and doing what I would otherwise do, though more slowly and for shorter periods and with a greater chance of a headache. But when my body temperature hits 102 degrees, my head sinks, my eyes close, and there is no possibility of a life worth calling normal. At 104, I lie in the private, sweaty flophouse of my bed and hallucinate. Likewise, when pain grows intense enough to force recognition, it demands complete attention. As I know it, severe pain is isolating and totally absorbing. I can't do anything but hurt.

What acceptance really means then is taking responsibility for constructing a life in the spaces between these moments of dysfunction, and adopting habits that will keep them to a minimum in intensity and frequency. It is a way of life that requires a great deal of patience, in the dictionary sense of "the capacity of calm endurance." The word "patient" is actually derived from the present participle of the Latin verb *pati*, "to suffer." To be patient, then, is, at the core, to be suffering. Acceptance does not eliminate that part of it. Peggy Evans compares living with diabetes to "walking a tightrope twenty-four hours a day." A newspaper feature on kidney dialysis quoted someone as saying that spending alternate days on dialysis was like having a bad part-time job. Phyllis Mueller thinks of her life as a Jekyll-and-Hyde existence and tries to be ready for whichever persona wakes up in the morning. Janice Willett sees her body, beset by Crohn's disease, as "a friend that I maybe haven't done right by," who, without "coddling," may turn against her.

For Peggy, balancing on the tightrope means following a regimen of diet, medication, and exercise that keeps her blood sugar at a healthy level. She has been taught a well-researched, theoretically sound system of maintenance, but putting it into practice means adjusting it, day by day, to her own body chemistry. Diabetes is one of the relatively few chronic illnesses that has a recommended lifestyle all its own, with a specialized vocabulary of "exchanges" and "glucometers." For other, less studied diseases, there are few practical guidelines to follow, beyond taking the prescribed medications. We may watch our bodies as carefully, but with very few clear expectations about what might go wrong. Limits are set by trial and error, and habits are adopted and then changed as new symptoms arise. Once we have an overarching diagnosis, we often attribute even unrelated problems to the chronic illness, confusing the pattern we are trying so hard to discern.

Body Consciousness

Determining the healthiest way to live requires a conscious awareness of bodily functions that often feels obsessive. Many people wake up in the morning instantly alert to their physical conditions. Susan Alm's very first sensation each day is pain in her joints. Louise Taylor usually expects trouble from her multiple sclerosis:

> When you open your eyes, is there going to be light out there? Are you going to be able to see? My first thought when I put my feet on the floor is if they're going to work.

And if they work and my legs are feeling okay and my hands are feeling okay, then I go about the day.

How breakfast feels on its way down is the first test for others, or what happens on the first trip to the bathroom. But morning is not decisive. Lunch imposes new conditions and starts a new test. The afternoon can bring a new round of fatigue or blurred vision. At its most intense, this body consciousness stimulates the imagination, posing yet another challenge: how to tell real symptoms from self-fulfilling anxieties.

Knowing the symptoms well, having the treatment ready, and following the regimen carefully do not necessarily ward off pain and suffering. Even responsible, cautious people like Peggy Evans and Don Welke have had serious complications through no fault of their own. Peggy describes what went through her mind when she developed neuropathy:

> When I was a new diabetic, they said, "Now if you stay on your diet and take your insulin, you won't have complications." And there were complications. Did that mean I had not stayed on my diet? Did that mean I had not taken my insulin? Well, I *had* always taken my insulin and I *had* always tried to stay on my diet, but evidently not enough. If I had tried harder, would I then not be getting these complications? I was ashamed and I felt that I had let the doctors down who had really tried hard to treat me and teach me. I think now it was because I was just very sensitive to the insulin. My body didn't utilize insulin as other people's did.

The protective bubble broken, Peggy had to start over, with additional limitations. The second time around, she had to face the fact that she had lost control over the course of the illness. More precisely, the *illusion* that she was in control was broken. It is quite common to feel ashamed or guilty when the illness worsens. Susan Alm's first thought when a new symptom appears is

"I must be doing this wrong." Thinking this way delays the unsettling admission that you do not and may never have mastery over the illness. Most of us would rather believe that mind has authority over matter, if we can only learn how to enforce it.

Loss of Control

Dealing with loss of control is the most difficult aspect of acceptance. The single most frightening feature of chronic illness is its uncertainty. The patterns you come to expect can change suddenly. The actions you take to protect your health do not always work in predictable ways. At times it seems that nothing you do really makes any difference. To deal with this loss of control sounds like a paradox. The term implies some deliberate process leading to positive results, but it does not suggest what that process is. Yet, in the negative, it becomes an indictment: He hasn't dealt with his heart condition. This implies that asserting intellectual or emotional control over the illness will compensate for the loss of physical control. But how do you begin to understand, feel comfortable with, or act in accordance with the realization that your life is out of control? In other words, how do you bring under control the news that you have no control? Realization—grasping the fact that it is real—may be as far as you get. But when Kathy Halvorson says, "I expect *anything* from my body," her tone of voice hardly sounds accepting.

Dealing with the loss of control is often interpreted as letting go of the wish for control and giving up all pretense that you can attain it. The importance of "letting go" has entered popular wisdom via Alcoholics Anonymous, which is frequently cited as a model for living with adversity. Many chronically ill people do find AA's Twelve Steps helpful, but they are not completely applicable to their situations. When alcoholics admit their powerlessness over alcohol, realize that their lives are unmanageable, and trust their fates to the care of a "Higher Power," whichever deity or supreme principle they believe in, the desired result is a behavioral change—abstinence from alcohol. To people unfamiliar with the AA philosophy, abstinence looks like a restoration of *self*-control. While the obsession with alcohol may never be overcome and the physiological risk of addiction is always there, the harmful consequences of drinking can be avoided. This is not quite the case with organically based or autoimmune illness. I could accept having a defective liver if a change in my behavior would eliminate the pain and fever. But what should I abstain from to make that happen?

Most of us want to believe that there is some concrete answer to that question and that a diligent—and controlled—examination of our habits will reveal it. We keep testing our tolerance for food, exertion, stimulation, and medication while trying to avoid serious risks. Again, I see that glass bubble inching along in new directions, very gently grazing the obstacles in its way. Gloria Murphy describes a tendency she calls "bargaining" after one of the stages Elisabeth Kübler-Ross named in her work on dying. "I was never bargaining with God; I was always bargaining with myself: If I clean the oven today, I'll be a real good girl and lie down tomorrow." Yet, as Gloria well knows, even forgetting the oven and lying down today is no guarantee against the next flare-up. My search for a means of self-control even relies on outright superstition. It takes quite a while before I am ready to wear the clothes I had on the last time I went to the emergency room. After getting sick while driving downtown, I changed my route the next time, on the chance that avoiding First Avenue would keep me well. Obviously, dealing with loss of control involves more than sound reason.

Aging may be a more appropriate analogy than overcoming addiction. Susan Alm thinks of the physical consequences of lupus as a little like aging prematurely. She finds herself comparing symptoms with her grandmother and sharing her resentment about the value that Western culture places on youth. Staving off physical degeneration with exercise, diet, creams, and drugs has become a social obligation. Freed from this mystique of eternal youth, aging is inevitable and simply must be accepted.

> I think feeling depressed about losing control is conditioned by a lot in our society, especially now that we have this craze for health and fitness. If you exercise and eat right, you can live to be 120, or at least when you're 40, you can look like you're 20. You supposedly have control over the natural aging process. The emphasis is always on youth, to the point that old age is evil. There's nothing about it that we say is worth looking at. I often feel that I'm so much older than my body, or my body is older than what it should be because it doesn't function right. When I talk to my grandmother, who is in her late nineties, I ask her how she's doing, and she will go through the same list of things that are wrong. The other day, she said, "You know, when you get into the nineties, some of the parts wear out." I thought, "Gee, in the thirties some of them wear out, too." She was really trying to resign herself to the same problems I was, to that acceptance that you're not perfect and you can't expect all the parts to work.

A Mind of Its Own

Treating your body cautiously does not always keep problems at bay. As Janice Willett puts it, "First you accept the idea that you have a disease and you can live with that, and then it does these unpredictable things. It has a mind of its own. It has a knowledge of its own, a process of its own." That valuable observation needs much more emphasis in the ongoing discussion of the body-mind relationship. This disease with a mind of its own occupies your body like some alien force, distorts your thoughts, and undermines your will. Margie Rietsma describes how she envisions this mind-body split:

> I guess I think about it as two parts: me and my body, as if my body were separate from me. It seems to me at times it

has its own mind. It does what it wants to do whether I want it to or not. I guess we're sort of at a compromise. I try not to put it through anything it doesn't want to go through, and it doesn't give me a whole lot of problems. I say, "Listen, I won't do this if you won't do that," and my body says, "Okay. You don't do that and I promise I won't do this." But sometimes it lies to me and does it anyway. I always used my body. I always counted on it. Nobody ever told me that I had any limitations. And now I find my body telling me that all the time: "You can't do that." I get real resentful: "How dare you? *I'm* in control here."

I have long thought of myself as a skilled practitioner of the mind-body split. My strategy for living with an unruly body has been to ignore it as much as possible. If I could avoid offending it, maybe it would leave me alone and let me live my life with gusto from the neck up. This was the version of letting go I could most easily accomplish, I thought. My body does not shift into static mode, however, and wait for orders from my mind. In an effort to relieve stress and distinguish it from oncoming pain, I began seeing a counselor who uses guided fantasy to accomplish an end similar to hypnosis. On one occasion, I came in complaining that I felt constricted in my upper abdomen, as though my liver were encased in a tight membrane. The sensation was like wearing a pair of pantyhose a size too small. She asked me to fantasize how I would free the liver from its confinement, and I began to imagine slitting the membrane open with a scissors. As I did, the opposite side of my abdomen started convulsing. There were real, physical spasms, and they hurt. "That's my spleen!" I cried, and suddenly a memory of an event in my childhood came back to me, almost as vividly as if I were reliving it. When I was about ten years old, a girl in the class behind mine at school died. We were told that she had fallen while climbing up a doorjamb in her house and her spleen had ruptured. I had never forgotten about that girl's death, but I did not remember it frightening me as much as it did in this visualization. The counselor asked me to envision myself at that age, and what I saw was a very unkempt girl with her shirt hanging out. My mother was telling me to tuck it in and to comb my hair, and I was insisting that I could not, because all my energy was needed to hold in my internal organs and keep them from exploding. I thought next of how I sit with shoulders hunched and midsection drawn in, often with my arm or hand across it as if to protect it from blows. For thirty years, I had been using the force of willpower to keep myself alive! Rather than surrendering control, I had practiced it to the extreme of trying to control involuntary bodily functions. Could that have made me sick? I wondered for a moment, but, no, my liver is clearly misconstructed and must have been from birth. At the very least, though, this subconscious effort at control added to the tension in that part of my body and, who knows, maybe even intensified the pain. Letting go means trusting that my body will not self-destruct if I relax my vigilance.

Qualified still further, acceptance means exercising what control you realistically can over how you live, and getting ready for chaos. Susan Alm says, "It's like being a mother. There's not a whole lot of control there, either." Robert O'Shea redefines control as relying on what you *can* know and comprehend:

> When you find out that you are chronically ill, you start striving for some kind of acceptance or serenity or whatever the word is. But you can't have that unless you're in control, and you're not in control unless you have knowledge. So I kept saying to myself, "All I want to know is the state of the art at this point, and where is Robert?" Given those parameters, you're in control, and then you can have a state of acceptance.

Caution and Risk

Once we know those parameters, each of us has to choose a way of life that suits our interests as well as the needs of the illness, and to put into place a form of medical care that we can call on when the illness rages out of control. To some degree, we also set the balance between a cautious style of living and reliance on medical intervention. Duane Barber pins his best hopes on his way of life:

> Since there's no cure for this thing, you have to take it upon yourself to take the best care of yourself that you can, and that means the whole picture: sleep, nutrition, exercise. If you have that tripod, I think you're well on your way to being able to resist any viruses that are around that would get you down if you have MS. I get about seven hours of sleep a night. I watch what I eat. The only time I drink is when I'm at home. My treat on late Saturday afternoon is a glass of wine, once a week. I make time to get to the gym. As part of my workout I do one thousand sit-ups a week. If I'm short on my sit-ups, I do them at home. I just think that being in condition is very important and reduces the fatigue level. In my situation, with my health, I have to have that kind of lifestyle to survive.

The same basic fact, incurability, leads Lily Washington to put her trust in the hospital emergency room. To Lily, asserting control over her life means taking the risks that the illness imposes on her:

> If there's not a cure on the horizon, if there's nothing I can do to totally eliminate it from my life, then there are times when I figure, well, what the hell? There are certain things I want to do and sometimes it means running yourself a little more than the average Joe Blow. According to the doctors, I should be living in a plastic bubble somewhere up in space to get away from all the stuff that I'm allergic to. I shouldn't have plants. I shouldn't wear perfume. I like plants and I have plants. I enjoy perfume so I wear it. I'll wheeze through a meeting and go to the hospital when the meeting's over.

Honestly confronting the choice between caution and risk is the first step in adopting patience as a way of life. Unfortunately, "patience" often connotes "passivity," a word to which it is etymologically related. In common parlance, "passive" means "submissive, compliant, not acting." Lifelong patience, however, demands action, in the form of staying attentive to the body and the emotions, sorting out evidence, weighing risks, making choices, setting limits, and recovering as much order as you can from the inevitable chaos. Sometimes we try to avoid this choice altogether by becoming passive and protecting ourselves against all risk. To maintain an illusion of normality, we surrender our entitlement to the limited activity we are capable of. Delores Garlid, for example, says she often refuses, out of both fear and pride, to go places where she expects she will have to climb stairs, even though she can usually manage them with effort. Many of us do opt out of the struggle from time to time and hole up inside our glass bubbles. We may think we have regained control, but we are only holding life at bay.

Active Patience

As you practice an *active* patience, you become increasingly familiar with how your body responds to your way of life. Eventually, the minute-by-minute hyperconsciousness of bodily signals that characterizes the period after diagnosis subsides into a daily check. Kathy Halvorson, for example, has paid enough attention over the years to know what she can usually expect each morning:

> I get up, and I'm tired. I have a hard time getting going, and so I push myself really hard for the first half hour in the morning. My body seems like it demands a routine. It calls out for breakfast at a certain time. If it doesn't come within an hour, I begin to feel sick to my stomach. So there's a food thing that I always have to maintain. I watch until midmorning for problems with my urinary tract, because if it shows up, it's often at that time.

So it goes through the day, making the framework on which Kathy constructs a routine that includes a full-time job, a husband and children, and several community obligations. Al Keski, whose multiple sclerosis affects his eyes most of all, has clocked the way his vision fades in and out during the day:

> The eyes fluctuate quite a bit. They undergo a drastic change during the day, from being quite well in the morning. If there's any kind of physical activity or any stressful situation, or if I get exposed to heat, they will get bad from, say, about eleven until about two-thirty or three. Then I take my afternoon coffee break, and I don't drink coffee because heat is a big factor. I'll have a can of pop, and things do get better at that point. If I have a reasonable afternoon, then about seven in the evening is when I'll do any reading for pleasure. Reading takes a lot longer. Needless to say, I don't do a lot of reading for pleasure.

Once you have recognized a pattern and see some order in the apparent chaos, you can at least choose how to fill out the pattern. But this restored control is still very tenuous. Any disruption in the pattern produces stress and anxiety, as Susan Alm knows:

> When joint pain is really bad and I can't sleep at night, then everything goes downhill. That will do it, right there. Or if the kids are sick and I'm up at night with them or something like that. I do require just a tremendous amount of sleep. My body needs a lot of rejuvenating. It works slower than others. If you don't get any sleep and when you get up in the morning you're in pain and can't get started, how can you make it through the day if you haven't filled up your reserves like you're supposed to?

Meeting the body's demands has to be the top priority or there may be no life worth living. Unfortunately, this requires more than a simple, conditioned response to unmistakable signals.

What the body demands is not always in its own best interest. Present comfort has to be weighed against continuing health. Do you, for example, feed an underweight body that has no appetite? Do you exercise a body that hurts? Al Keski's life is clearly caught in the balance: "I don't exercise enough and that's been bad, because any physical activity drives down my eyesight. So I'll avoid it. That's not right probably for the rest of my body, but I like to be able to see." Even if you read all your discomforts to mean "My body is trying to tell me something," you don't have to give equal credence to everything it says. When Bill Gordon's body, worn out by the fatigue that accompanies depression, wants to hide out in bed, he knows that the best course for the illness itself is to get up and stay active all day. Phyllis Mueller goes out to walk regularly, even when she's feeling "rotten." "It's not about what you feel like doing, it's about what you have to do to keep this body going," she explains. "I refuse to give up and be an invalid, and I think I could be without too much help. The difference between me and an invalid is that I keep walking." Besides maintaining physical health, exercise can produce the added benefit of at least symbolic control. Susan Alm, who has never thought of herself as a very physical person, testifies to this:

> I started swimming because I knew I needed some exercise and there was nothing else I could do with the joint involvement. The thing I liked about swimming was the diving, and I'm not a very good diver at all. The physical part of diving is really secondary. It's a mental exercise. You really have to think it through very clearly in your mind and know exactly what kind of dive you're going to do, where your body is going to enter the water, how you're going to be, and then you follow through with the physical part. That was the only time for years that I felt I had control over what I was doing. It gave me that sense of control that I felt I had lost with having a disease take over the whole of my life. It was clear to me

that that was why I enjoyed it, and it also made clear to me what it was about the disease that bothered me so much. It made me realize that not having control was the biggest loss.

A Day-to-Day Event

Each of these people wakes up in the knowledge that the new day may require great physical effort and enough mental concentration to sustain it. If it is a good day, physically, it is a precious commodity to be savored. It is often difficult to think beyond that one value packed day. The "one day at a time" approach of Twelve Step programs is very familiar to the chronically ill. It is impossible to overemphasize dailiness as a feature of living with chronic illness:

> One thing that has been a dramatic change is that I don't look too far into the future. I try and live each day as well as I can and be the best person I can be that day.

> My life feels like such a day-to-day event. That's a real difference between my husband and me and a source of conflict between us. He's always making long-range plans. My God, he talks about retirement! It's like each day is a new event for me. The days run together for him. A week just races by. A week is seven days to me. When I get up in the morning, it's like I know I'm alive again.

> I just take each day as it comes and I don't worry about tomorrow. I know that when I'm feeling good I should try to do as much as I can without overdoing, because sometimes I won't be able to do that.

> As long as I just go day to day, one day at a time—yesterday
> is gone, tomorrow is not yet mine, this is my day, this mo-
> ment is mine—things go real well for me.

> There were things that I wanted to do with my summer that
> I couldn't do just because of getting through the daily rou-
> tine, and that's about all I did. There are times in my life
> when all I can do is just get through the day, and that's it.
> You know, you really can't think beyond that.

Though the wisdom of it is obvious, living one day at a time is no
easy matter. The slogan "Today is the first day of the rest of your
life" conveys the cheery message that every new day brings the
promise of a fresh start. But it also asks you to rethink all your
options and make changes that enhance the quality and significance of your life. This can be terribly frustrating when you are
chronically ill: Here it is, the first day of the rest of my life, and
wouldn't you know it, I feel lousy! Living a day at a time works
best if you establish a routine, so that each new day has some
measure of predictability and doesn't get bogged down by seemingly trivial decisions that may, in fact, have drastic consequences.
Now that she is on disability and no longer has a job to go to,
Margie Rietsma is groping for a new routine that meets her
body's demands without confining her at home. Yet there are
times when the routine she has settled on is too demanding and
being sick seems sufficient activity in itself:

> There are times when just moving my legs to put something
> on I can wear is more than I can bear. The day before, I make
> up reasons to go someplace. I have to go here, I have to go
> there. Then I'll have an incentive to do it. But then some-
> times I ignore the incentive altogether and say, I'm not going
> anyplace, I'm just staying home today. I take mental health
> days. I just lock my front door and don't answer my tele-

phone, and stay away from people. I read, watch TV, sit in the bathtub, don't comb my hair, eat anything I feel like eating, just spoil myself a little bit.

Rather than a single daily routine, some people, like Gloria Murphy, live with a set of contingency plans to avoid letting the day go for naught:

> With MS you really don't know what's going to happen day to day, so I wake up in the morning and I test my parts. The ones that work, I use, and the ones that don't, naturally I don't use. If I'm not walking well that day, I can talk on the phone a lot, or I listen to music. If I'm not seeing well enough to read, I'll find something else to do. I've learned to compensate.

Once you know what the day has brought, it helps to voice your condition and make it tangible. "I have a headache today" announces to others, as well, that today's choices will be limited. Statements like this need not be heard as complaints or pleas for sympathy. When a headache is a familiar occurrence, announcing it is a simple statement of fact, like a weather report: This is today's limitation. Now that we all know that, let's work around it.

Redeeming the day by living as fully as you can within its limits rather than struggling in vain against them gives you back a semblance of control. Carla Schultz feels that her life has become more manageable since she has given up planning ahead:

> What I learned to do the two years I was sick after my daughter was born was quit planning. We love to have people over. We love to do things. What I would do instead is get up and see how I felt and then see if somebody wanted to go to the park with us or if I wanted to visit a friend or wash clothes. But if I said, "On Wednesday I'd like to go out for lunch," what if I got up on Wednesday and somebody expected me to be there and I had to push myself to go? So the technique

was not to plan. There are enough people that don't plan. It took the pressure off. If you're thinking ahead and planning, fantasize it out of your system, but don't do it.

While this can be satisfying in a private way, it is not always sufficient for life in the modern world. Living one day at a time puts you at a disadvantage when, in fact, work and social commitments require that you project yourself into a soundly planned future. Gloria handles this one with her usual flexibility:

> I don't look back on the past with a lot of remorse over time spent being ill, and I don't worry a whole lot about the future. I do plan ahead. I never, ever pass up a chance to plan something ahead, if it's a lunch out or a party or a trip. I plan and enjoy the plans and it very rarely happens, if it's something big, that I don't get to do it. I think there's a lot of determination and attitude involved in that.

Future plans, fulfilled or not, can be cause for anxiety. When I make big plans, I worry about jinxing myself. Airline tickets are the most worrisome. Yet I do not feel content with living one day at a time. I want to live consciously and feel I can make some difference in this imperfect world, but that is difficult to do with no vision beyond bedtime. It is frustrating to have to hedge and think, "What if I get sick?" every time you make a commitment. I feel stressed when I can't see my way clear to the end of long-term projects that I take on. I want to know my agenda. I want to solve problems before they arise. I remember the peculiar discussions we often had in my weekly writing group. One person would ask our advice about the wisdom of taking on an additional assignment. We would talk through its value to her and where it ranked in relative importance among the other things she was doing. Someone would usually suggest that she draw up a calendar, mark the days she could expect to devote to writing, then estimate how long each project would take and schedule certain days for it. It was a wonderfully rational approach to the problem, but there was no way I could ever apply it to *my* life. I have no idea which days, or how many, will be blocked out to accommodate illness. I compensate by working compulsively. Knowing that tomorrow may disappear in a Demerol fog keeps me focused on today's narrowly defined task. But there are days when the work doesn't go well and the precious time seems wasted. This adds to the stress, disturbs my sleep, and jeopardizes the next day's work.

I wish I had kept a schedule of all the times the illness has intruded on my efforts to tell about it. It seems as though each aspect has had to be lived afresh before it can be described truthfully. If the medium is to fit the message, maybe a book about chronic illness should include some plodding and semicoherent paragraphs, plus a few blank spaces to represent the days when no writing was done. Which symbol on the keyboard can convey the stress over time lost and money unearned?

Stress

Stress is a natural side effect of chronic illness, and each of these precious, value-packed days of ours should thus include some activity that will relieve stress, such as exercise, meditation, playing or listening to music, a hot bath (if heat doesn't cause problems), a telephone conversation with a good friend, a massage, or even just a favorite television program.

Just keeping yourself maintained consumes much of the time, attention, and energy you would otherwise devote to life's optional activities. In a healthy, energetic life, the tasks required to do justice to work, family, house, community, and your own spiritual well-being hardly seem optional, but chronic illness forces you to pick and choose. Everything you want to do must be reassessed and assigned a priority. Just how optional each activity is depends in part on the physical toll it exacts, but also on how much it contributes to the overall quality of life. Choosing among them is not always a matter of personal discretion, however. The world outside the glass bubble imposes itself, too. The examples people give to show how they have scaled down their activities are drawn more often from housework and recreation than from paid employment or family life. I see evidence of that piled all around my house. Physiological chaos, unfortunately, breeds environmental chaos, which is stressful in itself.

Living among healthy people unused to restrictions offers frequent temptations to deviate from the routine. Being asked to commit ourselves to events in the future breaks the habit of dailiness. Staying out past bedtime, missing a nap, or having a meal earlier or later than we are accustomed to wreaks havoc with the day's schedule and confuses the body's signals. A few hours of extra physical exertion may mean a few days of recovery. Travel and other activities that put us out of easy reach of medical care may even endanger our lives. There is not much room for spontaneity in such a life, and that alone is a source of stress. For a change, life seems *too* controlled. Kathy Halvorson misses the freedom to act on impulse:

> I wonder what it's like not to be concerned, not to worry that you can get to a doctor if you have to, not worry that you have a particular medication with you. When I went to Mexico, I had to take all sorts of stuff with me to be prepared for every infection that could come along. Now what's it like to just jump in the car and go somewhere and not have to plan? I really am very envious of that.

Pills and Other Accoutrements

Having to take medicine on schedule certainly does dam the flow of daily life. I saw this most clearly when I was on an intravenous antibiotic that had to be administered every six hours, even in the middle of the night. I could not keep the bag of solution out of the refrigerator for more than an hour, and I had to find a forty-minute period in which I could sit still with one arm incapacitated. People with diabetes learn to carry candy or glucose tablets with them and to pack a lunch if they expect to run over mealtime. Of all the elements of the daily routine, the one people seem to resent the most is being bound to a schedule of medication. When Lorraine Czerny forgets to take a pill, she blames it not on her memory but on a subconscious resistance.

> Now I'm on antibiotic therapy and it's just endless. And the amount of money you spend on medication: ninety-three dollars on one hundred pills, and that doesn't last a month! I take four of them a day, I try not to think about it. But there are times when you conveniently forget them, you know. The only reason you forget is that you subconsciously don't want to take them. Otherwise the habit is so ingrained.

Lorraine's medication schedule is, in fact, memory-boggling. Besides the antibiotics, she takes two pills a day to keep up her potassium level, one to regulate her blood clotting time, one pill one day and two pills the next day to strengthen her heart, one antidepressant at midday and two at bedtime, and a diuretic every third day. Whoever invented those multisectioned pill boxes deserves the Nobel Prize for medicine. Susan Alm laments:

> It bothers me to be a drug-dependent person. If I don't take that medication I could die. I mean, it's that simple. You're always dependent on taking the medication. You can't forget that. In that sense it controls your life to a certain extent. I don't like going out to lunch with my friends and pulling out three bottles of pills. It just bothers me to do that. But my doctor has been real good about finding medications that are compatible for me and that are timed-release so that you either take them in the morning or at night and don't have to screw up your whole day. When you have to take medication every few hours, you're reminded all day long that there's something wrong with you. I've got enough reminders of that, without having to take pills all the time.

Addiction to prescription drugs is also a frightening possibility. Rosemary McKuen recalls this worry, with the help of a journal she kept during the worst phase of her ulcerative colitis:

> There are pages and pages of journal entries where I am counting the number of Percodan I have taken. I took three drugs for eighteen months. I took Percodan three or four times a day, and sometimes I would double up on it. I was high, but nobody ever knew it. I'm pretty controlled. But I pretty much got through life during that period on Percodan. I took it even when I didn't need it because it made me feel better psychologically. Then I would get paranoid about that. I called the doctor a couple of times and said, "I'm scared about taking this Percodan," and he'd say, "You let me worry about that." He probably figured that when it was time to come off, we'd cross that bridge. In a way, I thank God I had it. It has created other problems, but I think the doctor was right. I might have been insane if it hadn't been for the fact that there was something to keep me pain-free.

Medicine reinforces the glass bubble, but also weights it down. Yet, without it, there might be no life at all, as both Susan and Rosemary recognize. Establishing a liveable routine may require new skills and special equipment. After her worst flare-up of multiple sclerosis, Louise Taylor had to relearn the simple household tasks she used to perform:

> They built up my eating utensils so I could feed myself, because I couldn't grasp them. And they put a carrot on a nail on a chopping board and had me practice chopping it. I had to practice getting in and out of the bathtub, and I thought, "Now this is dumb." They said, "Get yourself a kitchen cart and pile it with dishes or whatever you need and minimize the number of trips you have to make walking." None of that applied to me, I thought. "You'll be washing your own

dishes. Let's practice that." Well, I knew how to wash dishes, but it's different when you don't have any feeling in your hands. All of a sudden it hit me: When I go home, I don't want to be dependent on anybody, so I have to learn how to do things.

The wheelchair is, for many, a frightening symbol of degeneration. Asked to imagine the worst that can happen, people newly diagnosed with multiple sclerosis, for example, envision themselves in wheelchairs. Getting a wheelchair is what often marks the passage from invisible illness to obvious disability. The decision to do so is not always forced by desperate need, however. It is more likely to be a matter of judgment about how much the wheelchair might simplify or complicate life. Although it signals to onlookers that your mobility has declined, it does, in fact, increase it by letting you venture where you could not otherwise go. By expanding the options, it restores some control. For Gloria Murphy, Peggy Evans, and JoAnn Berglund, reliance on a wheelchair, formidable at first, has become just another element in the daily routine. All of them have learned to see it not as a place of confinement but as a tool that helps them stay active. I will never forget the day I saw Peggy Evans on her unsteady legs pushing her own wheelchair, which was loaded with packages that a healthier person would be carrying.

Selective Denial

To be honest, I had second thoughts about the title of this chapter. Maybe "Frustration as a Way of Life" would be more accurate. Neither "patience" nor "frustration" tells the whole story. With experience, most of us do acquire a capacity for endurance that is not always calm, but sometimes fretful. The truth of the matter lies somewhere between the concepts of acceptance and denial. We learn to accept, or acknowledge, the seriousness and the permanence of our illnesses, and then practice a selective denial. As one reader who takes three insulin shots a day put it, "I am thankful for a healthy sense of denial that allows me to forge ahead with hope." We can live as well as possible only if we ease up on the pervasive consciousness of illness to make room for all the other thoughts and feelings that a full life requires.

Few of us have the luxury of coming out from under the glass bubble altogether, though we may gain enough confidence to behave as though the bubble is shatterproof. Illness allows few delusions, but the focus can be adjusted. Duane Barber advises:

> You can't dismiss it from your mind. You know, right now I can feel the pins and needles. They never leave you, but you can try and cope with it. I like to use the word "minimize": minimize the illness. You can't banish it, but don't make the most of it. Make the most of something else.

With practice, some of the limits we place on ourselves become second nature and look less and less like sacrifices. Peggy Evans recalls:

> The first few years I was diabetic I studied it all the time. We were living in Canada, so I learned the gram measure and the cup measure of each food, and the protein, fat, and carbohydrate content, as well as calories. The dietitians told me I should teach it, so I guess I learned it pretty well. But I just do it naturally now. I just think that way. I serve vegetables at birthday parties.

In time, the daily routine begins to seem more like a preference than an imposition. The glass bubble is a comfortable place to take shelter against the stresses of ordinary life. Gloria Murphy was dismayed to read the headline on a newspaper feature article in which she was interviewed: "Victims of M.S. Slowly Learn to Cope." She thought she had described her life as a full and satisfying one with plenty of room for active choice. I, too, refuse to "cope" and prefer to "live." Carla Schultz believes that the pace of her life is well suited not only to her lupus but to her general well-being, and she recommends it to others:

> Get rid of the "shoulds." My shoulds are my goals and my ideals, but the house doesn't always have to be clean. I feel civic responsibility. Things don't go unless people cooperate and help. So if I felt strongly about something, I would pick the thing that was least stressful, like one evening of calling for the school board, but I wouldn't take chairman of a committee. It's easier now for me to think, "Is that something I really want to do?" Sometimes I think, "No, I really don't," and so I don't do it.
>
> My attitude is not "Live it up now because instead of this much time, you only have this much time." Rather it's "Take care of yourself and savor every moment so that you can enjoy more years with your family and of life." It gives you some sense of control to know that you feel better. You know how Buckminster Fuller talks about doing more with less? You maybe have fewer friends but get to know them better, have fewer activities but enjoy them more. So I can't really say I have regrets. I'm very much aware of my limitations and that, I think, I've accepted. I know that the penalty I would pay for trying to do everything and be everything for everybody would be just getting sick immediately, and being tired and achy.
>
> I've already outlived my expectations, which were that I'd never work, never get married, never have a family. These things evolved, and they've taught me not to set false limitations on myself. Don't let the disease control your life. Do what you can within your limitations.

Exercising a deliberate patience eventually pays off. A time comes for each of us when we can say, like Phyllis Mueller, "Hey, I had a good day, and I still don't feel well." Acceptance is as likely to come sneaking up on you in this way as it is to be sought and won. One day, after talking with me about the prospect of a liver transplant, my doctor walked me out toward the waiting room and said, "You've sure been through a lot in your young life. You just live from one trauma to the next, don't you?" Who, me? I thought. I guess if you look at my life objectively, from a distance, plotting the illness on a calendar, that's true. But, amazingly, I had never thought of it that way. I focus not on the traumas but on the recoveries, and see mostly light, interspersed with shadow, rather than the other way around. Illness is my normal condition. The glass bubble is a nuisance and I'd love to shuck it for good, but I still go places, do things, see people, and have plenty of surprisingly good days.

Chapter
10

The Good Patient

"I have to be the one to say, This is where I draw the line."

The chronically ill are a new phenomenon in medical history: a large population in need of frequent, long-term health care. Our needs can be difficult to fill, and they challenge some of the health care profession's basic premises. Sometimes this fact makes *us* look difficult and challenging, as well. Unlike the familiar type of the "good patient" who graciously dies or gratefully recovers, we keep coming back with the same old complaints. Phyllis Mueller finds that she aggravates doctors when she only wants their help:

> One doctor was very honest with me and he said, "You know, you are so challenging at times that I think it upsets people." He meant that they give me this and it doesn't work and they give me that and it doesn't work, and they feel challenged because they want to succeed. Instead of being angry at the medication, they become angry at the patient.

Allopathic medicine, as the standard practice in American clinics and hospitals is called, is fundamentally unsuited to treating chronic illness:

- Its mission is to cure, and doctors have only recently begun to see chronicity as a tolerable fact rather than a frustrating failure.
- The practice of medicine is divided into specialties by organs or regions of the body, and diagnosis and treatment are tightly focused on curing the ailment at its anatomical

source. Illnesses with wide-ranging symptoms make this work more difficult and pose strategical problems when one specialist disagrees with another.

- As technology has advanced, physicians expect to see graphic evidence of disease in blood samples or computer tomography. Pain and weakness that do not show up in laboratory tests are often dismissed as imaginary.

- The medical profession is a closely bound guild, with degrees and licenses, a cryptic Latin vocabulary, and an exclusive right to prescribe drugs, perform certain procedures, and discharge patients from the hospital. Physicians tend to be skeptical of laypeople who claim to have enough experience of illness to venture diagnoses or request specific treatments.

- The traditional relationship between doctor and patient is one of authority and obedience. A good patient is submissive, compliant, undemanding, and deferential enough to follow "doctor's orders" without balking. People who choose to manage illness on their own terms are occasionally "out of compliance," as physicians say.

Of course, this situation is changing. In the short twelve years since this book was first published, there have been some tremendous breakthroughs in medical attention to chronicity, thanks in large part to advocacy by the chronically ill themselves. More rheumatologists are familiar with the mysteries of lupus, and more gastroenterologists with the unpredictability of Crohn's disease. The American Medical Association has given its stamp of validity to chronic fatigue syndrome and fibromyalgia, and some hospitals and clinics offer special programs for patients with these diseases. Yet, as physicians themselves become more sensitive, the structure of medical care gets ever more difficult for the chronically ill to negotiate. "Managed care" institutions with their one-size-fits-all policies do not care much for patients who come in too often, use too many services, don't fit the treatment guidelines for their illnesses, request additional procedures, and just plain cost too much. Chronic patients are not the only ones complaining. Doctors, too, say that cost-based restrictions on treatment interfere with the physician's responsibility to do what is best for the health of the individual patient.

The Doctor-Patient Partnership

If the chronically ill have a common fantasy, besides getting well and living happily ever after, it is the ideal doctor. Ah, how secure you feel when you can trust your fate to one dependable person who truly cares for you, knows everything there is to know about your case, and will do whatever it takes to help you live better. Consistency of care from a doctor who is also easily accessible when you need help is vital. This is not the old passive reliance on doctor-knows-best, however. We may turn to medical science expecting certainty, but knowledgeable, compassionate doctors make no false promises. They know, and should level with us, that a disease is not a concrete entity, but rather an arbitrary "syndrome," a collection of symptoms that seem to have a common cause and to affect different human bodies in similar, but not always identical, ways. Ideally, the doctor-patient relationship evolves into a partnership between experts of two different sorts. The doctor knows the syndrome, but the patient knows how the disease affects one particular human body. To make the best decisions about treatment, doctor and patient need to interpret what they know to each other. Susan Alm feels that she has established such a partnership:

> I was approached in the beginning with, "Look, this isn't a cut-and-dried thing." I suppose if I had a disease and someone told me they were going to cure it and they didn't, I would look elsewhere. But I was told it was something I'm going to have to live with. We don't know why it came or what causes it. There's no cure. You can relieve symptoms, but you can't relieve the disease. I think also that the physician I go to

is one who's very involved in wellness and in allowing you to take control of your own health. He's there as a reference. You go in and say, "I've got this problem. What are you going to do about it?" And he'll say, "Well, if you have that kind of problem, there are these options. Which is going to work best for you?"

Once the relationship is in place, most of the people I talked with will readily follow the doctor's advice. JoAnn Berglund is emphatic about that: "I will try whatever the doctor I go to suggests. If he says to eat ground-up beetles, and if it works, I'd do it. I wouldn't like it, but I'd do it. I trust him that much." That doesn't mean we expect our doctors always to be right, much as we might like to invest them with supernatural powers. It is easy to slip into an old-fashioned hero worship when you are feeling low, not so much out of reverence as wishful thinking. Whenever my doctor assured me, "We're not going to let you die on us," I wanted to believe that he truly had that power.

Consistency of Care

When I first conducted these interviews, several people described the "doctor shopping" they had undertaken to find the one physician with whom they felt most comfortable. They visited more than one clinic, asked nurses who they would choose if they were sick, and evaluated both bedside manner and medical expertise. Fewer people have that choice now. Instead, the doctor-patient relationship has to develop within a complex institutional setting that may not even provide what the relationship needs to thrive: consistency of care, trust in patients' credibility, easy access to the physician, and freedom to make decisions.

Kathy Halvorson belongs to an HMO that assigns her to a different physician each time she calls. One of her chronic problems is infection of the urinary tract. When the infection recurs, she gets a nonrefillable prescription for a certain antibiotic. Even though the bottle it comes in is labeled "Finish all this medication unless otherwise directed by your physician," she usually saves a day's dosage for the next time, which she has learned is inevitable. That way, if she can't get in to see a doctor right away, she can at least begin treating the infection. On one occasion, a doctor she had never seen before reprimanded her for taking the antibiotic before he had a chance to do laboratory tests. "You sure screwed this up," he charged. "How will we ever know what this infection is?" "I know what it is," Kathy replied. "I've had it about five hundred times." "But I'm talking about *this* time," the doctor insisted. He was, of course, practicing medicine as cautiously as he had been taught. Diagnosis was the first order of business, and he was not going to proceed with treatment until he had lab results. Kathy, however, was approaching the problem the way any good chronic patient would. Her seeming recklessness was empirically sound, based on frequent identical experiences over a long period of time. She considered herself more qualified to interpret her symptoms than a doctor looking at her chart for the very first time.

My experience is the opposite of Kathy's. After many years with one gastroenterologist, I had tested enough antibiotics to know which brought my fever down quickly, which were ineffective, and which caused intolerable side effects. My doctor and a specialist in infectious diseases who had also treated me devised a "recipe" for me to follow when I felt that an infection was building in my liver. They gave me a prescription good for several refills of two complementary antibiotics and suggested that I keep some on hand. Yes, I was to call and inform my gastroenterologist, but in effect they trusted me to medicate myself. When I began having nasty reactions to the most effective drug, I had a long consultation with the infections specialist. He asked me not only about my symptoms, but also about my habits and schedule and the quality of life I sought. We talked through the peculiar challenges an infection in my liver poses, and he suggested that

I try a one-a-day, broad spectrum antibiotic new on the market and check back with him if I wasn't satisfied.

The health care institutions that refer to doctors, physical therapists, home health care nurses, and all as "providers" seem not to realize that these are human relationships of a very intimate sort. Besides providing a service, these people console, cajole, listen, remember, and establish trust. Over time, *if* allowed enough consultation time, our doctors get to know us, our families, our lives, our hopes, and the meanings we ascribe to our imperfect fate. This is an important context for treating not just the disease, but also the suffering individual in the most effective way. In meetings with groups of chronically ill people, I have heard the worry and sorrow of patients whose trusted relationships were broken when their employers changed health plans or their health plans reconfigured their "provider networks."

Getting through the Thicket

My own doctor-patient partnership of twenty-four years ended in the fall of 1998 when my gastroenterologist retired. We had developed a routine that greatly relieved my anxiety about getting deathly sick within minutes. If I felt pain or fever coming on, I was to call his nurse at the clinic, and she would relay the message to him immediately. I tended to hold off until I was sure I had legitimate reason to bother him, but he urged me not to hesitate, especially if I had shaky chills. This routine worked very well. I called, told my story to the nurse, and rarely waited more than ten minutes before the phone rang.

Before his retirement, we talked about who on the staff might take over my case, and I opted for a doctor who had followed me in the hospital a few times. She took time to talk to me, showed genuine interest in what I had learned about my illness, and paid close attention to nutritional deficiencies, which seemed like leading-edge health care to me. I thought often about checking in with her at the clinic, but it took a mild bout of fever in early

February 1999 to get me to the phone. When I dialed the gastroenterology department, my call was automatically routed to the clinic's general information line. A recorded voice offered me some push-button options, and I chose the one for appointments. The phone rang several times, long enough that I sighed in relief when I heard the receiver lift. My relief was premature. There was a quiet hissing sound and then . . . the dreaded music. This clinic has selected the most nerve-wracking music to occupy its patients while it keeps them on hold: New Age piano music with irregular trills and runs, up and down the keyboard, with no discernible melodic line to grasp onto. If you are already achy or dizzy or nauseous, the relentless key-tinkling is torture. I held the receiver away from my ear for several minutes until a human voice spoke. Confident that I was now on familiar ground, I asked to make an appointment with my new doctor. "Have you seen her before?" the receptionist asked, and I explained my situation. She checked my name, my birth date, my present address, and my insurance coverage, and then asked for my primary care physician. I told her that my gastroenterologist had been my primary doctor for twenty-four years. "The GI department is a specialty clinic," she explained. "Don't you have a family physician?" When I said no, she went silent for a moment. "The system is asking me for a primary physician," she said, sounding troubled, and then excused herself and abandoned me to the piano runs again. She must have found a way through that impasse, because she returned shortly to offer me my new doctor's first available appointment—seven weeks hence. It's a good thing I have additional refills for my antibiotic. My clinic is not the only one fortifying itself with bureaucratic brambles. Some HMO patients have told me that they cannot see the specialist who treats their chronic illness until they have seen their so-called primary doctor and received prior approval. This policy, meant to control unnecessary costs, delays treatment for those who need consistent specialty care.

In my case, hospital emergency care has become *more* accessible. Whether I have gotten more persuasive or just older, I am no longer subjected to the painful waiting I used to endure. I have many vivid memories of explaining my disease to the admissions clerk, the triage nurse, the nurse who checked my vital signs, and finally the doctor, only to find myself treated once again as an acute case of abdominal pain. When I could no longer tolerate the pain, I informed the staff that I usually get Demerol. Little did I know that requests for pain medication were interpreted as "drug-seeking behavior." When I found this out, I called a patient advocate, got a call from the administrator of the emergency room, and gave him the name of my gastroenterologist. The result was a new computer file of patients in frequent need of emergency care. My file would include a standing order from my doctor for Demerol. The next time I came in, however, the admissions clerk had no idea what file I was referring to, because I didn't know enough to call it by its computer code name. Since then, code words have not been necessary. In my twenties, emergency doctors quizzed me about my dilated pupils and asked again if I was absolutely sure that I was not pregnant. As a middle-aged woman well-versed in her medical history, I am finally *believed*. On my last emergency visit, I thought I might tough it out and avoid the Demerol. "You don't have to," the doctor said as the nurse rubbed my hip with a cotton ball. "You've earned it."

The Knowledgeable Patient

As often as chronic patients have to recite their medical history, it serves us well to know it by heart, to record episodes of illness, keep track of the medications we have taken, and have a vocabulary for the symptoms our illness presents. Good diabetes patients, for example, measure and record their blood sugar, give themselves insulin shots if the illness requires it, eat on schedule, stay fit with exercise, and recognize the warning signs of rising or falling blood sugar. Those of us whose diseases are more exotic or defy diagnosis or show great individual variation would like that clear guidance. Janice Willett calls Crohn's disease "the kind of disease where you find out bits and pieces as you go along, when you pay enough attention and make enough effort. You have to be very self-directed if you want to find out anything about it."

Janice, who lives in a large metropolitan area, can direct herself to an information meeting of the local Crohn's and Colitis Foundation of America. Organizations such as these, which generally have phone lines, mailing addresses, and Web sites, are the most convenient source of information designed for patients. Before illness organizations began to proliferate and before the Internet, the only recourse some of us had was to go to a medical library and look up articles about scientific research that we could barely decode. It is now possible to pull information on various diseases from the Internet in a matter of minutes—some written for physicians and some for patients, but not all of it equally helpful or accurate. It still takes some prior knowledge to determine the value of what you are reading. I look upon this self-education process about the same way I do auto mechanics. At a time when many women eager to be self-sufficient were learning how to repair their own cars, I decided there was a practical reason for specialized knowledge. Since I can't master everything, I would rather leave my car with an honest mechanic and spend my time writing. Likewise, I prefer to trust my doctor's knowledge of the mechanical workings of the liver. Still, I need to know enough about the disease to avoid flooding my engine or paying for a replacement part that I don't really need.

Those who go to the trouble of tracking down medical information want to be cautious yet cooperative participants in their health care. The more they know, the better equipped they are to seek treatment that is compatible with the way they live their lives. Unfortunately, managed care institutions have a built-in skepticism toward patients who want to make their own choices. The assumption is that prepaid customers will always help themselves to more than they really need. This distrust extends to physicians, as well, and obligates them to justify anything beyond what the typical case requires. Sometimes they have to absorb the additional costs themselves, or they might be offered a bonus for limiting their use of certain procedures. These policies breed suspicion between doctor and patient and weaken the partnership necessary for maintenance of good health, which is, ironically, the institution's professed goal.

Knowledgeable chronic patients, granted the right to choose, may, in fact, make *fewer* demands. When you know the limits of medical knowledge about your disease and what treatments exist for it, you know better than to expect a quick fix. You know, too, that a vain search with tubes and probes and gruesome liquids to swallow may be worse than the ache itself. When Kathy Halvorson tells her husband about some feeling of discomfort, he usually urges her to call the doctor, which she is often reluctant to do:

> I think that's the way a well person—a person who has really had good luck with their body—responds. I don't think he understands that you can't always get anything from doctors, that sometimes you just make it hard on yourself.

That is not so much an indictment of medical care as it is a realistic understanding that medical science is imperfect, as much speculation as certitude. When you realize that, you begin to learn which symptoms are worth reporting and which should just be tolerated or treated with other means, such as relaxation or a change in habits.

Vigilance

On the other hand, a terroristic illness can cause hyperalertness that is easily mistaken for hypochondria. When Lorraine Czerny made a second visit to the doctor for stomach pain that did not show on the GI tests, he asked her, "What are you upset about this time?" implying that the pain was psychosomatic. She got angry right on the spot:

He was treating me as a white-haired little old lady, and I resented that. I knew enough that this wasn't just a figment of my imagination. It occurred at times when everything was fine and dandy. I know when I get psychosomatic things because they disappear after something's been resolved. So this time I knew that it wasn't just a neurosis, and I wanted to find out. I thought I might be dying of stomach cancer. You get a bit interested, you know, when something's not right.

Symptoms that don't fit the familiar pattern *should* be reported, because having a chronic illness is never a guarantee against coming down with something else. I appreciate my doctor's response to false alarms. Once I felt a lump in the center of my chest and was waiting for it to go away when I happened to read that the Shah of Iran's fatal cancer had first appeared as a lump in the chest. My doctor felt it, smiled, and said, "That's your sternum." Then he drew me a picture to show how it curves out at the end. I had been sick for several months and had lost so much weight that my bones were protuding. I felt foolish, but he affirmed my vigilance and told me to come in anytime I noticed something out of the ordinary. "I'm always happy to relieve you of your worries," he said.

The good patient needs to be especially vigilant about medication. Physicians are not always well informed about side effects or contraindications or the dangers of combining certain drugs. I ask the pharmacist about the risks of each new drug or check the *Physician's Desk Reference,* which is now on the Internet, myself. Being alert to your body also yields clues to how damaging some medications might be. Margie Rietsma has tried countless medications for her arthritis and her multiple sclerosis, and has found that the treatment for one disease sometimes exacerbates the other. One day she got so frustrated with all the mysterious new discomforts that she gathered up her pills and threw them in the Dumpster behind her apartment building. "I'd rather hurt than put myself in jeopardy," she explained. "I've got to be the one to say, 'This is where I draw the line. This is enough.' "

Drawing the line on intolerable treatments is a privilege we rightly claim. If the disease can't be cured, our best hope is to live as comfortably as we can. Susan Alm decided to stop taking prednisone for her lupus, but, unlike Margie, she made the change gradually, under her doctor's supervision:

> One of the things that bothered me about it was the total dependency of that drug. I felt a great sense of relief to be off it. I was beginning to see long-term side effects and I just felt that I could live without it and be better off, even if the pain level was higher. You have to trade it off.

Many of us have learned the hard way that we can exercise our judgment and refuse treatment as well as assent to it. Rosemary McKuen remembers how she submitted to excessive and redundant diagnostic procedures that inflamed her ulcerated colon:

> Pain, abject pain. I would get so freaked out whenever they'd do these things because it was so intrusive. It was so humiliating. It would take me three times as long as the normal patient because I was so obnoxious, and I would cry. I hated it. I was so demoralized and humiliated. It never occurred to me to say, "The End."

Saying "The End"

Truly saying, "The End," drawing the line on the illness itelf, is a more drastic decision than saying no to unpleasant treatments. When Rosemary realized that she could be virtually cured by having her diseased intestine removed, her conception of her rights and responsibilities as a good patient changed:

> I had a discussion with a friend, and I guess it became clear to me, though it was never stated, "This is your decision.

From here on out, if you want to have the surgery, you have to make the decision." I think that if I had had a huge bleed, they would have gone in and done it, but in this chronic state, I was responsible for making the decision. One day I went in and the doctor said, "There isn't anything else I can do for you." I thought, "Wait a minute now. This was okay for a couple of years, but I'm not going to go through this the rest of my life."

Rosemary's moment of decision came five years after the onset of her illness, when the pain and disruption seemed worse than going through surgery and wearing an ostomy bag to catch her bodily wastes for the rest of her life. The right moment to proceed with radical, risk-filled measures is rarely crystal clear. Discerning it takes patience and courage and respectful cooperation between doctor and patient. Bill Gordon forced the decision by giving himself an ultimatum:

At the beginning of 1984, I said that I would not live to see another New Year's Eve. I didn't improve at all that year. I think my doctor was afraid with the New Year coming up that I might do something, even though I hadn't talked about it too much. There's just too much pain associated with this disease to handle much longer.

The doctor took Bill's hints of suicide to mean that he really would do anything to escape chronic manic-depression. He offered him three alternatives to death, none of them a guaranteed cure and all of them carrying risks that could worsen his condition: microsurgery to split the two halves of his brain apart, electric shock treatments, and an experimental drug. It was up to Bill, and he chose the drug. Fortunately, it worked and he has been mostly healthy ever since. Had this remedy been offered before Bill hit these depths, he might not have chosen it.

Alternative Care

Concern about intrusive procedures and harmful drugs, as well as the troubling state of the health care system, are turning more and more chronic patients to alternative forms of care. This was hardly the case when I first wrote this book. Back then, the most vocal proponents of herbal remedies, healing touch, and so on seemed to regard standard medical practice as irredeemably dangerous. This was alienating to people whose lives had been saved by high-tech medicine and pharmaceuticals. The philosophy behind that first wave of alternative care was a simplistic notion of the body-mind relationship that reduced it to mind over matter and offered absolutist answers to complex questions. What causes urinary tract infections? According to one pop healer, "feeling pissed off." My favorite statement of how body and mind interact comes from Herman Melville's *Moby Dick*: "Hell is an idea first born on an undigested apple dumpling." The thought of eternal damnation arises from a pain in the gut. I also believe that the notion of hell can upset your stomach, if you overstress yourself with worry about your salvation.

When I asked the people I interviewed about alternative care, only two had good experiences to report. Phyllis Mueller had taken just one short step away from the AMA's purview and consulted a chiropractor:

> I had gotten a name from somebody. He was highly recommended. And of course I didn't believe in chiropractic care, so I filed it away. Last spring I had a muscle spasm that just would not go away. My husband insisted we get that name and go see him. Within a month, the muscle spasm was gone. He had managed to alleviate that. And more importantly, he had believed in me and said, "Anytime your body gets that spastic or out of sync, you're bound to get depressed." He told me almost the opposite of what I had been hearing, that it's possible the physical causes the emotional

as much as vice versa. For the first time in my life, I can tell you the difference between stomach pain and muscle pain. I can differentiate between the colon that's inflamed, my stomach hurting, or the muscle pain. So I can therefore help myself a little bit because I know how my body is functioning now, which is something medical doctors sorely miss, in my opinion. So right now I'm going to go through chiropractic care for a while. I'm going to give that a fair shot. I'm going to try to believe in it, not blindly, but believe in it enough because it makes sense to me.

Kathy Halvorson has also learned to tune in more closely to her body through chiropractic care. While she still takes antibiotics for infections, she also follows a macrobiotic diet to relieve abdominal pain.

Standard care and alternative care are no longer an either-or choice, at least for those who can afford them. Some herbal remedies have been submitted to empirical testing and found either safe and effective or more toxic than the synthetic drug for the same ailment. Doctors have learned that movement and breathing techniques that release energy flow are not trickery but actually help people feel better. The health care industry is even beginning to tap into the growing market for these methods. My clinic now offers acupuncture and classes in qi gong, and my insurance plan covers a select list of chiropractors. Massage and visualization still come out of my pocket, but maybe not for long.

One change that has made me look more favorably on alternative care is that it is no longer the province of zealots in quest of perfection. Immigration has brought in trained practitioners from Asian countries with long histories of holistic medicine. My neighborhood now has a clinic run by a woman with both a certificate in Chinese medicine and a Western M.D. degree. Unfortunately, she is not in my provider network.

It may take activism by chronic patients to gain legitimacy for more alternative methods and to accomplish a merger of differing

views of health care. Public advocacy by and for AIDS and breast
cancer patients has certainly improved their resources. Following
their lead, we might pursue a no-fault health care system that is
based on compassion for the sick and shared concern for everyone's well-being and one that does not discriminate against the
chronically ill. Another worthy goal is to encourage more investi-
gation into environmental sources of illness, rather than seeking
the cause in human anatomy alone or in individual behavior. I am
counting on the deformed frogs in Minnesota's marshes to help
us with that task.

Time for Rest

There are times when active vigilance is more than our frail bodies and clouded minds can manage, and passivity looks enticing.
When daily life seems overwhelming, our escape fantasies may
even include being hospitalized. The hospital of my imagination
has green lawns and white wrought-iron furniture where the patients sit and drink tea in the afternoons, though the best I have
experienced in real life is a featureless white room with a view of
a cattail marsh. We who are frequently hospitalized in great need
and released with health temporarily restored do not see hospitals as dreary warehouses for the dying but rather as familiar
places of refuge. Nevertheless, we feel ambivalent about going
there. Esther Green says it well:

> Every time I go to the clinic they say, "Are you ready to go
> back in?" They can tell that my body is saying yes and my
> mind is saying no. One time they said, "We're not going to
> take no for an answer. You're ready to go in." I was glad that
> they forced me because I was just really tired—terribly tired
> and terribly weak. Sometimes I get that way right now—just
> so tired—and I say to myself, "When I go back to the clinic,
> I'm going to tell them I'd like to go back in for a rest."

It is not the physical confinement that makes us balk. Being ordered to bed is no bother when you are too weak to resist. The troublesome thing about the hospital is having your individual needs subordinated to the staff's routine. Questioning the orders or requesting a change in the routine can anger an already over-worked staff. Robert O'Shea tells how he handled that problem:

> It must just be very hard for people to be sick and be in dis-passionate surroundings. And I smile to tell you this. In the hospital this last time, there was almost a compulsivity about wanting to please. I mean, if you did a good arteri-ogram for the doctor, that was splendid. Or for the house-keeping maid to come in and say, "You sure keep a nice, clean room." I was happy to hear that. And you just love it, you know. Or you put out a lot of urine or you've got good veins. Gee.

Out of your element and afraid for your health, with your body exposed to a troupe of strangers, you may find that compliance gets you better care. Getting familiar with the staff has an in-valuable humanizing impact on the hospital stay. When a nurse from the intravenous team comes in and says, "How are your girls?" my tolerance for punctures rises a little. I'm relieved to know that I don't have to plead with her to use a size 22 needle or convince her that this particular vein is choked up with scar tis-sue. Familiarity may not completely ease the compulsion to please, however, as Robert also observes:

> When they come in for a procedure and they bring along your files, and you know that you're on your third manila folder, you think, "This is the trilogy of Robert O'Shea. What does all that mean? Will they grow tired of me? Am I be-coming a bore?" So you do a lot of soul-searching, which I think a person with chronic illness does more than some-body else.

Leafing through my files as I ride down to the X-ray room, I have noted the frequency of the word "pleasant" in the reports the doctors have written after examining me. At first, I felt as though I had earned an A in good patienthood, but over the years, the repetition has turned "pleasant" into a simple code for "doesn't complain." Knowing that has freed me from smiling at all times. In the interests of your own long-term care, the compulsion to be nice must give way to an assertive confidence that you understand your illness enough to monitor the course of your treatment.

A few attempts have been made to gear hospital care to people accustomed to structuring their daily lives around ever-present illness. For example, the privilege of leaving the hospital on a pass on weekends or in slow periods between tests and treatments was instituted halfway through my career as a hospital patient. The hospital I went to as a student encouraged postoperative patients to get up out of bed and eat at tables in an open area at the center of the ward. It broke the isolation and eased the transition to the more active life we would have to resume when we were discharged. I still have vivid memories of the people I met there. Gloria Murphy is happy to have found a hospital that, at the instigation of her neurologist, set up a special program for multiple sclerosis patients, who are grouped together on one floor:

> Everybody there is trained for us. Most of the people at that station have MS. We come in for treatment that lasts about seven to ten days, and we're encouraged to wear our street clothes. We have events during the day that we share together as patients. So it's a time for me to make friends and to see old friends. And the nurses there are people that have been there for several years, and I know them. It's almost like going to boarding school, except for the nausea.

Gloria's doctor has also organized a "celebration of progress"— as Gloria characterizes it, "a day of workshops and fun" that reunites people who have been in the hospital together.

The hospital-boarding school comparison is apt. They are both insular, protective environments where internal affairs loom larger than events in the world outside. The level of amylase in your bloodstream becomes more important than the hole in the ozone. Where chronic patients are in contact with one another, a kind of subculture is created. Once, long ago, I was hospitalized in a ward set aside primarily for patients with ulcerative gastrointestinal illnesses. The theory was that these illnesses had a strong psychological dimension and should be treated in a comprehensive fashion, with attention to personality profiles, family situations, economic problems, and so on. The patients were encouraged to live as normally as possible and to make some decisions for themselves, such as going home on trial visits to see if they were ready for discharge. I remember, especially, the teenage colitis patients who commiserated about their parents' high expectations, and the young mothers who confided to each other how hard it was to go home and face the stresses of child-raising. And I remember the literally sick humor that kept our spirits up: how we laughed until it hurt—which didn't take much—when one of the teenagers called out for a pizza with pepperoni and onions.

Spending time in a place where illness is the norm can be a very affirmative experience for someone who feels like a freak. Meeting people in the hospital helped Bill Gordon see his manic-depression as a genuine illness:

> I met a lot of people in the hospital—some were schizophrenic, some were paranoid, others were taking shock treatments for depression—and I felt a very strong bond between myself and the other patients. We did a lot of talking. At first I didn't feel like I belonged there, but later I told them I did belong there. I found out that these people—including myself—who were supposed to be crazy really weren't all that off-the-wall. It was interesting to sit down and share stories with other people who had mental illness, and to see what they had been through.

Managed care's efforts to limit hospital stays overlook this positive and reassuring aspect of hospitalization. Much as she tries to avoid having to be hospitalized, Susan Alm has one significant reservation about the emphasis on home care for lupus patients:

> There's both good and bad in it. You don't like to go to the hospital all the time. It's artificial and sick people go there! But in some ways not going to the hospital denies that there's something wrong. I don't quite know how to say it, but I sometimes need the reassurance that I really am sick because I can't do things. It's probably just me with this mental block of think-yourself-well. Sometimes I need a symbol that says, "Yes, that's right. You can't do that."

It's not just Susan. A hospital stay does legitimize your illness and lets you drop the pretense of good health and be just plain sick for a while. It decrees that your suffering entitles you to special privileges, at least now and then. Lying in bed and being cared for by others can be a very welcome respite from the strains of being invisibly ill in a culture that idolizes the self-made healthy.

A Health Care Package Worth Opening

Each time I go home from the hospital, no matter how relieved I am to be free again, I can't help being a little melancholy as well. I sort through the mail and find overdue bills that have accrued finance charges. I open the refrigerator and find the mushrooms shriveled into inky little lumps. The realization that I am on my own again hits hard: No one is going to shield me from the onslaught of stimuli that make up ordinary life. I have been declared healthy enough to go home, which means I ought to be healthy enough to function there. My doctor has written on my discharge papers, "Resume normal activity." But still I'm light-headed, my muscles have nearly atrophied, I have no appetite for what little food I have on hand, and I am scared to death that my body will malfunction again. Each time I wish there were a decompression chamber where I could spend a couple of days getting reacclimated.

I would like to see a halfway house for chronic patients—a place where we could get the medical attention we need without having to surrender our freedom of mobility or our right to make decisions. Easing slowly into the obligations we have to resume at home would prepare us for living on our own again. There are hospices for dying patients who want to finish their lives in a homelike environment but need constant care. How nice if there were something similar for patients about to resume living.

Another dream of mine is a multifaceted health center with a huge range of medical and alternative services and creature comforts, or at least an all-encompassing treatment plan suited to individual need. I did not expect that my sister Nancy would be the one to come up with it. When she was diagnosed with inflammatory breast cancer, a rare form described as "deadly," she felt devastated, until her responsible oldest child personality kicked into gear. She had recently retired from a second career in educational administration,where she had developed skills that could now be applied to the management of her health care. She set two goals for herself: to "get smart about it in a hurry," and to "find my power in a situation where I felt stripped of any power." First she went to the Internet and found a woman in her second year of survival who gave her leads on more information. She got help with a search of the medical literature, traveled to a clinic where research into her disease was being done, and got a second opinion and a list of treatment protocols. When she returned home, she requested more extensive testing.

She went ahead with chemotherapy, a mastectomy, and radiation, but complemented that approach with alternative care that would bolster her energy, immune system, and emotional health. A local resource center for women with cancer gave her coupons for six shiatsu massages, and a new friend with cancer took her to a volunteer-run alternative health center that provides free services to people with life-threatening illnesses. She scheduled at least two bodywork sessions a week, usually acupuncture for her immune function and some form of healing touch, massage, or energy work. The people who performed this one-on-one care were exceptionally supportive and helped break her sense of isolation. She also listened to a meditation tape every day, walked as far as she could manage, adjusted her diet, took nutritional supplements to counter the effects of chemotherapy, attended weekly qi gong sessions along with her husband, walked with her husband and children in the Race for the Cure, and spent time each day with friends.

Well before her one-year treatment anniversary, her immune system returned to normal readings. Her energy is at least that of a healthy person her age, her emotional health is "pretty good," and her relationships with family and friends are stronger than ever. Though there is no promise of cure and she describes her present status as an uncertain "what now?" she does feel that her self-administered health care program worked to keep her going through an extremely stressful experience. She knows that she is fortunate to have no job obligations, a loyal husband, adult children who are eager to help, and rare access to free care.

I doubt that many of us have the time or means or energy to replicate Nancy's approach or to sustain it over years of illness, but wouldn't it be wonderful if this were what "health care package" really meant? If only those who claim to "manage" our care would "provide" us with such a range of healing options. Good patients we would certainly be.

Chapter 11

From Patience to Passion

"Passion is its own reward."

Whenever I see people hug and squeal at the airport, engage in loud discussion with lots of gestures, or walk along in brightly patterned clothes and seemingly relaxed bodies, I wonder if I was born into the wrong ethnic group. Watching folk dances at an annual festival, I get caught up in the exuberance of the Eastern Europeans and the sinuous grace of the South Asians, but when the Northern Europeans come on with their stiff bodies and jerky hops, I grimace. Here I am, I think, doubly doomed—by illness and ethnicity—to a life of physical and emotional restraint.

As a chronic patient, I am rewarded for being nice, pleasant, accepting... As the granddaughter of Danish immigrants, I have heard over and over what calm, easygoing people we Danes are. We don't complain. We keep our troubles to ourselves. If we don't have something nice to say, we know it's best not to say anything. Shakespeare's *Hamlet*, which exposed the gloomy underside of the national character, is, after all, a tragedy. My grandmother used "Something is rotten in the state of Denmark" as a coded reference to things better left unsaid. In *Lake Wobegon Days*, a fictional memoir of growing up among transplanted Scandinavians and Germans in a small Minnesota town, Garrison Keillor relates a fantasy much like one I entertained as a teenager in another Minnesota town:

> Sometimes I imagined that we weren't really from Minnesota, we were only using it as a cover, disguising ourselves as quiet modest people until we could reveal our true identities as Italians. One day, my mother would put the wieners on the

table and suddenly my father would jump up and say, "Hey! I'ma sicka this stuffa!" She'd yell, "No! No! Chonny! Please-a! The children!" But the cat was out of the bag. We weren't who we thought we were, we were the Keillorinis! Presto! Prestone! My father rushed to the closet and hauled out giant oil paintings of fat ladies, statues of saints, bottles of wine, and in rushed the relatives, hollering and carrying platters of spicy spaghetti, and my father would turn to me and say, "Eduardo! Eduardo, my son!" and throw his arms around me and plant big wet smackers on my cheeks.

And what would a chronically ill Keillorini be like? A very demonstrative sufferer, moaning and groaning unabashedly with no qualms about being misjudged as self-pitying.

Behavior during illness is undoubtedly as much a product of culture as any other kind of behavior. A *real* Italian friend of mine, who does not speak vaudevillian English, comes from a rural area of Sardinia where old traditions linger on. She has described how people there behave when they are sick: they complain, they indulge themselves in suffering, they leave their hair uncombed and their bodies unwashed, they drop their usual responsibilities and expect others to wait on them. There are, she says, social rituals, like the rituals for mourning, that allow people with long-term illnesses to express such unpleasant emotions as sadness and anger. Accustomed to this in childhood, she finds strenuous efforts to seem healthy in spite of illness a little absurd.

The Right to Suffer

I don't mean to undermine the message of this book by offering invalidism as the best or most natural response. I would still insist firmly on the right to as much healthy normality as we can manage. But in claiming that right, we all too often surrender another: the right to suffer—not just to suffer physically, in a silent withdrawal, but to suffer emotionally, as well.

The Latin verb *pati*, meaning "to suffer," is the root of "patience" and "passivity," which are surely psychological aspects of suffering. It has also engendered another English word that is linked to suffering only when capitalized and sung as a mass: "passion." Passion is "the capacity for strong feeling," and it, too, is a psychological dimension of chronic illness. As our physical bodies experience the gamut from abject pain to deadening numbness to the pleasure of improved health, our emotions run a similar course. This aspect of suffering is the most neglected, however. It is obscured by the virtue of patience that the chronically ill are encouraged to learn. What social rewards there are go not to the indulgent sufferer but to the noble one, who knows that silence is golden. Emily Dickinson has described in poetry the suppressed passion that lurks beneath such a patient demeanor:

> On my volcano grows the Grass
> A meditative spot—
> An acre for a Bird to choose
> Would be the General thought—
>
> How red the Fire rocks below—
> How insecure the sod
> Did I disclose
> Would populate with awe my solitude.

If suffering, meaningless as it seems, is to have any redeeming value, it must do more than water the grassy lawn of patience. Passion is every bit as necessary to a full life. Suffering ought to set off the volcano and reveal the splendor of an "abandoned display of emotion," another meaning of passion.

Suffering Pain

I want to describe what I feel emotionally as I go through the cycle of sick-healthy-sick-healthy that is the course of my life.

Anything I say is subject to change at any time. I am used to feeling depressed or anxious or euphoric at certain points, but I can never really depend on that. My emotions do not well up in orderly sequence, one at a time. Conflicting feelings vie for ascendancy, giving me some freedom to choose—or to repress. The first twinges of discomfort that warn that something is awry in my liver are followed by a burst of irreconcilable emotions. The fatalist in me begins to despair, knowing that increasing pain is inevitable. The optimist takes regular, deep breaths, in the hope of easing the pain away. The rebel wants to flail at the offending organ, yelling, Why me? Why now? The good chronic patient dials the telephone to consult the doctor, but the terrified sickly kid bursts into tears in spite of herself. These warring personae fight it out until pain becomes intolerable. Then the fatalist feels vindicated, the optimist remembers that it seldom gets worse than this, the rebel groans in defiance, the patient pants her way through the hospital admission procedure, and the terrified sickly kid greets the doctor with a look that says, Do with me what you will. Just save me from this pain.

Pain settles the argument. There is no way to refute the evidence of pain. The reigning emotion becomes despair, which is probably the most difficult to describe, because it is so completely solitary. The worst pain I know is all-consuming. It erases other physical sensations and demands complete concentration. With no other sensations to measure it by, it becomes absolute—everything and nothing. As Emily Dickinson wrote, "Pain—has an element of Blank—." It creates a vacuum at the core that cannot be filled by any other emotions than hopelessness, helplessness, fear—the components of despair. Pain is extremely isolating. No one else can imagine or recall pain and feel it with the same intensity. While it lasts, it is all mine. It is like being enshrouded in my own body, unable to peer out, unable to feel anything but the body's immediate sensations. Sometimes a hand holding mine can at least keep me aware of my attachment to life beyond the pain and keep me from surrendering hope entirely. My voice can also break the isolation, even if all I can do is moan. Moaning does not relieve the pain, nor is it an involuntary mechanism. I can restrain it if I try. It is a reminder that I am still in there, still conscious and willful, but terrified of losing hold. Christ's words on the cross, "My God, my God, why hast thou forsaken me?" are the ultimate cry of pain. There is no greater despair than feeling that even God has abandoned you, trapped in your malfunctioning mortal body. The pain itself becomes all-powerful. I find myself talking to the pain, begging it to go away and spare me. The only way out of despair is to let go, to drift, trusting others to watch and hold on, or to mask the pain by numbing my consciousness of it.

After Great Pain

My generation pioneered, if you can call it that, in using drugs recreationally to enhance emotions and intensify vision, yet I was never even interested in smoking marijuana. I just didn't need chemical enhancement to know the depths of despair, nor could I imagine a greater euphoria than that which comes with release from pain. The smile on my face when the pain subsides is not a mask I wear for others, but an expression of supreme joy. Euphoria brings everything around me into sharper focus. I'm back and the world is beautiful. At least this is how it used to be. Over the years, the episodes of pain have become somewhat less intense, due in part to relaxation techniques. Usually the pain can be brought under control by Demerol. It eases away gradually as I get sleepy and a little disoriented. This has saved me from the worst despair, but it has also deprived me of the best euphoria, and I have to say I miss it. Instead of enhancing my experience, taking drugs has subdued it. I'm still happy to have the crisis over and done, but I'm relieved rather than ecstatic.

Even the old euphoria settles pretty quickly into a trusting relief. In a familiar hospital, with my treatment overseen by a doctor who knows my case well, I am content to drop my apprehensions and float on the assurance that, because I have recovered before, I will get better again. When I have been hospitalized elsewhere, I have missed this trust, which is so conducive to recovery. Instead, I have felt suspended in a state of anxiety, on guard all the time, fearful that the strange doctor might make mistakes or not take me at my word. In "my" hospital, listening to the red-winged blackbirds in the slough outside my window, I am much more at ease. Visitors ask me how long I expect to be there even before I have thought about going home. I am content with the solace that attentive medical care brings.

As I begin to recover, this contentment is broken by bouts of frustration, sorrow, and loneliness. The frustration is over the pace of recovery and the chance of setbacks. I can eat again, and my appetite returns with a vengeance. When I crave gumdrops I figure the worst is over. I eat my first meal cautiously and get caught unawares by nausea or abdominal cramps. The laboratory tests, too, show that I am not as healthy as I feel in the absence of pain. And then sorrow sets in, with the realization that my latest run of good health has ended. Knowing that I will never be free of illness reduces me to hopelessness again. If the day clouds over, so do my spirits, and I sit and cry the lonely tears of the incarcerated hospital patient. When friends come to visit, however, they usually find me pretty happy. Their presence eases the loneliness and soothes the frustration and, for the time being, I can come out from under the gloom. Another way to counter the sorrow is to project myself into the future after discharge. I imagine going home and relishing in the daily routine that I ordinarily take for granted. I am eager to do things I have been putting off and to plant flowers or paint to beautify the home I miss so much. If my physical recovery is going well, this daydreaming brings joy in the familiar and ordinary. If there's a setback, it feeds the sorrow.

Leaving the hospital is like embarking on an emotional roller coaster. First, there is the happy anticipation of being back to normal, but it is marred by anxiety about going off on my own and having to manage without instant help. I worry that it's too early and that the pain will come again as soon as I'm left alone. The terroristic nature of my illness takes on a new, heightened reality, and I panic. Sometimes I catch it in the hospital and can talk it through with a doctor or nurse or chaplain. Other times, it strikes late at night, when the list of appropriate friends to call has dwindled. As scary as it is, I prefer anxiety to depression, because it forces me to make contact with someone else who will help talk it through. If I don't do that, I slip into melancholy, a lovely name for a self-perpetuating sadness that feeds on awful thoughts about the worst possibilities. I don't know exactly what the old believers in "black humors" meant when they coined the term "melancholia," but what I call melancholy is quite distinct from a dull, listless depression. It is being on the verge of tears much of the time and having longings that you just can't satisfy in this state. My daughter found just the right expression for it when she was sick for a week at age three with a respiratory infection: "I feel so sad. I miss everybody."

Those first days home, I feel detached from the care and concern that come with being hospitalized, but the independence I long for is still beyond my capacity. It is a time when suffering passionately would serve my recovery well, but there are few opportunities to let the volcano erupt. I am supposed to be better now, and the practical demands on my life exhaust the energy that a good outburst would take. When I feel tense and ready to cry, I search for diversions like reading a novel, going outside in the hope that the beauty of nature will restore me, or giving in to fits of order by cleaning off my desk or alphabetizing the spices. Eventually, the bad humors pass and my balance is restored, but as long as the threat of ill health persists, it is a precarious balance. I am left with a muted sense of vulnerability that can turn to panic on quite short notice.

Sometimes, diversion doesn't work and I get depressed instead. By depressed, I mean a sense of being without purpose or worth, an emotional flatness, an obsession with misfortune that obscures beauty and other sources of joy, indifference to food, a tendency to withdraw because even dialing the phone takes too much initiative, a listlessness of the brain that makes it difficult to keep up my work or to remember what real emotional vitality is like. Depression is the least frequent and thus least familiar of the emotions I go through. It comes on when recovery is unusually slow or the episodes of pain unusually frequent. The worst case of it I remember accompanied that nine-month fever. It came close at times to the despair of pain, without the pain to provoke it. My usual remedies against depression only made it worse. Even the sunlight shining through the birch trees in a favorite vacation spot along Lake Superior seemed oppressive, because I couldn't enjoy it in the usual ways. I was too exhausted to walk in the woods and too chilled to sit on the rocks along the shore.

Because I am unaccustomed to depression, it scares me. But I am thankful that it scares me, because there may be no end to it otherwise. When fear intervenes, I am ready to get out from under. I can't say with certainty how I do it, or even if I *do* do it myself. Talking to other people and getting involved in their lives helps. Getting back to work helps. Singing helps. Doing something out of the routine helps. These days, Zoloft helps when nothing else does. Laughing helps. My sense of the absurd kicks in and I laugh at myself: Chicken Little, hunkered down, waiting for the sky to fall. I have just recovered from a potentially life-threatening infection in my most vulnerable organ. I have been spared again. Why waste my life bemoaning its imperfection? What helps most of all, of course, is feeling better.

Renewed Vigor

Just as release from pain brings euphoria, release from melancholy or depression brings a new emotional vigor. I used to notice it first in the new jubilance that my kids could arouse. Getting rid of my awful self-preoccupation brings the world around me into vivid focus. Events in the newspaper matter again and I get caught up in other injustices besides my own. I feel more compassionate and am eager to share friends' burdens. Objects take on symbolic meaning, and ordinary experiences seem laden with consequence. At work, both intellect and imagination serve me better than ever. It's a wonderful way to live, and I revel in it. I am like a fairy-tale hero imprisoned by trolls who has just escaped with the magic lantern that illumines life's shadows.

This high-energy state passes, too, subsiding into a contentment suitable for everyday use. Illness aside, I think of myself as happy, optimistic, and fundamentally secure, with a firm sense of purpose. Yet, I know this contentment depends on a little bit of denial. On the days that I feel well physically, I simply "forget" that I have cause for worry. Each episode survived has left me, in Emily Dickinson's words, a little more "enlightened to perceive / New periods of pain." Over the years, I have come to expect despair and melancholy and to wait them out in anticipation of relief and euphoria. I have learned how to sustain contentment and keep some disturbances in check. Still, like the pain that sets them off, these emotions do not appear on a predictable schedule. Sometimes I know enough to hang on tightly for the big plunge down the roller coaster. Yet, no matter how rationally I gear up for it, I can still get tossed over the edge.

Describing all this gives it an air of unreality—maybe even sentimentality. Does it really happen this way? Am I embellishing for dramatic effect? I have reconstructed this from memory—lots of memories—but there is no way to corroborate its truth. I can't rely on my journal, because there are long periods when the subject of illness is just too tiresome to discuss and I'm in no mood to write, anyway. If I ask people who have been around me during the illness, what they remark on is my emotional stability and how well I function through it all. I am good at smooth surfaces, I know. Also, there is something vital missing here. I have not mentioned feeling angry, because I still don't know quite where it fits. I think it is what fuels Emily Dickinson's volcano, and getting close enough to describe it means diving right into the hot lava. Am I capable of that much passion?

Cycles and Stages

My emotional cycle may not be all that typical. Its course is determined both by the unpredictability of Caroli's disease and by the fact that I enjoy remissions when the only symptom of ill health is anemia. People whose illnesses are gradually but steadily degenerative have little opportunity for euphoria—only relief if their condition is stabilized temporarily. Some people have long enough remissions to set consciousness of illness aside and let their emotions be governed by other joys and sorrows. Even those who see neither improvement nor deterioration but experience their illnesses as constant and unrelenting learn to invest their emotions elsewhere.

Elisabeth Kübler-Ross's book *On Death and Dying* gives a sensitive rendering of the emotional aspects of terminal illness. The *Time* magazine review quoted on the jacket credits Kübler-Ross with having "vanquished the conspiracy of silence that once shrouded the hospital's terminal wards." We whose illnesses are interminable thank her for that, too, and try to glean some use for our living in what she has revealed about dying. As I talk with other chronically ill people, I hear frequent references to "the stages of grief." It is reassuring to have them spelled out so concretely: denial and isolation, anger, bargaining, depression, acceptance. But for people whose illnesses go on and on and do not have a certain resolution, this is false reassurance. You cannot count on a linear emotional progression when your physical condition varies erratically. Acceptance is easily undone by nasty surprises.

In the preface to her book, Kübler-Ross wonders, "How many things are communicated non-verbally and have to be felt, experienced, seen, and can hardly be translated into words?" Unfortunately, readers are all too ready to simplify what is so difficult to express. Some people who use the stages to interpret suffering—their own or others'—become impatient and insensitive, as they wait for one unexpectedly tenacious stage to evolve automatically into the next. This reification—taking abstract ideas for concrete facts—is a risk inherent in all linear schemes. I would not be surprised to hear a sermon that identified the Seven Last Words of Christ by their stages of grief. Linearity is not the only problem. Seeing these emotions as products of terminal illness makes them, by association, pathological. Rather than inspiring true empathy, knowing what to expect may lead instead to a condescending sympathy: Don't mind him. He's just in the anger stage. The message we ought to get from the work on death and dying is that the emotions released by the certainty of death are authentic, essential human feelings worthy of being expressed while living.

The Catchall, Depression

Although chronic illness offers no uniform emotional course with distinct stages, the emotions themselves are familiar to most of us. Asked to identify and describe their predominant emotions, people I talked with emphasized anxiety or fear, frustration or anger, and above all depression, which seems to be the catchall term for despair, anguish, sorrow, grief, sadness, melancholy, loneliness—the emotions that do not evince rebellion but keep us trapped in gloom. For many, this depression originates in severe pain and the isolation such pain creates. Kathy Halvorson tells of feeling "the kind of pain where you lose your head and give up to it, and no matter who's around, it doesn't make any difference." Margie Rietsma says of the pain that wakes her in the middle of the night, "You feel like you're the only person in the whole world." When Esther Green feels this alone, she isolates herself from the rest of her family: "I just like to be all by myself, because I don't like to inflict my illness on others. I feel like I owe them an explanation, and I'd just as soon go off to myself. I don't want to be around them when I have these moods and attitudes, as they say." Retreating this way also helps preserve emotional energy. In a depressed state, there is simply not enough to sustain relationships with other people.

When depression becomes an everyday state of being, however, withdrawal is not a practical option. Susan Alm describes depression as an ongoing hazard in her life:

> Depression is really a constant thing. It's always there. It comes, I think, with dealing with the sense of loss, knowing that friends of mine will be able to do things that I can't do. That's a source of sadness. I don't believe I could even hold down a full-time job. It's taken me a long time to realize that. That Superwoman image is there, and other women can try to attain it. They can overachieve for a while and then fall back and everything is normal. But for a patient with lupus, all you achieve by trying to do it is a flare-up of your disease, and you frequently won't even accomplish the positive thing you're trying to do. You fall back so far that even normal life isn't possible, and you see yourself as a constant failure. You shouldn't continue that habit for life—of seeing yourself as a failure.
>
> Depression is also a feeling of helplessness—not being able to cope with doing things yourself. I recall one time when I actually had a kind of mind-body split, and I could watch myself. It became earlier and earlier in the day when I couldn't cope and I would just break down crying, because I really couldn't do anything. I couldn't do *anything*. I just couldn't function.
>
> It's a kind of heaviness, too, depression is. Things are just too much, they're weighting you down. You're almost catatonic. I can get into that. It's an escape in some ways because you can't cope with the difficulty around you, so you just turn off. Of course, having that sort of thing when there are little children you're responsible for is very difficult. It makes you feel guilty, because you're not being a good mother and you're not watching them, and you're very fearful that some-

thing could happen. I think that was the hardest part. I didn't mind the effect it was having on *me*. It's a double-edged thing: seeing that it was having a bad effect on my children was the worst and hardest part of it, but it also forced me to go outside of myself and to try to change things, which I don't know if you would do if you didn't have something outside of yourself to force you to do that. You might just keep being depressed until you're suicidal. You really might.

Rather than an intense experience of melancholy or loneliness, depression is as likely to be an absence of feeling. Lorraine Czerny barely knew she was depressed, and people around her didn't discern it because she functioned adequately in their company:

Last winter I realized that I was gaining weight, eating, and not doing anything in the apartment. I wasn't sewing, I wasn't knitting, I wasn't doing any of those things that I had started doing to keep myself occupied. So I finally went for counseling. Both my doctors thought I needed it. My energy was low. It took too much effort to do anything except sit and read and let the stuff accumulate around me. I wasn't weepy. I was probably more angry than anything else. I'm real angry, just plain angry, at times—when I have the energy to be angry. I think I kept up a front. Nobody suggested there was a change. It was sort of a surprise in the aftermath.

Bill Gordon's depression is accompanied by physical symptoms that keep him confined in an emotional vacuum:

Fatigue is a main physical symptom, plus unclear thinking, suicidal thoughts, but mainly fatigue. I get a depression that they call retarded depression where I just drag around. My whole body is retarded. My thinking process is retarded. Everything gets slowed down.

Both Lorraine and Bill could find some relief in antidepressant medication because their emotional state was diagnosed as a symptom of illness. For Bill, as a manic-depressive, emotional instability is the primary symptom and is attributed to a chemical imbalance in his brain that must be set right. Lorraine's cardiologist explained her depression as a consequence of heart surgery that he has seen in his repeat patients. "The brain is scrambled," says Lorraine, who has had surgery three times, "and there are some things that will never be the same, that I can't recover from."

Until very recently—probably until serotonin-boosting drugs like Prozac and Zoloft were developed—depression was seen not as a symptom of illness but rather as an emotional response to the presence of illness—and not a very useful one—for which you had to seek your own relief. As my doctor told me once by way of apology, "We can treat people who have abnormal reactions to normal stress, but not people who have normal reactions to abnormal stress." How you came out from under the gloom depended in large part on how you interpreted the emotion and its function in your life. Despair, depression, sadness, melancholy, and so on were classified as "negative" emotions, precisely the ones to be "eliminated" as you "accentuate the positive," to quote a Broadway tune. If they hung on too long, they became a source not just of solitary suffering but of social embarrassment.

Self-Pity

Many of us have been long accustomed to blaming ourselves for our flagging spirits. Lily Washington, who prides herself on defying her asthma, has moments of grief that she describes with a bit of contempt as "feeling sorry for myself." People who offer advice of the type "Just think how lucky you are to be alive" convey the message that feeling sorry for yourself is unseemly. As further reinforcement, there is the specter of the proverbial elderly relative who answers an innocent "How are you?" with "Just awful lately," and lures the listener in under the oppressive cloud.

Phyllis Mueller worries that her emotional suffering will degenerate into that kind of self-pity:

> You cannot have any self-pity. You just have to keep working
> to stay out of that bag. That's where I go down every time—
> is when I tell myself that this isn't fair. Well, life isn't fair. We
> all know that. And since I don't know what anybody else is
> carrying around with them, I'm not the one to judge that.

"Self-pity" is certainly in my vocabulary. In fact, I have edited the word out of this book several times. As I have tried to describe my own experience of illness coherently and truthfully, I have learned to interpret it in new, more subtle ways. I have caught myself calling melancholy self-pity and dismissing the slightest twinge of anger as self-pity. I have used the term in a self-mocking tone, I suspect to disguise my shame about not being able to stay perfectly composed. Hearing Phyllis talk about it has given me a different perspective. Yes, we all know that life isn't fair. Injustice is the great cosmic flaw that keeps us from experiencing life as truly good and beautiful. It is a fact to be mourned and decried. But how can we do that collectively if we don't do it individually, each time we experience injustice ourselves? Imagine being unmoved by the senility of your aging mother because the loss of human promise in a baby's brain injury is more tragic, or not grieving an accidental death because murder is more horrifying. Our own private afflictions, no matter where they rank among the world's horrors, are cause enough for grief.

Still, when we suffer these emotions, many of us feel compelled to endure them privately and overcome them on our own. Susan Alm's experience is typical: "Somehow it was conveyed to me as a child that depression was something you did not talk about, and it was something you made up, or you had to work it out yourself. It was a private sort of thing, and you didn't dare go for help for it." Withdrawing to protect yourself from exposure is common practice, whether it is actual isolation, like Esther Green going to her room, or an emotional shutdown such as Don Welke practiced by sitting silently in front of the television. In either case, the solitude may be overwhelming. When Kathy Halvorson lets her feelings show and doesn't get an empathetic response, her depression is compounded: "I start the whole spiral again. I'll say to myself, 'Why don't you just keep your mouth shut? Nobody's really interested. You are in this all by yourself, after all. They're not sick. You are.'"

Left alone with the depression, some people try to rationalize their way out of it. Calling it self-pity and measuring your misfortune against others' is one way to do that, but may just replace depression with guilt over feeling bad nevertheless. Telling herself, "Everybody has some kind of a problem. Mine happens to be physical," does not make Susan Alm any more content to wake up in the morning with instant pain. Seeking distance and self-control—leverage to lift the burden away—is another approach. Phyllis Mueller maintains a perspective that keeps depression short-lived:

> I think I am a fairly upbeat person until I've had just more than I can overcome. When I get overwhelmed with it, I get depressed and I'm just bitchy to live with. But I try to stay on top of it. I try to look down on it rather than try to look up and get through it to the top. It's very powerful and it would be easy to do, but I think that's my personal responsibility, not to let that happen, because I've only got one life, and if I'm going to go through it sick, then I'm going to go through it the best way sick I know how. The choice isn't sick or well, lady; it's sick and miserable or sick and somewhat happy. Well, I'll take somewhat happy.

Safety Valves

Norman Vincent Peale's line, "the power of positive thinking" has been around long enough to be a cliché, but it still works pretty well. Don Welke is a zealous advocate of the positive attitude, and even Bill Gordon says, "I have a feeling that thoughts can change that chemical balance in your brain. Thoughts themselves can change that." If positive thinking doesn't actually ease the depression, it can at least increase your endurance. This works best for people who have already experienced depression that finally lifted. A quiet, introverted person by nature, Don Welke tends not to get upset but to "let things ride and ride through them like on a wave." A phrase he has found useful while doing that is "Tomorrow has got to be better, because it can't get any worse." Sometimes, though, it does get worse, which doesn't necessarily negate the sentence. Each day, after all, brings a new tomorrow. Gloria Murphy repeats the assurance "This, too, shall pass," and even says it aloud to give it more conviction.

Because there are so few outlets for a full and honest expression of emotional suffering, many of us rely on safety valves to relieve the pressure that might otherwise set off the volcano. Writing in a journal has gotten Delores Garlid, Rosemary McKuen, and me through some of our worst moments. Esther Green takes the bus downtown and moves around in the anonymous crowd to break her isolation without betraying her feelings. She hopes that this diversion will also lift her spirits, and sometimes it does. But if it tires her too much, she comes home just as depressed. Even those who don't acknowledge any negative emotions can find them leaking out in barely detectible ways. Duane Barber is an example of this:

> I think I have been affected emotionally. I've been to a few funerals and I've noticed that I'm not as strong as I used to be when it comes to seeing somebody that I was close to die. As far as my own feeling toward myself in getting this is concerned, I never cried about it and never had any feeling.

The tear ducts are, of course, the body's own best safety valves. Even so-called sentimental crying—at movies or novels—can offer release for genuine, unsentimental depression. But crying is, for most adults, and for men in particular, a private act. We can do it in movie theaters with only slight embarrassment, wiping away the tears quickly before the lights come on and then smiling sheepishly at our companions. Crying on behalf of our own suffering is most frequently done behind closed doors, alone or with a trusted friend or a therapist, and even the red eyes must be camouflaged.

Delores Garlid distinguishes between "a healthy release crying and just a feeling-sorry-for-me cry." She can make herself do the first sort of crying by acting out physically, swinging a tennis racket against her mattress, for example. What Delores is seeking is the classical Greek notion of catharsis, which is a more eruptive release of emotion than simply letting off steam. It requires not diversion, but a confrontation with the awful emotion itself. Rosemary McKuen offers a moving illustration of catharsis:

> Last year I read *Working It Through,* one of Elisabeth Kübler-Ross's picture books. There was a woman with an ileostomy in it. Her biggest, deepest fear was that if anybody ever saw her stoma, if she ever had to expose and reveal herself, that she would be rejected. And so Dr. Kübler-Ross asked her to take her appliance off in front of this group of people who were there. She got the whole realm of experiences. One guy threw up. But it helped to face the absolute depths. And when I read that I just put my face down on the table and sobbed, because you do have those fears.

Humor has a cathartic effect for me, and, like Delores, I divide it into two kinds: the "make light of it" humor that tries to mask the emotion to avoid embarrassment and a healthy, bone-jingling laughter rooted in suffering. Before I went for a consultation with a member of the liver transplant team, I got my X rays and CT scans to carry along with me. I had long been curious to see what my liver looked like, but just hadn't taken time to check it out. I was also a little afraid of how I might react to such concrete proof of disease. It would end the slight hope that I might someday imagine the illness away. As I held the negatives up to the window, I thought, This is it. These must be stones, and there are the stagnant pools of bile. It's real. I expected a rush of emotions, but nothing came. I was as devoid of feeling as if I were looking at slides from somebody's vacation: Interesting enough, but you had to be there to appreciate it, and I guess I wasn't there. One evening shortly after, I dragged my children and a bag of toys along to a history lecture. I was listening as intently as I could, trying to ignore the kids, who were drawing at the back of the room. I felt a tap on my shoulder and my six-year-old handed me a piece of paper. On it was an amoeba-like outline filled with randomly scattered dots and spots of various sizes. "Here's your liver, Mom," she whispered. The two of us had to put our hands over our mouths to keep from exploding with laughter. When we got home, I put the picture on the refrigerator and showed it to everybody who came by. Of course, I asked myself, "Why is this funny?" and I knew the answer right away: If it wasn't funny, I couldn't endure it. After that, I could feel all the other emotions that I had expected the X rays to unleash.

The value of catharsis is that it allows you to face the emotion head-on rather than try to avoid, dismiss, or disguise it. But it is still a private enterprise and we seek it, usually, because we want to get the suffering over with, not feel it more intensely. Catharsis is a short-term passion in a life still sworn to patience. Most of our remedies against the negative emotions are premised on the belief that these feelings, no matter how understandable, either impede our progress toward acceptance or are only stations along the way, to be indulged in briefly, once and for all. Something very important seems to be missing here. It is the recognition that depression, melancholy, and the other "negative" emotions are necessary features of chronic illness. In some cases, they have a traceable physiological cause. In most cases, they are natural, appropriate responses to the particular misfortune of illness, inherent in this experience itself. They are not pathological, not evidence of failure to handle illness properly, but the human psyche's own mechanism for living through it.

A Surprising Gift

My own worst experience of depression was, in retrospect, my best, because it revealed that missing truth about negative emotions. It was harrowing, because I got to that point Susan Alm warns against, of feeling suicidal. I was not consciously planning to take my life, but I began to have sudden, unbidden fantasies in which I did. Images of myself walking into a lake with weights on my legs or lying in the garage under the car's exhaust pipe would flash into my mind at random. I kept the fantasies to myself as long as I could, partly because talking about them might make them real. Also, I already knew that advice to cheer up and look on the bright side wouldn't help, and I was afraid of being judged unkindly as emotionally overwrought. However, on a day when all the safety valves blew, I finally told my husband. He pleaded with me to forget it. "I don't want to hear about it," he said, meaning, I think, that it was too frightening to bear in mind. Next, I told my sister and we talked it over at the rational level where we both like to conduct our lives. But for several days afterward, she called to assure herself that I was still alive, and I felt responsible for having made her anxious. While both these responses were very natural, understandable ones, they left me with an even greater sense of taboo. I felt lonelier, too, knowing that my closest relationships could not accommodate this awful knowledge about me. I hesitated to tell my doctor, because I took pride in being the undaunted patient with the indestructible spirit. Besides, I didn't think my emotions were in his jurisdiction. But when I reached wit's end, I blurted it out over the telephone. His voice was surprisingly calm. "That doesn't sound like you," he said. "That's the illness. It comes from being so weakened." Just hearing that these suicidal fantasies were a consequence of my physical illness and not evidence that I was losing hold reassured me.

I felt even more assured a bit later when I talked to a minister who came to visit me in the hospital. His response almost knocked me off the bed: "That may be a real option for you someday. You should hold on to that and treasure it as a gift you've been given." What about burial at the crossroads? What about automatic damnation for self-murder? Never in my life had I expected a minister to "treasure" suicide. His words were very provocative, but also very clever, I realized later as I followed the train of thought they had provoked. He had approved my right to consider death as a way out of my suffering, and by doing so had affirmed the suffering itself. He did not tell me to cheer up but encouraged me to feel the pain and despair in all its intensity and to admit to myself that it was getting intolerable. By allowing me an escape, he also helped me to see that I didn't need to use it. He knew I wasn't really going to commit suicide, he admitted later, otherwise he wouldn't have said anything so risky. Now I knew it, too. The fantasies kept coming, but they had lost their power to frighten me. I could "treasure" them as a kind of psychic deliverance, while I awaited deliverance from the illness itself. I was still depressed, but I became more hopeful. It was a very instructive experience and the lessons still hold.

I do not mean to underestimate the dangers of suicidal depression. I have lost two sorely missed friends and a cousin to suicide and I doubt very much that this assurance would have been sufficient for their despair. When depression *is* the disease, as it was for them and is for Bill Gordon, the risks are very different. Bill does find some relief, though, in knowing that:

> Knowing that suicidal thoughts are a feature of the illness is, I think, the key. I tend to view the suicidal thoughts in the same way I would view a runny nose as it relates to a cold. It's just one of the symptoms. If I keep that in mind, and if I also keep in mind—and my wife will tell me this if I forget it,

which I do a lot of times when I'm suicidal—that the suicide thoughts always pass, then I can get through the episode. This is one of the hardest things for people to understand. There's a tendency to talk somebody out of it and to give bright and shiny advice about the future, which just doesn't help. The thing that helps me out the most is just remembering that it doesn't last forever.

Yet Bill's ability to remember and trust what he remembers is still adversely affected by his illness. To safeguard his life, he takes medication. In the midst of the suffering, it is hard to remember previous agony clearly enough to believe that you can endure it again.

The Volcano Erupts

There was one other time in my life when my suffering was affirmed and encouraged: when I went through the trauma of divorce. The frequency of divorce, coupled with the vogue for being "in touch with your feelings," had given divorcing people greater latitude to talk about how it feels. Friends were content to sit with me while I cried without offering advice or trying to cheer me up. They would take me out and walk me around when I was immobilized, and they were not dismayed if I didn't immediately snap out of it. They would laugh and do outrageous things with me when I needed that release. When all I could feel was hurt, they helped me get angry. Through it all, I was congratulated on how strong I was and how well I was bearing up, and there didn't seem to be any contradiction in this. If I failed to keep up the patient, smiling demeanor that I work at when I am sick, hardly anyone held it against me. Without that strained silence, divorce seemed more emotionally wrenching than illness has been. The emotions were mostly familiar ones, but I felt them more intensely, and I could not predict when they would come and go. When the worst was over, I realized that it had also been emotionally liberating. My capacity for strong feeling had been enhanced.

A significant part of that emotional liberation was getting angry. Anger was the one emotion that seemed unfamiliar. I felt not only the expected anger at the other party that nearly all divorcing people have to contend with, but anger at myself for past behavior that I now had cause to regret, anger at the fate that put me in this situation, anger at the social circumstances that complicate family relationships, anger at my upbringing and his for our respective idiosyncrasies, and anger at myself, again, for not being smart enough to figure this all out. Then, just when I was ready to declare the crisis over and settle into a new life, I got sick, and, boy, was I mad.

The divorce brought me into counseling for the first time. I took the Minnesota Multiphasic Personality Inventory, a diagnostic test for psychological abnormalities. Thankfully, I was assessed as normal, but there were peaks and valleys within that normal range. As the counselor interpreted it, "You have learned some rules about how you ought to appear before the world and will keep feelings in check to avoid breaking those rules," and "You suspect that you have been dealt with unfairly but do not allow yourself to acknowledge that openly or to express the feelings that it arouses." The truth was out. This, I thought, is the story of chronic illness. I have heard that story over and over from other people I have talked with. Anger is the most difficult emotion of all. The rules we have learned decree that we hide it from the world. The advice Esther Green would offer people newly ill is: "Always try to have a smile on your face. And if you're bitter or angry, keep it to yourself. If you're not healthy, people will like you if you don't go around with a nasty attitude." The gnawing, unspeakable feeling of being dealt with unfairly has been with Kathy Halvorson since age seven, when she was told how lucky she was to have recovered from polio: "I didn't know what to do with that except to feel grateful, but I remember feeling angry: So what's lucky about what happened to me?"

Why Me? Why Not? Who Else?

The suspicion that you have been dealt with unfairly leads you to the big existential question, "Why me?" Few of us really want to ask it, however, because we know it has no satisfactory answer. If you believe that you have been willfully afflicted by a punitive God, you have to admit to wrongdoing and make recompense. If you believe your illness is part of a divine plan, you get frustrated about unwittingly taking wrong turns. If you believe that misfortune falls randomly, you may be left with hopelessness: If there is no one to blame and no one to appease, where do you turn? Rather than ask the question explicitly, many of us try to restrain the feeling of injustice. Peggy Evans recalls her anger when diabetic neuropathy set in:

> It made me very angry—the condition did. It made me angry that I couldn't do things. I was not angry at the doctors, and I was not angry at God or anyone. It was just one of those things that happens in life, but I wanted to do what I wanted to do when I wanted to do it, and I couldn't. I pounded my knees and said, "I'm going to fight this."

"Just one of those things that happens in life." The phrase itself sounds like an attempt to minimize the injustice. It reduces anger to a knee-pounding frustration. Its impact is quite different from "One of the terrible things that happens in life," which might turn anger into a snarly discontent. Duane Barber is wary of such emotions:

> I haven't asked, "Why me? Why was I singled out?" I don't know—everything doesn't always come out even. It's not a fair world. I'm not bitter about it, which I guess you could very easily be. But if you're bitter today, you're going to wake up tomorrow morning and what are you going to do, be bitter again?

Well, what are you going to do if the anger and the sense of injustice are still lurking there? Some of us alter the question to
make it a just one. Rosemary McKuen says she came to illness believing in Murphy's Law: "If anything can go wrong, it will."
When she got sick, she slipped easily into a self-deprecating victim mentality that asked, "Why *not* me?" Others practice a
grandiosity that treats injustice not as disfavor, but as a kind of
selection. JoAnn Berglund, for example, sees it as a worthy form
of self-sacrifice: "If someone in the family has to have this, I'm the
one that's best able to handle it. My husband cannot cope with
illness, and you don't want your children to have something. I
handle it about the best of the five of us." I have rephrased the
question "What now? What do you want from me, God?" which
implies not penance but fulfillment of some unexplained mission. This is an attempt to find purpose in what might otherwise
be meaningless suffering, and to turn anger into exaltation.

When your tolerance for injustice is surpassed, you can no
longer evade the question. Curiously, both Don Welke and Phyllis
Mueller did their most vocal railing against injustice after being
injured in automobile accidents. Don Welke remembers:

> I suffered the most bitter part of my life in those three
> months because of the inactivity. The friends I had couldn't
> even come around. I'd be so bitter and cynical towards any-
> thing they were doing they didn't even want to talk to me.
> That had nothing to do with the chronic illness.

An especially reflective person like Phyllis would guess that the
bitterness did, indeed, have much to do with the chronic illness,
as it did in her own case:

> I was up half the night. I was tired. I was hurting. I wasn't
> happy very much of the time, and I was angry. It was an ac-
> cident that wasn't my fault, so we've really got a victim being
> a victim. I guess a lot of it was, God, why did this have to
> happen to me? I don't have enough crap in my life—now I've

got to go through this yet? I mean, isn't it somebody else's turn?

I'll Show YOU

When Phyllis acknowledged the injustice, the anger came spilling out over people she saw as more favored than herself, particularly her husband:

> I found that I got angry with my husband a lot, and I couldn't really tell you why. I still do when I have a sleepless night, and I think it's because he seems to be the picture of health, and I'm not. He has something that I want, and I wake up in the morning saying, "How would you like it if you couldn't sleep all night?" He does have a lot of compassion, I guess, because he'll say to me, "I could not go through what you're going through. I could not handle that." And I say, "Well, you would with a lot of practice." That's a sarcastic, snide response. I get sarcastic and cynical a lot when I don't feel well. It's sort of like the world owes me something better than this.

Families often get the brunt of the anger, simply by their proximity or because they make demands on us that reveal our hidden disabilities and show us injustice afresh. A sudden, misdirected outburst can be provoked by any kind of stress. This is how it works for Margie Rietsma: "I'll be sitting here and one of my children will be pestering me, 'Mom, can I have this? Mom, can I do that? Mom?' and I go, 'Jesus, leave me alone.' And it's not really them, because other times I don't mind. I'm already angry because I feel so bad."

When even the most intimate relatives and friends cannot emphathize with our more troublesome emotions, we feel the old injustice. Rather than sit alongside us and listen to our anger, they want to restore peace. This engenders a kind of I'll-show-you resentment, which led Louise Taylor to take her sister along to physical therapy:

> I didn't know how else to explain what was happening. It was unreal. It was humiliating. They put a strap around my waist so the therapist could hang on to me while I practiced walking. I could only walk the length of the parallel bars and then I was exhausted for the rest of the day. My sister sat there in total silence, so I didn't know what she was thinking. She didn't share, and we didn't talk about it. That was embarrassing for her, for her to see me in a whole new way. It's hard to explain why I feel so angry.

Reason, of course, tells us that our families are not to blame, and most of us try our best to spare them, though all of us fail occasionally. We find more distant repositories for the anger, such as cultural attitudes and the behavior of unsympathetic strangers. As her illness became more disabling, Gloria Murphy found herself more easily incited to anger by such things:

> I was very angry at attitudes: attitudes toward handicapped people generally, attitudes toward illness. Ignorance made me very angry: If you know I have MS, then please take the time to find out about it. I'll be glad to tell you if you listen. I had an experience where I had just got my handicapped parking permit, and I pulled into a parking space in a shopping center, and a man drove up behind me and honked. As I got out of the car, with my cane, holding onto a child on the ice, he got out of his car and started swearing at me abusively. "You're not supposed to park there," he said. I said, "But I have a state permit," and he said, "You're not sick enough. You don't need to park there." I've had lots of experiences being yelled at. One man yelled, "That's a crippled people place." I said, "But I'm a crippled people." He said, "Well, you don't look it." So that attitude of, "Well, you look well today" made me angry.

The Noble Sufferer

When even the special privileges that might rectify the injustice a little are denied, it's hard to keep containing the anger. I get livid at moral tales about exemplary martyr-heroes who behave in preposterously courageous ways. When I hear about quadriplegics who paint with their teeth, I want to kick them in the teeth. Some days I can't even brush mine. Very quickly, I realize that my complaint is not with the painter, and I redirect the anger toward those who expect such marvels of people who are ill. But who is to blame for cultural attitudes?

The responsibility is partly mine, too. I work to maintain an image of perseverance, and I enjoy the ego boosts when people tell me how strong I am. Yet, there are plenty of times when I want to crack that image open and confess, "I'm miserable." Constantly trying to live up to the noble sufferer status you have won for yourself leaves little room for anger. Anger that has no appropriate focus easily gets turned inward. It can engender self-hatred, with its force directed at the defective body that is the source of the pain. Rosemary McKuen remembers being angriest when she took a sponge bath after her surgery and saw the opening in her abdomen for the first time. She realized that she would have it for the rest of her life and she felt contempt for this body that had failed her. Kathy Halvorson has pounded her abdomen in anger rather than passively accept the pain she feels there. Bodily self-hatred can settle into a sense of unworthiness that makes the original anger seem even less justifiable. Feeling angry on your own behalf—self-pitying—triggers shame, and the shame is compounded when your illness makes others close to you angry, as it often does. Phyllis Mueller explains:

> I think my mother was angry when any of us kids got sick. She just didn't like having to worry about it, having to be responsible for it. So my memory is, when you get sick people get angry with you. I think I still carry that now, and that's

why I do the heroic things, because I feel less-than and I feel
judged when I don't feel well.

That may, indeed, be why many of us choose to be heroic: both to
avoid arousing anger in others and to subdue our own. Rather
than continue hating her body and what had become of it,
Rosemary tried to rise above the anger by turning her misfortune
into a calling. She began to speak publicly about her illness, offering herself as a model for others facing similar surgery. While
she believed firmly that she had neither caused the illness herself
nor done anything to deserve it, she still felt compelled to redeem
herself by showing how well she could bear the moral burden of
suffering injustice without rancor. One day, a wise and compassionate friend said to her, "You are, right here, right now, an acceptable person. You don't need that ostomy or that illness or
that sense of purpose to be an acceptable person." "That was the
most liberating thing anyone has ever said to me," Rosemary
claims. She was free to acknowledge that her suffering was simply unfair and without reason, and she could finally be openly
angry about that.

Someone to Blame

It is, nevertheless, difficult to feel that anger without someone to
blame. Having absolved ourselves of guilt and having learned
that being irritable with our families gives no relief, who is left to
project it onto but those who preside over our worst moments of
pain? Nearly all of us have some call for anger with doctors: a
faulty diagnosis somewhere along the line that prolonged the
suffering, insensitivity to our personal needs, an excessively long
wait for a brief appointment with a surly, hurried doctor who still
charged full price. Yet, the readiness to complain about doctors
and the intensity of feeling about them suggest that something
else figures here. The incidents that arouse the greatest anger are
of two sorts: (1) when doctors question whether the illness has a

genuine physical cause, thus challenging the legitimacy of our suffering, and (2) when doctors try out painful procedures that have no guaranteed results, thus increasing our suffering. As if we didn't have enough cause for anger, someone we turn to for help questions our integrity and asks us to bear even more trouble. Who wouldn't be mad? To be patient and smiling and cooperative in the midst of this takes great emotional restraint. Surprisingly, most of us manage that, but given a chance to talk freely with fellow sufferers, we let the anger rage. Even Phyllis Mueller, whose medical history is full of error and insensitivity, wonders at how easily her anger is provoked:

> I don't know if it's men or doctors or what, but I tend to lump it all in the same thing and say, "You're not treating me fairly." I feel demeaned. I think, "Am I getting paranoid about this? Am I just getting angry about everything?" But normally I'm not. When the illness flares up again, it all comes back and I have to deal with it again. On my good days, I like men, I respect doctors. I think, "How can I talk that way?"

Psychological Garbage

What do you do with anger that has no proper outlet? Are the choices really to fume indiscriminately or to keep it to yourself? Doing the first clearly has social consequences. But what are the consequences of repression? A theory current in popular psychology has it that anger turned inward becomes depression and that in fact depression *is* anger turned inside out. While anger turned inward easily disguises itself as other emotions, seeing it as the source of depression seems very simplistic. They are not mutually exclusive—one introverted and one extroverted, rising and falling like opposite ends of a seesaw. They can certainly coexist. And they are similar in their range of intensity. Depression can be an intolerably painful sorrow or an absence of feeling that even slows you physically. Anger can be a violent rage or a brooding discontent. Another pop psych theory is that repressed anger causes illness. This has some appeal, because it offers hope of controlling the illness by manipulating the emotions. I encountered this theory quite unexpectedly shortly after I had been in the hospital with pancreatitis. An acquaintance who had just been trained in a new form of psychic healing told me, with straight-faced conviction, that the pancreas is where anger is stored. "I know you have a lot of repressed anger," she said, "and I'd be glad to help you clear it out. Just give me a call." I was speechless and could only smile feebly as if to say, "Thanks but no thanks." Curiously, I was not angry. The anger came later, when I thought about how presumptuous it was to think she had the cure for a disease she knew absolutely nothing about. And did she really believe that healing a lifelong illness was like steam-cleaning a rug?

At the time this happened, I took her observation about repressed anger as an accusation, and I thought myself innocent. I was not tucking anger away in my pancreas. There simply wasn't any to repress. I honestly did not feel angry about my illness—melancholy, yes; depressed, sometimes; euphoric, enough to make it bearable; but not angry. A few years later, when I got angry about the breakup of my marriage, I found great stores of anger that I had never suspected. I learned what "repression" really means, and that it is not a conscious act. I still have not called to have my pancreas vacuumed, and it is not only because I doubt the efficacy of the method. I also question its underlying assumption: Emotions, it seems, are a kind of psychological garbage, and each of us is provided with a thirty-gallon can that must be emptied from time to time or we will rot from within. This approach justifies the expression of anger for its purgative effect; however, anger is not always experienced as catharsis or "clearing the air." Sometimes getting angry only makes you mad. In the case of depression as anger-inside-out, anger is justified because it relieves depression that might otherwise become self-destructive. But that leaves you with anger, again, which can be as intolerable and unshakable as depression. Neither of these theories admit the possibility that the emotions may not dissipate but hang on with greater intensity. Nor do they justify anger simply because there is good reason to be mad, and that is the crux of the problem.

Life Is Unfair

The best and truest justification for anger is that "life is unfair." Ironically, we use this phrase far more often to appease our anger than to provoke it. Injustice of any kind ought to make us mad as hell. As I was trying to make sense of my discomfort with popular notions about anger, I came across Stephen Mitchell's interpretation of the Book of Job in the first issue of the magazine *Tikkun: A Quarterly Jewish Critique of Politics, Culture, and Society.* I had read Job in bits and pieces and with great resistance, recalling Sunday school lessons about his unfailing faith, which I definitely could not imitate. Calling the story "the supreme poem of moral outrage," Mitchell presents a much more accessible Job: "You have heard of the patience of Job, the Epistle of James says, and it is this legendary, patient Job—not the desperate and ferociously impatient Job of the poem—who, ironically enough, became proverbial in Western culture." Mitchell goes on to show how Job suffers not patiently, but passionately, railing against God, arguing against God's sense of justice, demanding recompense. The amazing thing about the story is not that he gets angry, but that, in his anger, he never gives up on God, but continues to hold God accountable for what others dismiss as meaningless. What his suffering produces is a face-to-face confrontation with God that allows him to see beyond injustice: "When Job says, 'I had heard of you with my ears;/but now my eyes have seen you' (42:5), he is no longer a servant, who fears god and avoids evil. He has faced evil, has looked straight into its face and through it, into a vast wonder and love."

When Job's ordeal is over, his family and material goods are re-stored to him. It is a fairy-tale ending that can leave readers feel-ing cheated. After all, we cannot expect restored health as a reward for our own suffering. What use is there in the story then? I am hardly practiced at biblical interpretation or at finding prac-tical application for great religious truths, but something in me wants to follow the passionate Job's example. What would it mean to feel genuine moral outrage at the fact that life is unfair? Are there any benefits in that? In my life, the times when I have felt intensely angry rather than simply piqued and relentlessly de-pressed rather than sadly self-pitying have left me feeling wiser somehow. I am reminded that this is how you go about living a life that is, at the core, unfair. I have not been deprived of life but have been learning how to live it more thoroughly.

Naming the emotions "anger," "depression," "melancholy," and so on and recognizing their origin in physical suffering pro-vides the same ironic sense of relief that comes with having a con-fusing variety of symptoms diagnosed as a "real" illness. This does not mean the emotions will go away. I will still be anxious or melancholy or both when I get home from the hospital, but I know now that it is part of my restoration. There are other bene-fits in allowing yourself to feel these emotions. A derivative proverb has been pursuing me all through this chapter: "Passion is its own reward." Having strong feelings builds your capacity for strong feeling: the ability to feel "wonder and love" with just as much intensity as anger and to suffer compassionately with oth-ers who share this life of injustice.

The definition of "passion" that I have been groping for turned up unexpectedly in a quotation from a sermon by the Reverend Carter Heyward of the Episcopal Church:

> To live with passion is to live not above, or apart from, but within the dynamics of contradiction: in joy and sorrow, in caring and indifference, in courage and fear, in friendship and alienation, involved in the tensions that overload our senses

and jar our sensibilities and push us toward that cynical point, at which we can glibly thank God for our many blessings as we go on our way assuming that the world is cursed and doomed by some maniacal force that is beyond both human and divine control. Passion is that fully human and fully divine spark which leaps in the face of cynicism and burns with a commitment that neither God nor humankind is finished!

Living "within the dynamics of contradiction" allows greater latitude than Phyllis Mueller claims when she says, "The choice isn't sick or well, lady; it's sick and miserable or sick and somewhat happy." There is a third choice, which is much healthier emotionally: miserable *and* very happy.

When the full copy of Heyward's sermon I had requested arrived in the mail, I had been pondering Emily Dickinson's volcano, trying to make metaphorical sense out of experiences that lie beyond reason. What's at the core of the volcano? I kept asking myself, and the answer, in a tiny, tentative voice: divine spark? Heyward confirmed my guess and kept me pondering. A spark that is fully human and fully divine would, I imagined, give off both fire and light—both emotional intensity and clarity of vision. Another image came to me, this one very familiar, yet still amazing. In the cold of winter in the snowy, northern part of the world that I know best, there is a special quality of light that subdues color and turns trees, berries, people standing in the snow into starkly distinct abstract form. It is as though the gaudy, splashy nature we delight in during the summer has been reduced to the pure essence of beauty, which is light and shadow. The only emotion appropriate at such a sight is the one Emily Dickinson's volcanic eruption evokes: awe. If I can think of illness as my interior source of winter light, then a capacity for awe may be reward enough for a life of passionate suffering. My dual ethnicity—sick and Scandinavian—is not such a handicap after all. But I would rather be speechless with awe than silent for propriety's sake.

Chapter
12

Going on Faith

"Call it luck or call it grace, the resources have always been there."

"God never gives you more than you can handle." Chronically ill people who are used to talking in religious terms repeat this sentence as though it were established fact. As a proverb, it says a great deal about the human need to give life meaning. It is recited to counter doubts about whether current suffering can be endured: I must be able to handle this or it wouldn't be happening to me. It expresses a longing to find some lasting value in what would otherwise be mere misfortunes: If it is God's doing, it must have a purpose. It suggests that the universe does, indeed, have rational order: Even suffering is distributed fairly and efficiently. Said over and over as an incantation in the worst of times, it can be very effective, and several of the people I talked with would attest to its power.

Nevertheless, I cringe every time I hear it. It represents a change in how people who believe in a personal God perceive of God's behavior toward humanity: The old, wrathful God who struck people down with the whim of a tyrant has been replaced by a careful disciplinarian who won't hurt you any more than necessary for your own good. But I still don't like the premises on which the sentence rests: that illness happens in accord with a divine plan, and that you should never feel overwhelmed by it because it is always geared to your natural capacity. If you don't handle it well, it's your own fault. No longer punishment for sin, illness has become a test of endurance, and failure is reprehensible. Isn't that punishment, after all?

To my thinking, this proverb is too glib an answer to the profound questions that a lengthy experience of illness raises: Does illness ever bring suffering that simply cannot be handled by anyone? Is there any cosmic reason for illness to be so unrelenting? If there is a God, does God have any responsibility for illness? Is there any good to be derived from being chronically ill? When "Why me?" proves unanswerable, these are the questions that remain.

The Will to Live

My conversations with others who are chronically ill have left me with an age-old lesson freshly learned: No matter how fragile the human body, the human spirit can take just about anything. The lesson is reinforced every day in public accounts of lives disrupted by calamities that defy comprehension: torture, genocide, earthquakes that wipe out whole towns. Yet the human spirit does not thrive as well on continuing deprivation, like that associated with severe poverty or abusive family relationships. In both kinds of situations, however, there are people whose wills are quickly broken, never to recover, while others come through seemingly strengthened, to be awarded the title "survivor." What makes the difference? Students of human nature have speculated over and over about this, ever since the Neanderthals or somebody first coined the sentence that starts, "There are two kinds of people in the world . . ." The answer probably depends a great deal on circumstance, coincidence, accident, but the question still matters to all of us who feel ourselves afflicted. We can either succumb or survive, and we need to know what survival requires.

Popular mythology offers some answers, personified in the figure of the one-legged marathon runner that I have already taken exception to. The qualities this folk hero displays are physical stamina, stoicism, defiance of limitations, and single-minded commitment to a public display of such qualities. I have no quarrel with runners who lose a leg and decide to do whatever it takes to keep on running, just because they enjoy it so much. It is the exaltation of this behavior to Moral Example that bothers me.

Likewise, using the euphemism "challenged" to refer to people with physical disabilities surely makes illness a test of character. It's as if a line has been added to an old joke: A man who has had all his fingers broken asks the doctor, "Will I be able to play the violin?" "Oh yes," the doctor assures him. "That's funny," the man says, "I never could before." "Well, you'd better learn now!" the doctor orders. As unfair as it is, this image does appeal to many of the chronically ill, for understandable reasons. If you really believe there are two kinds of people in the world, you want to cast your lot with the ones identified as winners.

The winners I have met do not fit this image, however. Some of them look physically frail. They feel pain and they complain about it. They acknowledge their limits and live within them, like it or not. They live life in ordinary, unheralded ways, their minds occupied by work, children, dirty laundry, passing thunderstorms, the television news, and great existential questions. What qualifies them as winners is a demonstrated capacity to come through one ordeal after another with their will to live intact. In fact, the world is not divided into winners and losers, survivors and those who succumb. Chronic illness gives plenty of proof of that. Over any one lifetime of illness, there are moments of courage and moments of cowardice, moments of determination and moments of despair, moments of glory and moments of humiliation. That any of us survive these ups and downs is a miracle—a miracle that happens many times a day.

Strengthened Character

The people I talked with seem to attribute their survival, first of all, to facets of their individual characters that have been strengthened by life experience. "I asked the doctor," says Lorraine Czerny, "'Why do you suppose I made it? Is it because I'm a stubborn Czech?' There's a will to live that's very strong." Being single, she thinks, has firmed up that will. "When you're single, you have to do it on your own. The only person you can rely on is yourself. Other people can help you or sort of build up your morale, but it comes down to: It's you." A rigorous physical discipline keeps Duane Barber going and gives him a confidence in his self-control that is quite unusual: "I think I'm indestructible. It's silly, but that's the way I feel. Sometimes I feel so strong that that door could fall over and hit me and it wouldn't bother me." Phyllis Mueller draws on an inner core of strength that has been with her since childhood:

> The more I talk today, the more I look back and realize, I was really kind of a bullheaded kid. I just refused to look at limitations, I guess. I wasn't going to sit down and never have any fun. I always questioned authority, too. I attribute where I am today to that rebellious streak, to my refusal to look at the great authority and say, "Yes, you know best."

A healthy skepticism is to be highly recommended. Trusting in the truth and authenticity of your own experiences, as Phyllis does, strengthens your will far more than adopting without question the conventions that society imposes on sick people. Public rebelliousness in league with a private tranquility may be the ideal. Don Welke credits his survival to the fact that he doesn't "get shook up about these things." "I'll make it home. Somehow, I'll make it home," he says.

A sense of humor is, of course, invaluable. Gloria Murphy's is the kind that flaunts her illness. She laughs about her sons decorating her wheelchair for special occasions and racing her through shopping centers. Phyllis Mueller has a special talent for self-irony that sees her through. When her doctor warned her that a new medication might make her "squirrelly," she said, "Well, who would know?" I can trust a whimsical sense of the absurd to kick in when things get too ponderous.

When these internal resources flag, other sources of support seem to turn up. Many people describe how the moral support offered by friends makes the difference between surviving and succumbing. Where family is close and the relationships firm, family members are the most immediate source of comfort. Peggy Evans has certainly found this to be true. "One resource was given to me by my family. I don't even need to ask for it or look for it—it is there, more supportive than I knew, as long as they understand what is happening." Peggy goes on to say:

> And the other is faith. It has been very interesting to me that as the busyness of the temporal world shrinks and is not in my life so much, that the world of God is more in my life. My world is no smaller. It hasn't shrunk. There's just more room in it for God. Faith seems to be there when I need it. It is just there and I know it is there.

More Faith Than Religion

The combination family and faith was frequently cited by the people I interviewed as the best guarantee of psychological survival. Many people see faith taking a larger role when other resources fall short. Such is the case with Sandra Stieglitz, who lives in near isolation to protect her health:

> Faith plays a tremendous part. You know the saying, "There are no atheists in foxholes." My religion, my faith, was always very vague, and the sicker I got the more I turned to God. Because of some near-death experiences I've had, it has slowly evolved into something more and more important: more faith than religion.

More faith than religion. The distinction is important. Among the people I talked with, those who readily stated a religious preference were no better equipped for chronic illness than those who didn't. Membership in a religious institution and the devout practice of that institution's rituals do not promise survival, nor does lack of belief spell doom. I know plenty of optimistic, strong-willed atheists and agnostics who handle misfortune quite well. I certainly do not have the evidence to claim that the "foxhole" of chronic illness breeds believers, yet nearly everyone in my group of interviewees expressed belief in some cosmic center that gives coherence to life and is a source of strength when life is difficult. For some, it is an inherited religious creed central to their upbringing. For others, it is a conviction born of experience with illness itself. Some talked with ease in the vocabulary of their religions. Others borrowed terms from Jungian psychology or the Twelve Steps to describe their faith. For several, this was an awkward topic to discuss, because their faith is very privately held. This group of people does not, of course, reflect the broad religious diversity in the United States, but neither do they have a uniform understanding of what God is or how God works in the world.

Sandra Stieglitz identifies her religion as Jewish and her faith as nondenominational. A solitary descent into the depths of illness leads many of us who are spiritually inclined to focus on a cosmic power or first principle or ground of being that is not limited by religious doctrine but transcends all our efforts to name it and define it. Faith in this unnameable thing is "just there," as Peggy Evans attests. Sandra's illness keeps her at home, unable to participate in public worship. Peggy's mobility is often limited, too. They each have private rituals they can follow to sustain their faith, but Peggy has found, to her surprise, that her faith is not dependent on them. Even though she rarely prays or reads the Bible, she feels connected to that divine essence. It seems that the God who "surpasses all understanding," to borrow the vocabulary of my religion, becomes a more palpable presence in the lives of many people who are chronically ill, regardless of their religious allegiances.

Despite our different creeds, we who survive on faith seem to share a belief that we will endure even if our worst fears come true because there is a guiding force beyond ourselves to see us through. Also, we believe that enduring will be worth the pain because life itself has purpose. In the middle of my divorce, a woman divorced just two years before passed on a bit of wisdom she had been given by an elderly neighbor: "Things works out, honey." In Christian Scripture, it is stated by the apostle Paul as, "We know that all things work together for good to them that love God, to them who are called according to God's purpose." I prefer the clarity, simple conviction, and universality of "Things works out."

The Tune without the Words

What Paul is describing in the eighth chapter of Romans, where the passage quoted appears, is a concept called "hope." If the difference between surviving and succumbing—not physically, but psychologically and spiritually, can be described in one word, "hope" is surely it. But what is hope and where do you get it? Again, I call on my favorite source of scripture, Emily Dickinson:

> "Hope" is the thing with feathers—
> That perches in the soul—
> And sings the tune without the words—
> And never stops—at all—

Sometimes the clamor of the world around you or your own cries of pain drown out the tune, but that doesn't mean the feathered thing has stopped singing. Sometimes you have to strain very hard to hear it.

In my first year of college, newly exposed to classical music, I had a terrible time identifying pieces that sounded familiar and recalling the melodies of compositions I *would* recognize if I heard them played. Then a dorm-mate taught me to sing, "This is the symphony that Schubert wrote and never finished." The opening of Beethoven's Fifth Symphony is "Dot, dot, dot, daaash," Morse code for the letter V, the Roman numeral for five. My problem, I realized, is that tunes without words escape me. For me, then, religious faith works like a mnemonic device. When I no longer hear the sound of hope, words like "God," "grace," and "forever" help me recall the tune. But that being perched in the soul keeps on singing, regardless of our attempts to name it. It is significant that Emily Dickinson, too, has put "hope" in quotation marks. Robert O'Shea, at ease with religious terminology himself, suggests that the names we use are not what matters most: "Call it luck or call it grace, the resources have always been there."

Setting Words to the Tune

Setting words to the tune seems to mean more to the chronically ill than the simple acceptance of denominational doctrine. Illness itself brings a fresh encounter with the questions that doctrine tries to answer. One of the big ones for people who suffer loss of bodily functions and risk early death is, "What happens to us after death?" There is, not surprisingly, much interest in published accounts of people who have been revived at the last minute and report seeing a bright light or hearing voices or traveling through tunnels. For some, a religious conviction that there is life after death has been important in facing the crises that come with illness. Don Welke says that is what settles his nerves before surgery. Gloria Murphy has been helped by believing that "life is a journey and illness is part of my journey and the outcome will be everlasting life." Phyllis Mueller wants to believe that she will be rewarded later for the pain she is suffering now. "I ain't going through this for nothing!" she says. Donna Schneider, currently quite fearful of dying from her illness, wonders whether people who believe in personal rewards in a hereafter have an easier time subduing such fears:

> I have kind of mixed emotions, because Judaism differs from the other religions in the fact that my life is here, now, today. I don't have too much to look forward to when I go. My reward is here and now for living a good life here and now. My memory will always be perpetuated. That part of

us never dies. It's kept alive with the kaddish prayer. The purpose of it is to keep you alive in others' memories. But I'm not sitting out there and listening to what's going on. Dust returns to dust. Maybe for another religion it's easier to be more accepting.

But being raised on the Protestant Sunday school notion of celestial bliss does not turn death into a welcome rite of passage complete with awards ceremony. I myself have thought of that heaven as a rather dreary place. Once I had a dream about going there. It was like a huge cocktail party, and I found myself standing around trying to make small talk with Ralph Waldo Emerson. Now that we could see concretely what transcendence meant, there was no longer any point in talking about it. People who do not believe in individual immortality do not necessarily fear death. One reader tells me that he is not troubled by death because it *is* a physical reality, a truth, and "truth is the best we can hope for." At sixty-six, with three critical heart operations behind her, Lorraine Czerny is still seeking answers to the question "What happens to us after death?" Sunday mornings she attends services at a mainstream Protestant church, but she has also spent a few weekends meditating at a Catholic retreat center, and she reads popular books about Eastern religions, in an effort to hone her personal faith:

> Religion really is basically within yourself. The church is nice—the music in the Sunday service is lovely—and it sort of brings you to a place where you realize why all this is going on. When I had my first heart surgery, I met two other women who both had young children. I went to visit them a couple of times afterwards. But they died, leaving those children, and it made me feel a little guilty. A friend of mine recommended Edgar Cayce's book, so I read that. That gave me some idea that satisfied a hurt or a hunger to know why those women died and I lived. It gave me an answer that the

regular church couldn't give me. The answer was that through karma they were taken away. They had finished this particular portion on earth and they were fulfilling their karma by dying early, and I still was going through living out my karma in this life. You go through certain stages to reach perfection. It's sort of weird. But it worked for me. It didn't make me antichurch. It really hit chords and really made sense. I suppose if I read it before I had surgery I would have thought it was kooky.

Searching for explanations that "hit chords" in harmony with the tune you hear within seems to be a common response to chronic illness, though none of the people I talked with had ranged very far afield. For most, it means selecting among religious tenets and practices that are at least compatible with their own traditions and reshaping them to suit the spiritual needs that illness arouses. For me, this means seeking a divine female presence that feels more healing to me, as a woman, than the image of God as father that dominates Christian tradition, and looking back to my ancestry, Old Norse mythology, for images and values that resonate. Continuity with the past can also foster hope. "Even though I'm not a particularly observant Jew," one reader writes, "I do derive a great deal of strength from being part of the Jewish People." Rosemary McKuen has searched earnestly for the most fitting way to express her faith. Raised Catholic and now a student at a liberal Protestant seminary, she started attending a charismatic Christian church during the worst phase of her illness:

I really needed the emotions, I guess. When I speak of my relationship with Christ during my sickness, I was in a very companionable state. I would write everything I felt in prayers. I'm not exactly sure now about that. My relationship with Christ is different now. Then God was my brother, my father—all the people I didn't have around me to be close to, to communicate with. I've come to feel a little more distance. I still have that same love, but I also have a sense of being responsible for working things out intellectually, too.

Bill Gordon sustains his hope by attending somewhat revivalist seminars on personal motivation, but he describes this as a temporary, makeshift approach necessitated by the illness, not as a permanent change in the nature of his religious belief:

> Some of the things are just a little bit too positivistic for me, but still I can just take from it what I want and leave what I don't want. I still pooh-pooh this sort of thing to a certain extent, but I need it, damn it! I'm a depressed person. So whatever I can get to help me become a little more fired up on life, I'm going to take that. About where I normally fit in is with what goes on at my church, which is positive, too, and doesn't go overboard. That's where I want to be, but to get there I've got to go somewhere else and be around people who are a little more rah-rah.

Out of her reading and her life experience, Phyllis Mueller has molded for herself what she laughingly calls "a kind of Abraham Maslow religion," after an influential psychologist:

> All I think the requirements are anymore are, number one, don't hurt anyone else knowingly, have a good social conscience, and two, be the best you can be. You are here for a prescribed amount of time, and don't waste that. Be the best you can be, heighten your awareness, learn all you can, cultivate this neat person.

Faith Communities

This outlook has certainly helped Phyllis survive a life of pain and anxiety, but she would like her religion to live up to the requirements of her faith, and thinking it deficient leaves her feeling both sad and angry. She goes to mass nearly every Sunday, wanting the nurturance that a worship service offers, but she feels little solace in the Catholic Church, which, she says, is "kind of messing up God for me." Her disillusionment is due, in part, to turmoil about the church's stance on social issues, but also largely to what she sees as the institution's failure either to help her come to terms with her illness or to comfort her in her suffering.

> I don't think being sick has brought me anything by way of religion. Normally, from what I hear, it's "I've found God," or "I was born again." Well, I'm still waiting. I feel angry sometimes with God. I think, he's deaf, you know? I think I believe in God, but there's another element in there. I'm confused about the church's role in all this. The few priests that I knew I thought to be rather self-centered individuals, and I'm not into hearing a stock sermon on how I should feel and how I should possibly even pray and offer this up. Some of the younger ones today are very good. A lot of them have had a lot of psychology and they see this all differently. But the older priests? I wouldn't bother. I would just call a good friend, who could probably give me just as much insight really, and more support.

Bill Gordon found himself not only confused and angry, but fearful: "I sometimes get the feeling that I'm going to be punished because I get so angry at God for letting this happen." In contrast to Phyllis, he did seek advice from several different ministers. Their willingness to talk through the questions, whether they had firm answers or not, brought him some relief. Not everyone expects a discourse in theology, however. Donna Schneider's ambivalence about the role of religion in her life is traceable in part to feeling neglected by her rabbi, who never called to ask how a diagnostic operation he knew she was having had turned out. What may be forgetfulness or a simple breach of etiquette takes on greater dimensions when the offended party is in spiritual need.

Each of these people sees the clergy as the legitimate interpreters of the faith, the ones who control access to the resources that the religious tradition provides. It is easy, then, to feel shut out when their help and concern are not forthcoming. It was this feeling that prompted Gloria Murphy and several others to form a lay ministry group to work with parishioners in personal crisis. Hospital chaplains can, of course, offer both wise counsel and consolation because of their familiarity with illness and their daily experience with spirit-boggling problems. Nevertheless, there is something symbolically significant about attention from your "own" clergy. I remember a day when I was sitting in my hospital bed staring at my first tray of real food and trembling with fear that eating it would upset my liver function again. In walked the senior pastor from my church. I should say not "walked" but "wafted," because with him came an aura of calm that set my trembling to rest. He may have been trembling for his own reasons, wondering what he was possibly going to say to me, but he didn't need to say anything. He carried with him the invisible baggage of a long tradition of faith and hope, and his presence was a reminder that I belong to a caring community of people who share a common outlook on human nature and the value of life and who stand by each other in crises.

In the past five to ten years, religious institutions have begun paying more deliberate attention to the common needs of the chronically ill and the disabled rather than responding to members' illnesses as isolated crises. In part, this may be a response to the shortcomings of the health care industry, and in part the result of observing the unity of physical health and spiritual health in the religions of recent immigrants. I have been invited to participate in services of healing prayer and to talk to congregational committees charged with designing special programs. These might include one-day workshops, adult education classes, and ongoing support groups for people facing illness. A few houses of worship even employ nurses who check on homebound members on behalf of the congregation—a practical synthesis of body and spirit. For Christians, the emphasis in the Gospels on Christ as healer poses a challenge that is met with Oral Roberts–style faith healing on one end of the spectrum and, on the other, scholarly assurances that rational explanations can be found for what only *appear* to be miracles. I am holding out for something in between: subtle miracles, maybe.

A God Who Falls Short

No matter where or on what day of the week you look toward divinity, there is always a great risk in setting words like "God" to the tune that plays in your soul. God comes alive and must be called to account for your suffering. Sandra Stieglitz finds herself caught in a paradox: The more she believes in God, the more she worries that God might fall short of her expectations:

> The thing I've got to say to myself, I guess, is God has gotten me this far. There's never been anything I couldn't handle somehow. I guess I just have to trust that it's going to work out. In the back of my mind, I think, I do believe in the existence of God, but there have been concentration camps in this world. There have been horrible atrocities. I really don't know how much I can count on God. The terrifying thing is, I have learned how much the body can endure, and how much pain we can be in and still live.

This terrifying thing Sandra has learned is that belief in God, even though it may be your ultimate resource for living with illness, does not spare you from pain. If God exists and God is good and all-powerful, why is there such suffering in the world? How stunned I was that lesson-packed first year of college to find that I had not invented this problem. It already had a name, "The Ontological Question." As a fourteen-year-old confirmand memorizing Luther's Small Catechism, I had struggled over the admonition, "We should fear and love God . . ." How could we fear and love someone simultaneously? I've learned since that every act of loving brings with it the fear of abandonment. It's no different at the cosmic level. Loving God as the source of hope means, quite naturally, fearing that God will abandon you to hopeless suffering.

Being sick frequently and interminably personalizes the ontological question and keeps it active: How can I, why should I, believe in a God who will not heal me, no matter how fervently I pray? If God loves me, why does God leave me in such misery? The underlying question is not so much "Why me?" as "Why does this happen at all?" It is often expected that a life crisis like illness will provide definitive answers. At the least, there should be a reward for suffering well, like the one Phyllis suggests: an unmistakable invitation into God's protection, which some Christians call being "born again." If illness itself doesn't do it, then recovery certainly should bring a spiritual renewal. Bill Gordon was surprised to find that it hasn't worked that way for him now that his depression is under control. "You'd think that I'd be so grateful after having my health problems solved that I'd get down on my knees and pray every night, but I don't. I think it's because it's not really over yet. I've still got so much to do to get back to where I was." Given the nature of chronic illness, there is no precise moment at which you can say, "Thank God, that's over." Al Keski, a devout Protestant who sees his faith slipping as his health deteriorates, talks about "losing ground." Ordinarily a football term, it takes on new significance in a religious context: Faced with more suffering and no satisfactory explanations for it, you run the risk of losing your very "ground of being." What if the feathered thing in the soul just plain flies away?

While the unrelenting pain and despair of chronic illness can shake the very foundations of faith, some people do become more actively religious at times when their personal hold on God is tenuous. My return to church was by no means a "born again" experience. I simply decided to work harder at maintaining a relationship with God that had never been severed but had become a little strained through neglect. When I first got sick and was struggling with the meaning of it all, I had nowhere to turn. I had left the Lutheran Church as a teenager, alienated, in part, by an uncompassionate minister who offered rigid, simplistic solutions for complicated life crises and social problems. It was illness that finally drove me back to church at age thirty—Presbyterian this time—wanting some formal sustenance for the faith that had, nevertheless, stayed alive in a religious vacuum. I just needed help staying on key as I sang along with "hope." Ironically, it was after I was well into an active church membership, and sick again, that I experienced my worst "dark night of the soul." The ontological question burned with the same intensity as my fever. Prior to this, I thought I had found an answer to it: that God had afflicted me and then spared me, again and again, in order to keep me working steadily toward some ideal, fulfilling some destiny that was uniquely mine—only I hadn't been told what it was. I prayed and prayed, always the same prayer in essence: Make me well. It went unanswered. Instead of getting angry at God, I felt unworthy of better treatment. I thought that I must have failed to carry out my half of this undefined bargain and did not qualify for renewal of my lease on life. But thinking that way left me feeling blasphemous. I could not believe in a God so vindictive as to make me guess my destiny and then punish me if I guessed wrong.

To free myself from the ontological dilemma, I had to question its assumptions: "Does God exist? Is God good? Is God all-powerful?" About this same time, the sermons I was hearing and the books I was reading were also questioning God's omnipotence. It was consoling, for example, to be told that God's silence was only a sign that God was still weighing options and figuring out how to answer my prayers without throwing the whole universe into chaos. When people asked why God allows nuclear weapons, the most reasonable answer was that stopping the arms race is in *our* power—God is not responsible for nuclear war. Into this new theological atmosphere came Rabbi Harold Kushner's best-seller, *When Bad Things Happen to Good People*, which several of the people I interviewed had also read. The message that affliction is not God's will, but that evil befalls people at random, without regard to their own behavior or moral condition, was liberating to those who wondered what they had done to deserve illness. Reading that God's failure to heal illness was due to God's incapacity to eradicate evil rather than the sick one's unworthiness restored some lost self-esteem. The book's reception across the religious spectrum suggests that it did much to nourish that basic core of hope. Yet, as much as I concurred in the book's view of affliction, I finished it feeling a bit bereft. For one thing, Kushner had rejected the image of the beautiful tapestry being woven with our lives, its pattern still visible only to God. I rather liked that one and had frequently used it to comfort myself: even if suffering seemed meaningless, some cosmic good might yet be revealed. As hard as I had worked in my own life to reconcile the mysteries of religious faith with the "knowns" of science, I was not ready to give up on a divine manipulation of nature in my own case. It wasn't enough to be told that what God offered me was strength—not at a time when I had so little of it. The Kushner book left me still pondering the questions it raised: What's God for, then? What good is an impotent God? And what can such a God possibly offer in times of illness?

God Our Fellow Sufferer

My life has been full of quiet epiphanic moments in which I have been certain of God's existence and God's mercy. One such happened, appropriately enough, at church, which is not where they usually take place. It was a noontime service on Good Friday, and we were singing the beautiful, poignant hymn that is a recurring motif in J. S. Bach's *Passion According to St. Matthew*: "O Sacred Head, Now Wounded." When we came to the line, "Mine, mine was the transgression, but thine the deadly pain," I started to cry uncontrollably—not voluble sobbing, but a steady flow of tears. The words "deadly pain" had caught me and held me. "I know what that is," I thought. The deadly pain is mine, too. I was overwhelmed as never before with memories of all the pain I have ever suffered, and I realized, as if for the first time, how much of my life that pain has claimed. Yet, at the same time, I felt buoyed up, even "ecstatic" in the religious sense of the word. There was something wondrous about being able to focus on the pain and let the emotions run. I wondered if this was what medieval mystics meant when they claimed to have experienced Christ's passion. Certainly, this was something more than an annual, ritualized sorrow over the crucifixion.

There was an organ postlude after the service, so I could sit unobtrusively, dabbing at my eyes with the few shreds of Kleenex I had dug out of my purse, while others left the sanctuary. Religious ecstasy would create quite a spectacle at my decorous church. When I finally walked out, I found a friend waiting for me. This friend resists the central Christian doctrine that Jesus died for our sins. She does not appreciate martyrdom, especially not if it is preordained by a God who could come up with a kinder alternative. When I explained briefly what had happened, she asked rhetorically, "And what's your trangression?" It surprised me to realize how little that question mattered. This was not a case of "Why me?" Though we were in the habit of long, rambling theological discussions, we put this one aside and walked out into bright sunshine, talking about ordinary things. I couldn't have made any more sense of this experience just then.

Reflecting on it later, I learned what this Good Friday had given me. There were two insights of great value. The first: how wonderful it is that human beings have the capacity to forget. I knew that if I had to carry with me always the cumulative memory of pain, it would be overwhelming and impossible to endure. I thought of people I had talked with who found fault with themselves for practicing "denial." I remembered Louise Taylor's cynical tone of voice when she described her response to a flare-up of multiple sclerosis: "When it went away, I swept it under the rug: one more experience that didn't really happen and wasn't too bad, anyway." How fortunate for Louise, I thought, that she can do that. So often, we are reminded of the importance of remembering: of learning from the past, of recalling injustice to fire zeal, of proclaiming our heritage. But the capacity to forget is also a gift to be grateful for. Our survival depends on it.

The second insight was nothing less than an answer to the troubling questions, What's God for, then, if God is not all-powerful? What responsibility does God have for illness? The answer that came to me was Christian in origin, because it is the tradition in which my own spirituality is rooted and so its imagery and vocabulary are familiar. On that Good Friday, the central Christian symbol of suffering, the crucifixion of Christ, took on deeper meaning for me. "Jesus died for our sins" was transformed into "Jesus died because there is sin," with "sin" understood to mean not human beings' individual offenses but evil that exists in the world despite God's will to destroy it—evil that we each partake of in grand and petty ways. The message of the crucifixion is that God cannot spare us from pain, but loves us enough to want to know our suffering firsthand, to know how to comfort us. Jesus' death on the cross was not a payment for human misdeeds, staged in a gruesome way that would shame us into confessing so that we might be given another chance. It was an entirely merciful choice to side with humanity against inconquerable evil. It was a horridly painful human death, not eased by divine miracles. Even Christ could not be stoical about suffering. He prayed for a last-minute escape. He begged for water when he felt dehydrated. He moaned. I do not agree with theologians who say that he was "merely" fulfilling prophecy by quoting the twenty-second Psalm when he cried, "My God, my God, why hast thou forsaken me?" That cry of rage and abandonment, no matter where its formulation came from, is the most compelling evidence that Jesus felt pain. This particular epiphany left me with the comforting conviction that God is with me in the worst of it, knows my pain, and willingly bears it. There could be a nicer ending to the Jesus story, but I am grateful for this one. God as Fellow Sufferer does far more to sustain me than the Almighty Lord and Master. And there is the Resurrection, after all, for those who want divine intervention. For me, the Resurrection keeps on happening. It is the newly strengthened hope that sings out as euphoria when the pain is over.

By no means do I offer the crucifixion and my understanding of it as the only or the most nearly complete answer to the questions about God's responsibility for illness. All religions presumably have ways to account for personal suffering. In times of illness, people in search of explanations turn to the ones their own traditions offer. Who believes what and how devoutly matters less here than how each of us selects and reshapes the religious tenets available to us to make sense of illness and mold a workable faith. In describing that process in my own life, I wish I could be certain of offering "something for everybody," but I know that is impossible. There is no language in which to talk neutrally about religious faith. Even the word "God" carries specific connotations and cannot be used as a general term for the metaphysical aspects of existence. I offer my case as an illustration only, to show that illness and the troubling questions it raises can and do challenge, reform, and even enrich religious belief, and that this renewed faith, in turn, aids endurance. Some readers may see resemblances to their own journeys of faith. Others will feel as though they are reading a foreign language. Limited though this interpretation of suffering may be, my own story of illness would not be complete without it. Faith has been critical to my survival.

My Good Friday epiphany was hardly a unique moment of truth. I could have arrived at the same interpretation of the crucifixion—but without the indelible impact—by singing certain Lenten selections in the Presbyterian hymnal or reading any of various theological works. One that I have read since is entitled simply *Suffering*, by the German Lutheran theologian Dorothee Soelle, whose work on that topic I first encountered in Harold Kushner's book. Soelle writes:

> Is it necessary for this symbol of suffering, of failure, of dying, to stand at the midpoint of the Christian religion? Has not

an overemphasis on the cross in theology and piety resulted in the fact that a "God who justifies misery" was and is worshipped in society?

. . . But the cross is neither a symbol expressing the relationship between God the Father and his Son nor a symbol of masochism which needs suffering in order to convince itself of love. It is above all a symbol of reality. Love does not "require" the cross, but *de facto* it ends up on the cross. . . . The cross is no theological invention but the world's answer, given a thousand times over, to attempts at liberation. Only for that reason are we able to recognize ourselves in Jesus' dying on the cross. . . .

. . . Love does not cause suffering or produce it, though it must necessarily seek confrontation, since its most important concern is not the avoidance of suffering but the liberation of people.

Life is imperfect. This is the most important lesson that chronic illness teaches. Life offers us both joy and suffering, and not always in balance. To have one, we must make our peace with the other. That is the reality we live, the reality we cannot gloss over or pretend away when we are sick.

God Accepts Imperfection

Soelle uses the word "love" interchangeably with "God." In the course of the interviews, I learned what this can mean from a few people who believe firmly in a God who loves totally and unconditionally, who is love itself. Gloria Murphy, for example, lives day by unpredictable day trusting in the mercy of a loving God:

Every morning I say a little prayer just offering this day in prayer. "Please accept where I'm at today, and I will accept whatever comes to me today, or help me to accept it." You may have noticed in the bathroom a poster that says, "There is nothing that will happen that you and I together can't handle." And that's getting old. It's been up there for years. I won't take it down. I also find that my faith is a very healing thing for me, because I know it's always there, it's a constant and it's not going to go away. I feel as though the Lord totally accepts me where I'm at. He accepts me if I'm happy and he accepts me if I'm sad, and that's okay. He's a merciful Lord. I don't think I've ever doubted that. Not ever.

The poster over Gloria's bathtub—the tub she fell into trying to pretend that multiple sclerosis did not limit her—is a meaningful restatement of the proverb "God never gives you more than you can handle." It converts God from the disciplinarian who metes out suffering into a steadfast and willing sharer of burdens: the divine Fellow Sufferer.

Gloria's understanding of God's unconditional love was not new to me, but hearing her say these words had a fresh impact. Even though I recoil at the feudal-sounding, exclusively masculine "Lord," the notion that "the Lord totally accepts me where I'm at" struck me as a great relief from many of the psychological burdens that chronic illness brings with it: shame about being imperfect, guilt about imposing on family and friends, embarrassment at not being able to contain fears and disappointments, humiliation at not being able to overcome physical limitations. I remembered a time when my husband read to me out of the Psalms as I lay on the couch feeling miserable. The message I heard then, too, was that God invites us all in, without qualification, to be sheltered and comforted. God does not inflict illness upon humanity, nor does God demand perfect achievement of those afflicted. A God whose name can also be Love cares for each of us as we are.

Conversations with Rosemary McKuen about her decision to enter the ministry have also reinforced this sense of an unconditionally loving God. "It is the love-against-all-odds nature of God which I feel called to share with others," Rosemary explains.

Illness has not been Rosemary's only source of suffering, and she has not always been so certain of God's loving presence in her life. As her vision of God has changed, her mode of prayer has changed with it, from an urgent "Help me" to a more patient "Lead me in the right direction." Likewise, I have dropped the "Make me well" that left me feeling like an unworthy beggar and replaced it with variations on the theme "Thank you for staying with me."

It was at first a surprise to hear that Peggy Evans, so firm in her faith, seldom prays at all. She herself is surprised at how easily her faith has been sustained: "I guess ultimately, when you just get down to the very basics of it, God is there and God accepts us and God's grace offers everything." Yet, there is something about Peggy's demeanor that can be described as "prayerful." It is a rapt attention to life and its meaning that is a kind of wordless prayer, an always open line of communication with God. As I think about how the nature of my faith has changed over the course of my illness, I am not really surprised by Peggy's admission. I rarely fold my hands and shut my eyes and compose the long monologues to God that qualified as prayers in my Sunday school. While I can't say that I pray constantly, as Paul advised the early Christians to do, I seem to be praying moment by moment, every time I think how fine life is, in spite of it all. It seems as if the pervasive consciousness of misfortune that I had the first years I was sick has given way to an appreciation of the overall value of my life.

Grace and Gratitude

There is a special word in the vocabulary of Christianity to describe God's rapt attention toward humanity: *grace*. It is a divine love and protection freely given, unsought, unearned, "just there." If I were to ask myself a question that I asked of the people I talked with, "What resources do you draw on to keep going?" my answer would be "Grace." It is an intangible, metaphysical answer, but it stands for some very real sources of support: There are close friends, truly "created in the image of God," who are willing to share in my suffering, plus a worshiping community that seems to care about my welfare through no merits of my own. In times of trouble, solutions have appeared "miraculously," which is only a slight exaggeration. These advantageous coincidences can be seen either as divine intervention or as a natural result of a growing attentiveness to life—a kind of divine guidance. Most amazing of all is a feeling of buoyancy that is barely describable. Just when I expect to be immobilized by pain or fear, I start to "float." It is grace that carries me along and keeps me from succumbing. Recently, a visual image has attached itself to this feeling of buoyancy. Sometimes I have sought it through meditation and other times it has appeared on its own. With my eyes shut, I begin to see a field of beautiful purple light, with concentric circles and winglike shapes moving toward the center, drawing me in. The circles and shapes are a soothing gray and seem to have a soft, downy texture. I like to think that what I am seeing is Emily Dickinson's "thing with feathers." But, see it or not, I know "hope" is there.

Freely bestowed as it is, grace does not require a response. Yet, it seems to invite one. The first is its linguistic offspring, gratitude. By contrast, illness makes you appreciate your better moments, and eventually, unless you are constitutionally sour and cynical, you become grateful. I have learned from Kathy Halvorson, who finds solace in the promise of each new day, to review the day at night and make note of all that has been good in it. Another friend selects one pleasant surprise from each day's events—one thing he could never have predicted when he woke up in the morning. This redeems even the seemingly dreary days and helps sustain hope.

An Unconditional Love of Life

In her book on suffering, Dorothee Soelle calls for a response to grace that goes beyond this celebration of life's best moments.

She suggests that if God loves us unconditionally, then we ought to love God unconditionally. If God stays by us and suffers with us, we ought to stay by God and love life even as we suffer. Interestingly, she calls this complete love of life "acceptance," the catchword for coming to terms with illness:

> The prerequisite for acceptance is a deeper love for reality, a love that avoids placing conditions on reality. Only when we stop making conditions that a person has to satisfy before we yield ourselves to him, only then do we love him. . . . The same thing is true of the relationship to reality, that is, of love for God. It cannot be made dependent on the fulfillment of certain conditions.

To love reality replete with suffering, you don't have to like illness one bit. Soelle makes very clear her opposition to the masochistic tendencies in Christian doctrine. You don't show your love for God by enjoying pain. In fact, her book is also a call to social action that could alleviate much of the suffering in the world.

As I have moved toward this notion of acceptance—from a preoccupation with illness to gratitude for all that is good in life to an unconditional love of life—I have also moved from sorrow and fear to a glossy-surfaced contentment to a true joy in living. The distinctions are very subtle and not always recognizable, and I am never really sure of staying put in any one state. I am beginning to see yet another transition: a progressive change in my attitude toward suffering, from *suffering indulgently*—feeling like the only one afflicted—to *suffering patiently*—practicing a stoical silence that sometimes even denies reality—to *suffering passionately*—honestly acknowledging pain and despair and expressing moral outrage at its necessity. Beyond that lies a fourth possibility, which I think of as *suffering the Passion*. To me, this means accepting the double truth that Christ's death symbolizes: Suffering is central to the human condition. It is not an aberration, not deviant, it simply is. And suffering can be endured, because there is a divine presence in the midst of it. With that acknowledged, I can even affirm my illness—a very private, personal suffering—as my own share in life's condition: not an aberration, not deviant, simply a way of life. As long as I can hear the voice of hope, the sign of God's ever-loving presence, my life need not be diminished by illness.

The question I asked most stubbornly for the first twenty years of my illness was, "What am I supposed to do with this, anyway?" Slowly the answer came. Just live it, pain and all, with attention and purpose, and it will bear its own rewards. I still remember and treasure a scene in the movie *Chariots of Fire* in which the Scottish hero Eric Liddell is upbraided by his sister for postponing their long-planned mission to China in order to run in the Olympics. To justify his decision, he says, "I believe that God made me for a purpose, but he also made me fast, and when I run, I feel God's pleasure." I held onto "feeling God's pleasure" as the key to my vocation—the destiny that I once presumed God was commanding me to fulfill by allowing this cycle of illness and recovery to continue. That deep feeling of pleasure that comes with doing something you feel called to do, that suits your talents well, and is in accord with your conscience may be destiny itself. Learning to feel God's pain has made me much more attuned to God's pleasure.

Happy and Still Sick

Whether or not religious belief is an element in your psychological survival, there is plenty of good to come from accepting reality without condition and living life intently, despite being chronically ill. Phyllis Mueller remembers just when her orientation changed: "The first day I ever realized you could be happy and still sick was a real red-letter day. I think that was the beginning of some kind of recovery for me emotionally." Experiencing chronic illness can alter your perspective on all that life offers and call your priorities into question. Many people I spoke with gave examples of this. For Susan Alm, it is finding a kind of cosmic pleasure in small pleasures, which has begun to soothe her frustration about not achieving her original career goals:

> One of the things that has helped me is a very small comment from our pastor who has encouraged me to get more involved in some things in our church. They were all things that I would love to do but have never considered important: domestic things like arranging flowers and making things beautiful. His comment was that one of the main ways we come to know God and to understand him is through beauty. It just struck me that nobody had ever told me that before. There is a way in which you find a sense of spiritual well-being in creating a beautiful environment in which to live, or for people to grow up in, or things to look at. That is an important thing to do in life, and I had never thought about it that way before.

Robert O'Shea drew up a model for how the change in priorities works: a "ladder of values":

> I think that the lower scale is property. It is very, very natural to people to want to amass things—not bad or greedily, but just comforts which we need. I think the second value is sex, the ability to express what it is to be a woman, to be a man. It's not just sexual action, but the total female identity, the total male, and I think that is a real value. I think the next value is life—not just living, but creating: the quality of life, having direction, purpose, awareness, all those things that make our life worth living. Philosophically, it would take another big jump to the next value: truth, meaning, intellectual inquisitiveness, all those things that qualify us to be thinking, reasoning people. At the top of the scale is that very elusive word called "conscience"—to live according to those principles and values that you think are good. Now what happens if you're ill but still able to work and go about your life is that a lot of things change. All of a sudden what has

just been kind of a philosophical ladder, you begin to find yourself climbing up a little bit, and you say, "Well, do I really need that car? Is it important that I should worry about that mortgage, because it's taking a lot of energy that I don't have?" And so somehow you're not as conscious of, umm, "Miller time" as you used to be, you know? You still know the value of all those things, but you're not going to make a mortgage drive you into the grave, because you know that there's something out there much more significant.

Freedom from the Curse of Perfectionism

"Miller time," the image Robert groped for, is a slogan in a beer advertisement and symbolizes the carefree state of satisfaction that American commercial culture passes off as true happiness. Chronic illness, unless denied, defied, and overcome, disqualifies you for such untroubled happiness. Yet, as I watch some of my peers, caught up at midlife in "Miller time" but still feeling unfulfilled, I can't help but wish a good chronic illness on them. Lived fully, the experience of illness can free you from the curse of perfectionism that makes happiness conditional on having everything just right. Bill Gordon learned that his lifelong and much rewarded tendency to push himself until he had done things perfectly was actually hazardous to his health. The inevitable failures fed his depression. Like so many of us, he has had to face his shortcomings and try to forgive himself for them. Perfectionist tendencies show up often as a desire for complete control over the course of life, which is impossible to maintain when your body seems to be disobeying the laws of nature. Learning to let go and take life as it comes is one of the benefits chronic illness offers. This change in perspective leads to a happiness that is not diminished by the imperfections of the world around you. As Robert O'Shea put it, "A cold cup of coffee isn't the problem that it used to be."

Smug as it sounds, many people can testify, "I am a better person for this." Esther Green says that knowing how it feels to live in a malfunctioning body has made her more tolerant of other people's behavior:

> I think I can look at other people in a different way instead of criticizing them. Everybody has got a reason for what they do. I really don't think a person who's sick can be critical. There might be times, you know, when people would rather not be around me because of my illness, so I really can't be critical.

Phyllis Mueller has gone through a similar change:

> I am a much more compassionate person than I used to be. I really was very judgmental of people. I was extremely introspective and zeroed in on my problem: look at poor me. I kind of like who I'm becoming. I'd like to be this person *without* the pain, but on the other hand, if I didn't have the pain, I wonder if I would have become this person.

Suffering with Others

"Compassion," usually regarded as a kind of moral achievement, is one of the "luckiest" or most "gracious" consequences of living with illness. The prefix *com-* in Latin means "with" and adds a dimension to suffering that turns it from a private to a shared experience. The ability to "suffer with," to identify with others' suffering enough to care for them truly, benefits the one showing compassion as well as the one being treated compassionately. As Phyllis indicates, compassion takes the focus off "poor me," the solitary victim of illness, and highlights the commonality of suffering, thus breaking the isolation. Being the frequent recipient of others' care gives you the chance to learn how best to care for others.

Compassion is not just given and received, it is shared. Sharing in others' suffering makes your own less shameful. It allows you to be more vulnerable, to expose your suffering to others who want to be compassionate. Gloria Murphy says, "I had always been a listener. I had never, ever been someone who shared myself too much before MS. But now I enjoy sharing myself, and I do think it helps others." Compassion inspires you to seek solutions for suffering, or at least ways to ease it. Though there are times when illness, at its worst, isolates you from the world, in the long run it can engage you in life's purpose. Suffering together with others sustains the shared hope that humanity will endure. Through the gift of compassion, the experience of chronic illness offers protection against apathy, an indifference toward life that means, literally, "not suffering."

None of this philosophizing is intended to suggest that chronic illness is a blessing or that it leads to a privileged state of exaltation. Life can be lived fully and unconditionally without such provocation. Being strong of faith and hoping fervently do not ensure a spiritual glory that transcends the physical symptoms of illness. Loving beauty will not cure the inflammation in Susan Alm's joints. Ordination will not restore Rosemary McKuen's missing intestine. Nor does reciting Emily Dickinson poems stave off liver malfunction. A whole chorus of people swathed in silver linings would still join with Phyllis Mueller in saying, "I'd like to be this person *without* the pain." I remember my incredulity when I read that the fourteenth-century English mystic Julian of Norwich had prayed for a bodily sickness so that she might know Christ's Passion. "You can have mine," I said aloud. But I understand completely how, given that sickness, she could arrive at a faith that proclaims, "All will be well, and every kind of thing will be well." Somehow, "things works out" in a forcibly examined life judged to be worth living.

This chapter opened with "God never gives you more than you can handle," a proverbial statement that rankles me. Another pet peeve is "There but for the grace of God go I." It expresses pity rather than sympathy and does it from a comfortable and uncomprehending distance from which the value of the other's life cannot be discerned. Often, we who are chronically ill are urged to rely on the sentiment this proverb contains—to ease our own suffering by comparing ourselves with others who have it worse, a habit that betrays a lack of compassion. There is only one thing I can say in response to such thinking. The experience of chronic illness, examined through my religious faith, has led me to a different observation altogether:

"Here, with the grace of God, I am."

Chapter
13

Facing the Future

"What was it Scarlett O'Hara said? 'I'll think about that tomorrow.'"

Robert O'Shea, who had heart disease, died of a heart attack at fifty-three. Death came quickly, without warning, in a period of apparent good health. It was, for me, a sobering reminder that those "interviewees" are real people with fates that continue to change, for better and for worse, apart from their more static presence in this book. Writing about them does not put their lives on hold. His death also brought the grim realization that a wise and accepting outlook on illness does not make the illness itself less perilous. Robert's heart disease had led him to examine his most deeply held values and to make significant changes in the way he acted on them. He had started a new career and committed himself to marriage after many years alone. Yet, neither that nor his exuberant optimism nor his strong religious faith won him time to live out his renovated life.

Robert's heart disease (like Caroli's disease, lupus, and diabetes) was never regarded as a "terminal" illness, but only as "potentially life-threatening." The difference between the two is one of time and degree of predictability. The terminally ill are "given," as the expression goes, a number of months to live and, presumably, to tie up loose ends before they die. For the potentially threatened, today's potential may be tomorrow's sorrowful news, or it may wait until next year or the next decade. Of course, all human life is terminal in that sense. "I could walk out of here this afternoon and get hit by a truck" is repeated with the frequency of a cliché. Yet when someone resorted to that line in a group of chronically ill people I was meeting with, a chorus of voices protested that healthy people "don't have to live with it all the time." Death itself is a universal certainty, but one that most people disregard until illness brings it to consciousness.

Whether you fear it, feel reconciled to it, or even sometimes wish for the release it offers, death looms ahead of you, obscuring the future and serving as a backdrop that casts your life in stark relief. Even Lily Washington, who tries her best to be nonchalant, has flashbacks to her grandmother's death from asthma and is reminded that she, too, faces that danger. Being told that your illness will not kill you does not always eliminate the worry. As Gloria Murphy recalls: "People don't die from MS, they live with it. But I was more worried about all the X rays I had had. Something else would happen." That initial fear subsided, until something else did happen: an attack of angina that led to the discovery of coronary artery disease.

> I spent the summer kind of sitting and staring because a lot of fear set in again—a fear of my body. I had thought that whatever happened I could handle, but there's something about the heart. Being the only one you have, it needs to beat. I was told to call 911, the emergency number, and get a paramedic unit if it happened when I was home alone. That was really hard to accept—the fact that, gee, if I'm really this ill, what is going to happen to me? Well, now I've gotten over that sort of fear. I just don't really think a whole lot about it.

Not thinking a whole lot about it may be the best way you have to protect your sanity. It is psychologically hazardous to live in constant anticipation of death that may come tomorrow or in twenty years. A life suffused with mortal fear is hardly worth preserving. So you set the fears aside, at least until you have new reason for concern. Like depression, melancholy, anger, and other emotions, anxiety about death returns when provoked.

The Blank Wall

In my twenties, newly diagnosed, I expected an early death. The doctors told me that my life expectancy was shortened, but they did not know enough to specify by how much. The only certainty on which I could construct my life was that I would get worse and eventually succumb, and I guessed that would happen before age thirty. I lived those first years on edge all the time, constantly aware of the danger. In dramatic moments, especially after a heavy dose of the Scandinavian literature I was studying, I imagined myself ducking out of reach of the icy fingers of Death. When I tried to set the fears aside and simply live into the future as I had done before, another image of death intervened: a blank, white wall, with no frame, no mortar lines, nothing from which to determine its dimensions or its distance ahead of me. The wall became a great source of frustration. Whenever I tried to make plans, it blocked my way. It forced me into living day by day and kept my ambitions in check.

Then, to my surprise, I turned thirty—and thirty-one and thirty-two. I went for three years without a single episode of illness, after a decade of anticipating one every single day. I had outlived myself, and I might even be getting better. There was no longer sufficient cause for fear. The specter with the icy fingers stopped following me. I knew it would thrill him to catch a promising young woman and turn her life story into a tragedy, but what could he want with one already over the hill? Death just short of forty is premature, but the sentimental value has depreciated considerably. My perception of the white wall changed, too. Sometimes I have the sensation that it is moving ahead of me, keeping a steady distance. I am no longer sure that it is a wall. It may just be a blinding light, an optical illusion that obscures my vision of the future without denying me entry.

After turning thirty, I tried to think of each day as a bonus and not rue my losses, but by my fortieth birthday, I had upped the stakes again. Freed from anxiety about dying, I felt that I had barely started to live, and I wanted enough time to do it properly. Sophie Tucker's "Life Begins at Forty" could have been my theme song, and that decade was jam-packed with writing, child-raising, teaching, public speaking, and attempted romance, all of it still disrupted from time to time. Now that I am beyond fifty, I am back in the habit of dailiness and have eased my pace. I fret about wrinkles and age spots, yet have to acknowledge that what they symbolize is a precious gift. I worry less about death than about osteoporosis and Alzheimer's disease and try to pin my hopes on quality rather than length of life.

Prepared but Not Ready

About a year and a half before his death, Robert O'Shea recalled his feelings the night before heart bypass surgery:

> If you're able to get your house in order, I think you can handle anything, and my house was in order that night: You're lucky, Robert. You've had time to talk to people. Your bills are where they should be. If this is what's going to happen, fine. I think the cruelest thing that could happen to us is to die without that preparation.

In one sense, he suffered that cruelest thing by dying so suddenly, but someone as reflective, even prayerful, as Robert O'Shea could hardly be called unprepared. He knew that sudden death was a likely possibility, though he chose not to belabor it. As he said to me once, "This is the neat thing about chronic illness: You have time to reflect. Not to be martyrish about this, but it can be very, very positive. In fact, it's almost like an expensive luxury, and part of the cost of that luxury is knowing that two weeks from now I may have a heart attack." I would guess that we who face such a possibility and mull it over from time to time share a common orientation toward death: usually prepared, but never really ready.

Lorraine Czerny's life is a good example of that stance. Lorraine's heart was damaged following scarlet fever at age four. At thirty-five, she began to get extremely short of breath and to retain fluid. Of course, her heart was immediately suspect. The doctor she was seeing considered the problem permanent and irreversible and predicted that she would be bedridden until death. Lorraine's sister, who worked in a hospital, had heard about new methods of heart surgery being performed at the University of Minnesota and suggested that she look into it. Her doctor was reluctant to refer her there, thinking her too old to be a good risk, but she was insistent. Yet, even with the hope that the surgery offered, she was reconciled to an early death:

> Before the operation, I felt very comfortable. I felt like I was being carried along. And when I went into the operating room, I was more curious than scared, because I had never been in an operating room and I had read enough about the surgery to be very curious about the whole thing. Then, when I woke up after the surgery, I said, "Oh, darn it." I've never been frightened of dying since then. Don't ask me what happened. I have no recollection of why my first thought after surgery was "Oh, darn it." I don't know if anyone was near me or if I said it aloud or not. And then I forgot it. I just went on with the business of living.

This contentment lasted as long as she could overlook the uncertainty of her condition.

> I was very confident that I would be all right. I was very happy, and I knew that it wasn't a cure-all. But I went back to the clinic afterwards for a checkup, and this one doctor emphasized, "Now, look, you are not cured." What he did was put a fear in me that wasn't there, because I had accepted that this would be temporary and that they had no knowledge of how long it would last. And what he did was make me anxious. Now why did he have to say that to me?

> He was trying not to make me too optimistic, but he took
> the joy out of the fact that I was better than I was before.

Not expecting to live long, Lorraine did not give much thought to
the future. She took jobs that she liked, even if the pay was too low
to allow much savings, and she used that to travel. For eighteen
years, she lived a normal, healthy life, yet still prepared for life-
threatening illness: "I never knew quite where I was, if I was okay
or I wasn't okay," she remembers. Then, at age fifty-three, two of
her valves closed and she went into surgery again. Her condition
was critical and her recovery long, but she did survive. This time,
though, she had to stop working. "I asked the doctor how long I
had: 'Do you think I have about ten good years left?' He thought
that sounded reasonable. And I was asking that because of the
money, to know how to pay what little bit of money I'd saved."
Just about ten years later, she had surgery for the third time, becoming one of the first survivors of a triple valve replacement.

> I was right in my assumption about having ten years left, but
> I was wrong in forgetting that technology does move rapidly.
> When they said ten years, that was all right. I was pretty set,
> and I was starting to get things in order here. Well, then they
> said they could replace an aortic valve, too. Well, I woke up
> in surgery and there I was. And the doctor said I'm in better
> shape now than I have been in years, probably to where I was
> after that first surgery, when I was thirty-six.

Before each of her operations, Lorraine talked matter-of-factly
with the nurses about the likelihood of dying in surgery, and each
time recovery surprised her. When she talks now about the
course of her life, she even sounds a little miffed about outliving
her expectations. Because she had so little savings and had to re-
tire early, she lives in subsidized housing and can't afford a car.
She has an insurance policy she could cash in, and if she only
knew her life expectancy she would parcel it out over the remain-

ing years. As prepared as she is to die, however, Lorraine is not yet ready to forego what chance she has for additional life. She still wants to travel, and she talks about finding a job to supplement her Social Security income. Asked if she would consider another operation at her age, she ruled out a heart transplant and said she didn't think she could handle more valve surgery. But then she checked herself: "I say that now, but when the time comes right down to it, I probably would go through with it."

Robert O'Shea, prepared for what he described as "a whole new life," was overtaken by death, which was not really unexpected. At the same age, Lorraine Czerny, prepared for death, took a chance at life and was surprised to have more of it than she had made provision for. Either of them could have identified with the psalmist who pleads, "Lord, make me to know mine end, and the measure of my days, that I may know how frail I am." It is not, after all, the inevitability of death, but the uncertainty of its timing, that complicates our decisions about living.

Preparing for Life

Uncertainty itself—the mystery of an aberrant biological process—is a major aggravation. Having no certain expectations for the future makes it difficult to plan for it. Susan Alm, who has lupus, describes her frustration at not having a prognosis to go by:

> Not all cases get really bad. It's just a very unpredictable disease, and that, to me, is one of the hard things to deal with. I mean, if you get certain kinds of cancer, you know your chances are one in eight million of surviving. You know that disease is going to progress along a certain route, and it might take longer or shorter, but at least you know what you're up against. And the fear of the unknown is always worse. I just really don't know what will happen. So to counteract that kind of fear, you just arm yourself with as much knowledge as you can about the disease, and that's about all you can do.

Living one day at a time, necessary for the maintenance of a reasonable level of health, also helps to stave off anxiety about the course of the disease. "I do not get into futuring," Delores Garlid says firmly. "I try to deal with today. That doesn't mean that I don't know the reality of what may happen. And yet, each day I get up and I walk." Likewise, Don Welke, who is well aware of the many, diverse ways that diabetes can affect the body, says:

> I never thought of diabetes as life-threatening. I wasn't thinking, well, I'm not going to be here tomorrow so I'm not going to plan anything. I'm just going to live day to day. See, everything in a diabetic just starts going to pot after a while. I've got another twenty or thirty years to live, and I'm going to live, so I've got to figure out a way to make all this stuff last.

Don's determination to take things as they come and then do whatever is necessary to survive suits his personality very well. Not all of us can face danger so calmly. Some of us try not to acknowledge the most fearsome possibilities. For JoAnn Berglund, this is total confinement in a wheelchair or being moved to a nursing home. "Maybe it's not facing reality, but I'm not going to think about that. What was it Scarlett O'Hara said? 'I'll think about that tomorrow.'" Others of us—and this certainly includes me—are natural-born worriers. Peggy Evans says, "I've learned that the worst things that happen to you are the ones you never worry about. The things you worry about never seem to happen." Worrying, then, is a roundabout way of bringing your fate under control. Al Keski makes a habit of expecting trouble: "I handle most situations by preparing for the worst. Then anything less than that is a relief." This tendency has gotten more pronounced since the MS was diagnosed, and he is trying to curtail it:

> Basically, I've always lived in boxes. I've built my stack of boxes and I knew which one the next one was and everything was well contained within that. I could plan ahead. When I was in college, the first quarter of my freshman year I had all

of my classes singled out through senior year. Now all of a sudden the tops are off all those boxes. I've lost that control.

I don't like to consider myself a worrier, but my wife says I am. I like to think ahead and consider the options. It's crossed my mind thinking about the house here, that this is a poor layout for somebody in a wheelchair. We've talked about that: What would we do in that situation if I became limited to a wheelchair? I guess we'll have to cross that bridge when we come to it, which we may never. I feel very fortunate in some ways. I've had an opportunity to do most of the things I've wanted to do. I guess I feel I've lived a good life so far, and it didn't happen to me when I was twenty. So I'm trying to think of the positive things rather than the negative things.

Al's wife does not share his worst-scenario approach to the future and this has become a source of conflict. One of his biggest worries is that he will be unable to work and the family finances will be depleted. He wanted to make provision for that by setting money aside and taking out insurance policies, but his wife did not want to talk about it. "I think there is some barrier there about facing the options that could happen," Al surmises. With advice from a counselor, they finally did sit down and work it out so that he could rest easier and spare her his agonizing about it.

From his wife's perspective, Al's concern about the future seems overdrawn. If your desire to control your life is especially strong, the uncertainty of illness can easily push you toward excessive and unwarranted worrying. Lorraine Czerny thinks her concern about having enough money for her remaining years is a little neurotic, but, she adds, quoting her doctor, "As long as you know you're neurotic, it's all right." Ignoring the hazards is no healthier, however. Deciding whether to wrestle with the unknowns or avoid the fray altogether is parallel to choosing a mode of life that protects but also limits you, or one that leaves you unrestrained but puts your health in jeopardy. Louise Taylor says:

> It's a decision that you can never really feel satisfied with. Some days I say, "Push yourself and do what you can today because tomorrow there's a chance of blindness, there's a chance of paralysis." I don't know if I'm hurting my life by pushing myself. I think about it a lot. I ask myself, "Because of this illness is my life shortened anyway?" The doctors won't say. They can't predict the outcome, so they don't want to set up that trap. My gut feeling is maybe my life will be shortened by this, so therefore make the most of each day. You never quite know what to do. What I'd like to be able to do is just—I don't know if "let go" is the right word—but reach that point where I can just start living and stop being afraid that it's going to happen again and alter my life again.

Letting Go of Fear

It is, however, impossible to "let go" of something that you have never once held in your hand. Keeping it there long enough to examine it and say farewell makes all the difference between letting go and just plain denial or repression. As a practiced worrier, I would maintain that worrying thoroughly before setting a concern aside reduces the risk that the fear you have abandoned will come back to haunt you. Our prehistoric ancestors scratched pictures of wild animals into rock surfaces, presumably to capture some of the animals' strength so they could more easily hunt them down. Facing our worst fears exerts a similar psychological magic. Honest talk about death is critical to anyone who expects to meet it soon, but difficult to practice. A few years ago, my parents told my sisters and me, very timidly, that they had bought themselves a cemetery plot, so that "if something happens," we would have fewer arrangements to make. What did they mean by

"something"? I teased them. And why the "if"? Isn't death inevitable? Saying the word "die" is not a cue for the Grim Reaper's
entrance. To feel as prepared as I hope Robert O'Shea did, it helps
to say the words, draw up the will, pick out texts and music for
the funeral, and talk to family and friends about how this feels.
That done, you are also prepared for a less troubled life, however
much remains.

Voicing other worries can have the same demystifying effect,
as well as help you figure out whether the worry is helpful or
self-defeating. Many of us have very precise reasons to feel apprehensive. Esther Green worries most about going blind, a real possibility, and choking on her food, because her esophagus gets
constricted. She has changed her eating habits and alerted her
family so that if it does happen, they can take emergency measures. Louise Taylor has practiced being blind by feeling her way
around the house: "At first I thought, 'This is stupid,' but then I
thought, 'No, you'd better start preparing for what might be
real.'" Louise and I share the worry that our battered veins will
collapse, making the use of intravenous medication very difficult.
The one manifestation of diabetes that frightens Peggy Evans the
most is kidney malfunction. Once that fear is acknowledged, she
is ready to put it aside: "I think it's not too helpful to imagine how
I would feel and what I will need at that time. I've done it, but I
don't benefit." Donna Schneider, whose kidneys are diseased, lives
in dread of needing dialysis, and she does let the worries run. Her
job as a social worker forces her to face the possibility:

> I'm the lucky one who always gets the dialysis patients. The
> first time it happened to me, I said to my boss, "Do I have to
> go?" I couldn't help thinking, "Someday this could be me."
> Here he was, a seventy-eight-year-old man with a shunt in his
> arm and his wife trying to manage with the great big book
> that they give you on special diets: two ounces of this and
> one of that. On the one hand, I thought, "Gee, without the
> dialysis, he's gone." But every time I hear dialysis mentioned,

I get a twinge. Right now, the government pays for kidney dialysis under Medicare. But with all the cost cuts, will my name be put in a hat and will I be one of the lucky ten? Or will they not look at me at all because I'm over fifty? Am I going to have a say in what happens to me, or is it going to be the dollar that has the say? I do worry about it taking everything the family has.

Phyllis Mueller's anxiety about the future is as wide-ranging as her illness:

I worry about where I am going to be ten years from now. Am I still going to be sick? Am I going to be able to keep working? I don't want to be confined to the house. I want to be able to get out with people. I worry about that sometimes. I worry about my health getting worse. I don't worry so much about whether I'll get better, because I've been able to manage things as they are now. But I worry about a decrease in my health and how I would handle that. I'm sure everybody thinks about that. If I found out tomorrow that I have to add one other disabling thing to my life, I would be very depressed. I would have a real hard time coping with that. I think I'm doing okay with where I am now. I've reached some kind of acceptance with that, but, God, don't pile any more on me. That would scare me. That would upset me a lot.

Asked if there was anything they did not think they could adjust to, several people identified a single fate-worse-than-death: losing their minds to the illness. For Kathy Halvorson, it is an unsubstantiated fear provoked by illness still not understood: "When my arm goes numb, what does it mean? Is something moving toward my brain? You get all sorts of scary feelings." Susan Alm has some basis for worry in her medical history:

There have been times when I've really been concerned that the disease was affecting my thinking process. To me, that is the most frightening part of it, because I'm probably more metaphysical than physical. That's my self-image. If you want to hit the taboo thing, that would be it. Not using your hands is one thing, but not using your mind . . . It has to do with a kind of swelling I get at certain times. My body gets real swollen and I just can't think. I keep telling my doctor I have edema of the brain. It doesn't happen real often, but when it does it really bothers me.

In the aftermath of the Demerol I take for pain and the intravenous Valium I have been given as an anesthetic, I have felt spacy in a way that would be hard to bear as a permanent condition. Whether it had its origin in my body or was drug-induced, the inability to link words together in a sustained thought is one of the worst things I can imagine. But now I am rethinking that, too. My mother has lost that very capacity to Alzheimer's, but still she laughs, shows affection to her family, and has her joyful moments.

Earlier in her life, Janice Willett suffered from clinical depression, and she says, with no hesitation, that mental and emotional pain are far worse to bear than any of the physical pain she has experienced with Crohn's disease. Although it is worrisome to think of illness affecting her mental stability, the fact that she has endured that before lessens her fear of physical problems:

I remember having the obstruction in my intestine and being in the emergency room, and the pain was pretty severe, and I kept telling myself, I can take this. This is not as bad as the emotional terror and deep depression. Because I have experienced these, I somehow feel that I can take whatever my body dishes out.

Having come through it before is the firmest foundation most of us have for optimism. Don Welke believes that each episode endured has left him better equipped to handle the next one: "You definitely get stronger. You get used to handling it. You seem to get more fierce, I guess, emotionally, with each thing you go through." Esther Green says, simply but firmly:

> If somebody told me I was going to wake up and have these problems, I think that I would just deal with it. I can't think of anything I wouldn't actually be able to cope with, because I have been through an awful lot in these last few years. I would just deal with it like I'm doing, because there's no way you cannot deal with it. There's only one way, and that's to end your life.

Suicide and Euthanasia

That "precious gift" that I was given in my worst depression—the realization that suicide could free me from suffering—is, of course, available to everyone, but few people volunteer that they have considered it. Bill Gordon talks openly about it, because thoughts of suicide are a manifestation of his illness, and being matter-of-fact about them defuses their power. Al Keski broached the topic cautiously, adding his reasons for not choosing suicide:

> I don't think there's any person along the way at some time or other who doesn't contemplate suicide—no matter how lucky you are, no matter what the situation. Not that I've ever seriously contemplated it, but yet you do think about it. I think you just look at the obligation you have to your family and how they would get along. It wouldn't be fair, that's the problem.

Al is undoubtedly right in assuming that everyone has thoughts of suicide. Even the serenely accepting Peggy Evans has had them: "At one point I was even thinking, now, in the future when I get all these kidney problems, which is going to take more courage: to live with that or to end it all? Now that's getting pretty low,

I guess, but I did think that way." Peggy found, as I did, that she could not comfortably entrust those thoughts to anyone else:

> I did mention the thought of suicide to a friend who had come up to visit me, and she was so horrified at the thought and didn't want to talk about it. I did not mention it to anyone else, because I assumed they would react the same way. It was in the future. It was not immediately threatening. It was something that I thought I might think about someday, feeling that worse was to come. I don't think about it now that I'm feeling better and can do more, but I'm sure it must still be there.

It seems only natural that a serious deterioration in the quality of life or the prospect of dangerous or painful medical procedures would bring on fantasies of escape. That is all that thoughts of suicide amount to for most of us. Telling others that we have considered that option is a way of expressing fear that we will not be able to endure the worst that might happen. When such worries afflict us, pie-in-the-sky promises do not help. Carla Schultz remembers trying to console her mother after her father's death with that helpless banality, "Things just can't get any worse." Her mother's response: "Honey, things are never so bad they can't get worse." The next day Carla, barely recovered from a flare-up of lupus, came down with pneumonia. What the people in whom we confide at such times can offer is simple agreement that the condition of our lives may, indeed, become less tolerable, plus assurance that they will stand by and help us bear it. When Delores Garlid tried to talk with her daughter about "what if?"—which for her means becoming immobile and totally dependent—her daughter answered, "You know, Mother, that I will be here and will do what I need to do. I don't want to talk about it, but I will be there for you." Even without a full-blown conversation, Delores was satisfied for now.

Of course, there are situations in which death seems preferable to further suffering, regardless of how faithfully family and friends lend their support. It is a little sobering to think that two historical figures I especially admire, Charlotte Perkins Gilman and Virginia Woolf, committed suicide rather than live out the course of their illnesses. Gilman left a note claiming a right to suicide that ended, "I have preferred chloroform to cancer." Woolf, fearing she would not recover from another episode of a recurring mental illness, wrote to her husband, "I can't go on spoiling your life any longer." When thoughts of suicide come close to realization, both physical condition and style of living need to be reevaluated. If you don't have the clarity of mind to think through alternatives to death, then others need to intervene. Shortly after the onset of her kidney disease, Donna Schneider caught herself thinking almost constantly that it would be better to kill herself and get it over with than to suffer indefinitely. She sought counseling, but was not helped. After "many, many crying sessions" with her husband, who was very understanding, she had an honest talk with her doctor and learned that the suicidal depression was a side effect of the drug she was taking. An adjustment in the dosage took it away. It seemed a simple solution to a life-and-death crisis, one that could have been found much earlier.

Esther Green touched on an even greater taboo by recounting a conversation her husband and daughter had, in which he asked how she thought God would look on a person who "gave somebody something in a mercy killing." Family members who resent the illness's intrusion into their own lives may well wish you dead on occasion and even entertain fantasies of murder. Those who stand by you in your worst moments of suffering certainly wish for the power to release you from it, and euthanasia is one way of taking control. To think about it is quite natural, to talk about it, bold, and to act on it, greatly controversial. Dr. Jack Kevorkian has been practicing "assisted suicide" for years, outside the law, and the state of Oregon has recently approved a "right to die" measure. One concern I have about making suicide and euthanasia easy and legal is that people may take recourse to them prematurely. One of Dr. Kevorkian's first patients was a woman with a fairly new diagnosis of MS who had hardly had time to learn that the illness is bearable and can even go into remission. A frightening issue raised by disability activists in Oregon is that public funds for euthanasia are available to impoverished people who are ill or disabled, while these people have very limited access to antidepressant medication and home health care. In this case, euthanasia nudges too close to eugenics. We "apostles of imperfection" still have much to contribute to this debate.

Worst- and Best-Case Scenarios

Worrying your way through the worst scenarios and making practical arrangements for all contingencies still does not relieve life's uncertainty. Suffering, no matter how patiently, with a chronic illness does not protect you from other misfortunes. Obvious as this seems, it often comes as a surprise. Gloria Murphy remembers thinking, as the doctors were describing the condition of her heart, "Gee, I have MS. I can't have a cardiac problem. I already have something. Are you sure you've got the right person?" As Rosemary McKuen explains, "There's always the possibility that I'll get sick with something else. But you always feel that, well, I've paid my dues. I put in five years with ulcerative colitis and that should count against anybody else's normal lifetime of disease." Compared with all life's other unknowns, a chronic illness that has become fairly familiar begins to look less like chaos. Its presence, no matter what its prognosis, is at least something to count on. Given a choice, I would rather die from Caroli's disease than be gunned down by a sniper or poisoned in a nuclear accident. At least I know what signs to watch for and what to do when I see them. In the meantime, that proverbial truck is still careening down the street at random, ready to run down the next person who unknowingly darts in front of it. On this score, I'm with Scarlett O'Hara: I'll think about that tomorrow.

While everyone with a chronic illness lives at risk of getting worse, some of us also face the prospect of getting better. Of the many, many doctors who have examined me, none has ever been able to determine exactly what sets off the infections in my liver. But that, to me, is not the biggest mystery of my life. Taking illness as my normal condition, I wonder far more how I happened to have three three-year remissions: one when I was settling into an exciting but demanding new job that offered no security to settle into; another when I was adopting a second child, floundering about for a new career, and going through a divorce; and the third while my children were adolescents, both my sisters were diagnosed with cancer, and my parents sold their home of forty-three years and moved one hundred miles to a senior complex in my neighborhood. Obviously, stress is not the variable factor.

Diseases given to unexplained remissions do offer hope, though remission is a precarious thing to count on. As Al Keski prepares for the worst, he also tries to keep in mind that "There's nothing normal with MS":

> You hear about individuals who are bedridden who, after several years, start getting better and get out of bed and are mobile again. So the mystery of the illness is even greater, knowing that whatever level you end up at, the whole thing could still turn around. The uncertainty goes both ways. There's nothing definite. But there again, there's my box with the cover falling off.

Indeed, it happens. The future to be faced is not just degeneration and death, but also restored health. Louise Taylor, long accustomed to an annual hospitalization with MS has, for no apparent reason, skipped a year. Norma Bellisch, a recently divorced mother of two young children, living under considerable stress, compares her current condition, at thirty-five, with how she was at seventeen, when her multiple sclerosis was diagnosed:

I was losing my vision and having walking problems. I could hardly talk and I was numb from my toes all the way to the top of my head. I was looking at it then as real critical and I never thought I'd live for a few years beyond where I was, because everything was going all at once. At the time I was very pessimistic, not knowing what was going on. Here I am now, seventeen years beyond that, and my health is good. A few years ago, I thought I could never ride a bike again, and here I can ride around the whole area, with the baby on the back. I take my daughter into the city for Suzuki lessons twice a week in all that traffic. People say they're just amazed at what I can do. I can look into the future now and think, I should be the same way I am today. I can't say that I'm hindered in any way right now.

Lupus, too, is given to unexplained remissions. Carla Schultz explains:

The strange thing about lupus is that it's not unusual to document miracle cures. I had these *terrible* exacerbations. I was on the borderline to last rights, and then to be healthy! It's real hard to . . . well, I don't know if you can process that.

"Processing" a new state of health is, ironically, much like "accepting" a new illness. It involves, once again, shifting your place on the spectrum from healthy to sick, forging an identity that fits you, and adopting new habits. Lorraine Czerny finds herself at sixty-six healthier than she has been in thirty years and very surprised to be aging, a fate she never expected:

My trouble is that for years I never thought I would live beyond sixty. Well here I am at sixty-six, and I can't get adjusted to the fact that when I look in the mirror, here's this wrinkled face. I think, "My gosh!" I want to do things and I can't walk or run. You just pick up and want to go, and the mind is still young, and the body refuses to function that way. It's a strange feeling. I've gotten to the point where people get up to give you seats on the bus or hold you under the arm when you're walking or doing something you feel perfectly capable of doing. Gad.

There is a wide choice of new identities: healthy, formerly sick but cured, still sick but in remission, still sick and barely avoiding danger. Bill Gordon wants to see himself as cured, now that he has found a medication that keeps his condition stable, but his doctor emphasizes that his dependency on the drug is continuing evidence of illness. Without it, he would be back where he started. After the ostomy, Rosemary McKuen was ready to declare herself cured of ulcerative colitis, but doctors speak as though she is still vulnerable to whatever caused the illness. "I'm just as vulnerable as anybody else," Rosemary maintains. She is even at something of an advantage, because she has had the experience of being chronically ill and knows how to respond should it happen again:

> I want to be better prepared. If I ever had to confront a disease again, I would approach it completely differently. It wouldn't be something that happened to me. I wouldn't be a passive agent; I would be active. I never, never want to go through that experience the way I did. I'd go to the ends of the world to find what I could do to avoid that, and I would know when to say no. I would try to learn everything that I could about what's going on in this camp and that camp.

At the other end of the spectrum is Rachel Ryder, who has gone for more than twenty years without an epileptic seizure. Her doctor has suggested that she go off medication, but she is, to use her own term, "psychologically dependent" on the security that comes from swallowing a pill each morning. Some of her habits show that she still anticipates seizures. For example, she will not swim in a pool without a lifeguard, and she always stays along the edge. In order to trust in her apparent good health, Rachel would have to "let go"—of her identity as a secret epileptic and her fear of the terrorism that marred her adolescence.

Stalling for Time

The question "Would I really be healthy?" is one I have pondered as I have thought about a possibly impending liver transplant. When my doctor presented it as a genuine option and not just the science fiction marvel I had taken it to be, I began to dream my way into a future of wondrous possibility. Friends offered to bake me a chocolate cheesecake as my postoperative initiation into good health, and the fantasies spun on from there. One day, I was driving near the airport when a plane lifted off, nose upward, and crossed the highway in front of me. I was struck by the wanderlust that such a sight always provokes, but this time it was followed by a new sensation of freedom. Imagine buying plane tickets without fear of jinxing myself, I thought, and boarding the plane without anxiety about getting sick away from home. I felt as free and easy as Wendy in Peter Pan: "I can fly! I can fly!"

Attending a support group for liver transplant recipients—both actual and potential ones—brought me back to earth. At my very first meeting, a woman told about cutting her vacation short and going to the hospital because something about her medication had gone awry. A transplant may do nothing more for me than replace a chronic illness with a permanently abnormal physical condition. I would be trading the danger of a life-threatening infection for the possibility of constant minor infections, a side effect of taking antirejection drugs that suppress the body's immune system. I would be trading sudden trips to the emergency room for regular trips to the laboratory to have my blood tested. With veins like mine, that would be an ordeal. I would be trading one antibiotic pill a day and occasional intravenous therapy for antirejection drugs, steroids, diuretics. Most of the people I met who had survived transplants had been ill with primary biliary cirrhosis, and, in the jargon used by transplant surgeons, they were "end-stage" cases. If organ donation becomes more standard practice, I may have the luxury of waiting for the most propitious moment. But that requires knowing just when the trade-off will be to my advantage—and knowing it in time, before a deadly infection sets in. In other words, I should wait as long as I can, but not too long, or I may not survive the surgery. The surgery itself is a frightful thing to face. I have not yet worried my way through it, but as I watched a movie in which the heroine gradually lost consciousness to an anesthetic, the reality of the transplant struck me and I thought, "I don't want to do it."

At present, I am stalling for time. What I hope for is nothing more miraculous than another three-year remission. Transplantation is developing so rapidly that an additional three years ought to tip the balance of that awful trade-off. But what I really, really want is a remission that goes from three years to four to five and beyond. Even if it is only remission and not cure, how wonderful it would feel to be free of the symptoms of illness. The fears would probably persist, even if they never materialized. I suspect I would be more like Rachel Ryder than Rosemary McKuen, not quite daring to trust my good health and let go of my identity as chronically ill. Though it would be wonderful to finish each day feeling good, some features of chronic illness would be hard to surrender: euphoria after pain, the excuse to take time out for reflection, and the periodically renewed certainty that life's imperfections can be endured.

High-Tech Hopes

The advances in medical technology that have turned terminal illness to chronic also bring hope of recovery. Don Welke lives on that hope. Without insulin, he would not have survived childhood. Without laser therapy, he would be blind. Without kidney dialysis and transplantation, he would be dead of uremic poisoning. As a high-tech success story, he is ready for whatever else science offers: "It's just like changing parts. I'm a cybernetic person. Technology will keep up with me and I'll keep going. So I don't have to worry about it." Don's forecast may seem a little glib, because it leaves out, for the moment, the many negative dimensions: the risks to be weighed, the ethical questions to be resolved, the pain and suffering to be endured, and the ever-present possibility of failure. JoAnn Berglund talks with less bravado about undergoing experimental chemotherapy:

> I hate it. I get so tired of it. This time I was really sick with nausea. It took longer than it was supposed to. I was so sick I said, "Couldn't you just quit now?" Dr. White said, "I told you you were going to be sick." I said, "I know, but you never can tell anybody how sick they're going to be." All I can do is just hope that I can keep it at this level. I'm hoping that I'll be stabilized and that the chemotherapy will hold it at bay. And each month that goes by, there's a chance of a new discovery. That's all I can hope for.

Asked if there was any procedure they would refuse even though it held out hope of a cure, nearly all of the people I talked with declared themselves, in theory, willing to consider anything. Practice, too, seems to bear this out. Esther Green says, "I don't know if I have been a real guinea pig or just overanxious, but I never actually said, 'No, I won't.' Because I'm just so anxious to find something that would hold me for a long, long time." Gloria Murphy has thought through several options to replace the steroid she takes now, should that stop being effective:

> Using Cytoxan, which is chemotherapy, means loss of hair and all that. One of the nurses was talking to me about that because I was having a hard time and not progressing real quickly. She said, "How would you feel about Cytoxan?" and I said, "I really don't know. I'd have to think about that." They also do plasmaphoresis, which is the blood washing, and that I'd probably do. I don't know if my feeling about Cytoxan is the vanity thing, with the body image, you know.

> But if it came down to the fact of not being able to walk or use my arms or feed myself, I'd probably give in and do it. And I think my husband would probably be real insistent about it. It would be "go for anything."

An exception to the "go for anything" approach is Peggy Evans's reasoning about having a kidney transplant:

> While my children were growing up, I was willing to do anything to survive. Now I don't know how I feel. I think it might depend on when I need it. I'm thinking of the triage aspect of choosing who is to get what. I'm not sure that I would feel that I wanted to take a kidney that someone else younger who needed it more would have. My husband and I have talked this over, and I think a lot would depend on when it was and how we felt at the time.

Peggy's concern about the ethics of claiming an organ that could be of benefit to someone else arises, in part, out of a sense that her life has already been sufficient:

> When I became diabetic, I had a four-year-old and a one-year-old, and I remember asking the doctor what the longevity outlook was. He said, "Well, pretty near normal." I thought to myself, "If I can raise these children up to be twenty-one—the age of maturity—I will be very grateful." Not only did I raise them to twenty-one, but I had a third one and he's twenty, and they're all very healthy, and I feel very fortunate. My main responsibility in life is over because they're brought up. I can just enjoy life, and I do. I have my own philosophy, that because I've had life taken down to the very basics of life and death several times, that after that everything is gravy. It may be lumpy, but it's still gravy.

Vying with this feeling that someone else may be more entitled is a natural desire for continued life. When Donna Schneider heard

Peggy Evans talk about her reservations, she said, "I am not that generous. This is the only life I've got, and I want every day of it that I can get for me." There is actually not much distance between Peggy's view and Donna's. Both of them qualify their statements about the use of radical procedures with "probably" and "I'm not sure." The truth is that no one wants to declare an intention once and for all without reserving the right to reconsider, in light of present circumstances. Donna tells a story about a ninety-year-old woman who had instructed her children not to allow surgery or special life supports if she became ill, because she wanted to die naturally, with dignity. The next time she went into the hospital, however, she was conscious and she consented to surgery herself. At what would otherwise have been life's last minute, she changed her mind.

Peggy's mention of triage—allocating medical resources according to who would benefit the most—unsettled not only Donna, but the rest of us who met that day to talk about the uncertainty we live with. In the United States, greater awareness of the need for organs and a national policy on the selection of recipients may alleviate concern about robbing someone else of a chance at life. The global perspective is far more troubling. We who expect that our lives will be saved by highly technological intervention easily forget that there are many areas of the world in which dehydration is still a leading cause of death. As much as I want to live, I also wonder whether prolonging my life is a just use of scarce medical resources. Being the beneficiary of advanced technology probably ought to carry with it a responsibility to promote greater funding and better distribution of basic, sanitary health care.

The Hard Decisions

Also discomfiting was Peggy's admission that, in choosing whether or not to go ahead with treatment, you are choosing whether to live or die. Worse, you may be choosing to live only at the risk of dying in the process. And as Rosemary McKuen realized before ostomy surgery, the big decisions ultimately belong to patients, not doctors. Few people have the strange privilege of voluntarily undergoing treatment that will either kill them or prolong their lives. It has always amazed me that others seek out such risks, defying rough seas, winter storms, or wild animals for the thrill of challenging death. I get all the adventure I need just living in my defective body.

Because they cannot be made conclusively in advance, these life-and-death decisions, when they do present themselves, must be made quickly. You prepare for them best by keeping a measure of the quality of your life and being clear about your minimum standards. When I was at my weakest and most feverish, I questioned whether a life that went on that way was worth the effort it took to live it. If this is what the rest of my life is going to be like, I thought, then I don't even care how long it lasts. I felt useless, and even the daily routine of getting dressed and eating was too much for me. Knowing that was going to be a permanent condition might force the choice. Many of us fear arriving at that state without the mental faculties needed to make the choice. It is important to discuss with family and close friends, in healthier and less anxious moments, the question of when and under what circumstances you would rather forgo treatment than have life prolonged. Then, if they find themselves in the unenviable position of having to choose for you, they can do so with clear conscience.

My sister Joey's death from lung cancer has become an exemplary model for me. Her final months were horrid. Every breath was a painful effort and she could no longer speak. The words she mouthed to us let us know that the quality of her life was not worth sustaining. The day it became clear that death was imminent, her husband took her to the hospital intensive care unit. For twenty-eight hours a respirator and dopamine held off death while the family and her closest friends came in to say good-bye. She was lucid and free of pain. When someone offered her ice chips, she smiled and mouthed, "Coke." When we had all taken our turns at her bedside, she made the decision to unhook the respirator so that she could die, with her husband and children there to see her through. The day I lost my sister was also, ineffably, the day I got her back. It was a wondrous gift she gave us.

Last-Day Living

Staying attuned to the quality of your life is essential to living well with chronic illness. When you know that you have less time than you otherwise expected, or at least fewer good moments, you are inclined to live more deliberately in the time you do have. The habit of "dailiness," which helps us take pleasure in the moment, is not always easy to achieve, and it is easy to forget in times of remission. If we are lucky, we have enough reminders of life's fragility to jog us back into attentive living. I once attended a presentation on the care of terminally ill patients where the speaker handed each member of the audience three sheets of paper with large circles drawn on them. The first challenge was to imagine we had one year to live and to show graphically, by dividing the circle into different-sized pieces of pie, what we would do and how we would apportion our time. Next, we imagined ourselves with one month to go. On the third sheet, we laid out plans for our last day. After completing mine, I looked over my neighbor's shoulder and asked friends what they had put down. It was no surprise: foreign travel, finishing big projects postponed for a lifetime, going off on spectacular adventures. One person described her last day as a feast of her favorite fresh fruit enjoyed in the company of friends assembled from around the world. "Well," I laughed, "you must not be planning to die of a gastrointestinal disease." My own answers were the ones that surprised me: no big trips, no farewell extravaganzas, nothing out of the ordinary. Being certain of death, I would probably live just as I do now, in the face of uncertainty. Only the allotment of time would shift a little: I would try to spend more of it with the people I care about the most, and I would have more fun.

I seem to have already benefited some from Robert O'Shea's legacy: the dearly bought luxury of taking time to reflect. To be prepared, if not ready, for death, you live every day as though it were your last. Unfortunately, that sounds trite. It is usually interpreted to mean "get all you can out of life" or "burn your candle at both ends." But rather than packing all the excitement of life into one day, which you can hardly manage with pain or limited energy, this last-day consciousness forces you to decide which of life's many options matters the most. The wisest way to live and die is to let the candle burn at its own rate and use the flame as you have chosen: to see by, to expose a hidden injustice, to fuel a passion, to warm a child's cold hands, or just to roast marshmallows.

Afterword

Twelve Years Later

Letters I receive from readers often mention people whose stories are told in this book: "My experience is just like Louise Taylor's," they will say, or "I could really identify with Phyllis Mueller's frustration." Though I could not reinterview everyone (the original interviews took nearly three years), I did want to give readers who grow attached to these "characters" the latest news about their lives, as of February 1999. Some have moved, married, or divorced and could not be located, but those I did find were just as generous about sharing their lives as they were the first time.

SUSAN ALM has a second illness: Crohn's disease. She has recently recovered from a long, critical episode of pancreatitis and is thriving in a new line of work as an architecture history consultant on church renovations.

LORRAINE CZERNY, who wasn't sure if she could go through another surgery, went ahead anyway and had a replacement valve replaced. Since then, she has made three trips to visit relatives in the Czech Republic. She describes herself as "relatively pain-free with knees that work," thanks to recent knee replacement surgery, and is ready to resume her pace of church activities, concerts, plays, and traveling. "My biggest problem," she says, "is that I'm going to be eighty soon. That shakes me more than the various surgeries!"

At seventy-one, PEGGY EVANS has also outlived her life expectancy. Her diabetes is still severe and has taken its toll on her mobility and her vision. She is now legally blind and can no longer read or drive a car, but she can see well enough to paint and has taken up watercolor. Peggy maintains her serenity and her joy in life, relying for support on "the three F's: family, friends, and faith," which also make her life worth living. "My husband, especially, handles my condition well and apparently without worry," she says, "but is ever on the alert to remove or bridge the bumps and boulders in my path (literally and figuratively)."

"Strange as this may sound," DELORES GARLID says, "I have come to the recent realization that my MS is a gift I cannot give back. For someone who thought my life had ended when I was first diagnosed, I certainly have been proven very wrong. Instead, through having MS, I have found a very special purpose for my life." For the past thirteen years, she has held a full-time job with the National Multiple Sclerosis Society, and she feels "passionate" about helping people who share her disease. Her health has held steady, with only mild effects and no major flare-ups.

BILL GORDON has been mostly well since he started on Tegretol at the time of our last interview, but he has to guard against stressful situations. "I am still finding where I fit back in the world," he says, and that has been difficult. He has been employed at times, but has had to give up jobs when they become too stressful. This has put him in serious financial difficulties. He was divorced nine years ago but child-raising kept him in daily contact with his wife. Last year, they remarried on their twenty-sixth wedding anniversary.

ESTHER GREEN passed away in 1990 at age sixty-four. I saw the obituary in the newspaper and went to the funeral, which was packed with mourners. Obviously, she was much loved.

Forty-seven years after the traumatic childhood illness that opens chapter 6, KATHY HALVORSON returned to the Sister Kenny Institute for an evaluation. For the first time, she felt that her symptoms were validated, understood, and explained. She is indeed experiencing the long-term effects of childhood polio. She maintains her health with stretching exercises, chiropractic care, and massage as well as standard medicine. Massage, her chiropractor says, is a lifelong necessity because it not only relieves pain but reinvigorates her neurological connections and increases blood flow to her knotted muscles. Though she still keeps her illness quite secret, she will soon be speaking to staff members at her clinic about postpolio syndrome. Kathy still keeps up with a demanding full-time job.

AL KESKI has not had a flare-up in ten years, but he does have some vision problems and occasionally uses a cane. While his health has held steady, his life has changed drastically. Shortly before the passage of the Americans with Disabilities Act, his employer down-sized, starting with the sick and the aged. He had to fight to collect his disability insurance and now lives on Social Security disability and a ten-hour-per-week job that he can do at home. He was divorced two years ago after twenty-eight years of marriage. He figures that his illness contributed to the divorce, not only by complicating his married life, but also because the new demands it placed on his wife ultimately gave her more confidence and a stronger sense of herself and her own goals.

ROSEMARY MCKUEN is "enjoying a very, very good health." A Presbyterian minister, she has been serving interim pastorates in small churches and takes time between assignments to write.

PHYLLIS MUELLER finally has a diagnosis: Four different specialists agreed that her symptoms point to fibromyalgia. Even her history of digestive problems can be attributed to this musculoskeletal disorder. The diagnosis is a great relief, not only because it gives her some certainty, but because an illness recognized by the AMA entitles her to health care that her HMO previously refused. She does not get coverage, however, for the chiropractic treatments and massage that ease her pain. Though she never has a sustained period of feeling well, some days are easier to handle than others. She is "not so panicky" as before, more frustrated than angry, and more willing to work with her limitations. Her outlook on life is just as vigorous and realistic as always: You live the best you can because "you're not going to get another shot at it."

GLORIA MURPHY still tests her parts each morning, and some of them don't work as well as they used to. She goes into the hospital once or twice a year, to the MS "boarding school" at Fairview-Riverside Hospital in Minneapolis. "With each flare-up," she says, "I lose a little more." She can no longer read books and she uses her scooter whenever she leaves the house, but she still keeps up her vocation of educating people about MS and offering support to others who are sick. She speaks at churches and schools and facilitates a support group at her church for people with chronic illness. Gloria calls herself "a huge believer in the power of prayer," and is working on a book of short writings about living with illness.

"Who is this insecure, neurotic woman?" RACHEL RYDER asked herself after looking back to see what she had told me twelve years ago. She feels she has grown a great deal. "I'm still not the poster person for epilepsy," she says, "but I don't keep my illness as big a secret." The most dramatic change in her life and her sense of strength came about when her husband suffered a brain injury that left him debilitated for the five years before his death two years ago. The family dynamics were completely altered. Rachel became both breadwinner and caregiver, and children who had grown up and moved away came back home to help. When she looks back on those five years, she wonders how she managed it all, and she suspects that her struggle with epilepsy in adolescence helped her to carry on and keep life as normal as possible. Rachel is contending now with grief and loneliness and says, "I am still in the process of reinventing myself."

After worrying for years about the prospect, DONNA SCHNEIDER went on dialysis at the end of 1994. She goes to the hospital three days a week for three-hour treatments. Donna has decided against a kidney transplant because of her sensitivity to medications and the possibility that her disease could affect the new kidney as well. The same year she went on dialysis, her husband had a heart attack and bypass surgery. "Some days," she says, "we don't know which one of us is the caregiver." Her life has really changed, but she's adjusting to it and still manages to travel as long as she can arrange dialysis away from home. She quit working when she started dialysis, and now has time to enjoy her two granddaughters. She also puts in some hours at her "favorite charity," a local gambling casino. When I wished her a big win, she laughed and said, "No, that would spoil it. It would take away the hope."

Ten years ago, a friend suggested that CARLA SCHULTZ try Chinese herbal medicine, including a detoxifying agent and nutritional supplements. One year later, all her lupus bloodwork had returned to normal, and she has relied on the herbal medicine ever since. She had already given up cortisone, which had caused her hip joint to deteriorate so that it had to be replaced. Though she still tires more easily than the average person, she is otherwise healthy enough to work three days a week and keep up an exercise regimen.

SANDRA STIEGLITZ wrote me in February 1999 that her health had been in steady decline, and she had a "severely compromised immune system with no apparent hope of any recovery." Because her heart was failing, she had entered a hospice program. "Dealing with the illness isn't the hard part," she wrote. "The hard part is spend-downs—who will pay what—and getting care. I am forced to fight the system, which isn't healing or positive. A day at a time, I will get where I am going and then have peace." Peace came on March 16. Sandra was fifty-two.

LOUISE TAYLOR's health has gotten more complicated, but she has gotten better at living her life. In addition to MS, she now has diabetes, her family's disease, and lupus, so she has to be careful to monitor her symptoms and to make sure that medication for one illness doesn't exacerbate the other. On the positive side, she has learned to detach her identity and self-esteem from her job title. Five years ago, her neurologist convinced her to quit her job and go on disability. She has discovered that the skills she used in her job can be applied to other endeavors that are important to her. Louise says that in the past she "pushed away" relationships because she expected lovers to abandon her when she got sick. She understands that now and has a stable relationship with a

woman who already knew about her illnesses. Louise has published an account of her diagnosis in an anthology and now feels
motivated to keep writing what she knows about life.

At the time of our interview, JANICE WILLETT's symptoms of
Crohn's disease were growing in frequency and intensity. When
she had to be hospitalized for six obstructions within eight
weeks, she knew it was time for more surgery. Since then, for
three years, she has been symptom-free and no longer even has to
restrict her diet. "I remember the first time I ate a salad again,"
she says. "I was in a Perkins restaurant and it tasted so good that
I felt like standing up and shouting with glee, 'Janice Willett is
eating a salad!' but I knew the audience wouldn't quite get it."
Her doctor predicts that the surgery should hold her for about
ten years. In the meantime, she is trying to learn all she can about
Crohn's and its treatment and how her emotions might affect it,
and she appreciates having the good fortune to be well most of
the time.

Index

About the Author

After a ten-year academic career in Scandinavian languages and literatures and women's studies, Cheri Register returned to her true vocation, writing. She has also published a book on international adoption entitled *Are Those Kids Yours?*, two books on Swedish women's literature, and many essays in periodicals and anthologies. Her next book is a documentary memoir about working-class life in a Midwestern meatpacking town.

Cheri also teaches creative nonfiction writing at the Loft Literary Center in Minneapolis, Minnesota, and does freelance editing, as well as public speaking on chronic illness. She has adapted her work life to suit the needs of a congenital liver disease, Caroli's syndrome.

She has a Ph.D. in Germanic languages and literatures from the University of Chicago, and she lives with her young adult daughters, Grace and Maria, in Minneapolis.

Other titles that may interest you . . .

FINDING THE JOY IN TODAY
Practical Readings for Living with Chronic Illness
by Sefra Kobrin Pizele

These daily meditations address the physical, emotional, and spiritual challenges faced by those who have a chronic illness, helping them regain peace of mind by focusing on the joy to be found in each day.
384 pages   Order no. 5489

CHRONIC OBSTRUCTIVE PULMONARY DISEASE (COPD)
Practical, Medical, and Spiritual Guidelines for Daily Living with Emphysema, Chronic Bronchitis, and Combination Diagnosis
by Mark Jenkins

This book presents the symptoms, causes, and progressive nature of COPD and describes how to apply Twelve Step concepts to help those who have COPD meet the daily challenges of living with this disease.
180 pages   Order no. 1370

CHRONIC ILLNESS AND THE TWELVE STEPS
A Practical Approach to Spiritual Resilience
by Martha Cleveland, Ph.D.

This interpretation of the Twelve Steps integrates beliefs and behaviors that help people cope with chronic illness through a hopeful prophesy and commitment to spiritual wellness.
222 pages   Order no. 1024

HIGH BLOOD PRESSURE
Practical, Medical, and Spiritual Guidelines for Daily Living with Hypertension
by Mark Jenkins

This book presents basic and essential medical information on the symptoms and causes of high blood pressure, as well as the spiritual aspects of the Twelve Step program that can help those with high blood pressure make positive changes in attitude and behavior to address the challenges presented by this disease.
180 pages   Order no. 1368

Hazelden offers titles on a wide range of behavioral and medical chronic illnesses. For price and order information or a free catalog, please call our telephone representatives or visit our Web site at www.hazelden.org

HAZELDEN®

1-800-328-9000   (Toll-Free U.S., Canada, and the Virgin Islands)
1-651-213-4000   (Outside the U.S. and Canada)
1-651-213-4590   (24-Hour Fax)

www.hazelden.org
15251 Pleasant Valley Road
P.O. Box 176
Center City, Minnesota 55012-0176